QUALITATIVE ANALYSIS USING ATLAS.ti

Software is cut and dried—every button you press has a predictable effect—but qualitative analysis is open ended and unfolds in unpredictable ways. This contradiction is best resolved by separating analytic strategies—*what you plan to do*—from software tactics—*how you plan to do it*. Expert ATLAS.ti users have unconsciously learned to do this. The *Five-Level QDA®* method unpacks the process so that you can learn it consciously and efficiently.

The first part of the book explains how the contradiction between analytic strategies and software tactics is reconciled by "translating" between them. The second part provides both an in-depth description of how ATLAS.ti works and comprehensive instruction in the five steps of "translation." These steps are illustrated with examples from a variety of research projects. The third part contains real-world qualitative research projects from a variety of disciplines, methodologies, and kinds of qualitative analysis, all illustrated in ATLAS.ti using the *Five-Level QDA* method. The book is accompanied by three sets of video demonstrations on the companion website: www.routledgetextbooks. com/textbooks/5LQDA. Although this book uses screenshots from the current ATLAS.ti Version 8 (for Windows), it is still fully applicable to users of older versions. Mac users should watch the video 'The ATLAS.ti Mac Interface'.

The *Five-Level QDA* method is based on the authors' combined 40 years of experience teaching ATLAS.ti and other software packages used as platforms for conducting qualitative analysis. After many years observing their students' challenges, they developed the *Five-Level QDA* method to describe the process that long-time ATLAS.ti experts unconsciously adopt. The *Five-Level QDA* method is independent of software program or methodology, and the principles apply to any type of qualitative project.

Nicholas H. Woolf has worked as an independent qualitative research consultant, coach, and trainer since 1998. He has conducted or consulted on numerous research studies, from single-site to multinational studies in various fields in the behavioral sciences using a wide range of methodologies, from highly structured content analyses, to evaluations, grounded theory–style projects, and interpretive phenomenology. As a trainer Nick specializes in teaching qualitative analysis using ATLAS.ti. He has conducted 285 workshops at over 100 universities and other institutions, primarily in the USA and Canada, for more than 3,000 PhD students, professors, and research and evaluation consultants. In 2013 Nick introduced *Five-Level QDA* in his keynote address at the first ATLAS.ti users conference in Berlin (Woolf, 2014).

Christina Silver has worked at the CAQDAS Networking Project at the University of Surrey, UK since 1998. She is responsible for capacity-building activities and has designed and led training in all the major qualitative software programs, including ATLAS.ti, Dedoose, MAXQDA, NVivo, Transana, QDA Miner, Qualrus, and Quirkos. Christina also works as an independent researcher, consultant, and trainer, supporting researchers to plan and implement computer-assisted analysis and contributing to doctoral research programs in several UK universities.

Developing Qualitative Inquiry

Series Editor: Janice Morse
University of Utah

Books in the *Developing Qualitative Inquiry* series, written by leaders in qualitative inquiry, address important topics in qualitative methods. Targeted to a broad multi-disciplinary readership, the books are intended for mid-level to advanced researchers and advanced students. The series forwards the field of qualitative inquiry by describing new methods or developing particular aspects of established methods.

Other Volumes in This Series Include

Mixed Methods in Ethnographic Research
Historical Perspectives
Pertti J. Pelto

Engaging in Narrative Inquiries with Children and Youth
Jean Clandinin, Vera Caine, Sean Lessard, Janice Huber

Interpretive Description
Qualitative Research for Applied Practice, 2nd Edition
Sally Thorne

Qualitative Ethics in Practice
Martin Tolich

For a full list of titles in this series, please visit **www.routledge.com**

QUALITATIVE ANALYSIS USING ATLAS.ti

The Five-Level QDA® Method

Nicholas H. Woolf and Christina Silver

 Routledge
Taylor & Francis Group

NEW YORK AND LONDON

First published 2018
by Routledge
711 Third Avenue, New York, NY 10017

and by Routledge
2 Park Square, Milton Park, Abingdon, Oxon, OX14 4RN

Routledge is an imprint of the Taylor & Francis Group, an informa business

Library of Congress Cataloging-in-Publication Data
Names: Woolf, Nicholas H., author. | Silver, Christina, author.
Title: Qualitative analysis using ATLAS.ti : the five-level QDA method / Nicholas H. Woolf and Christina Silver.
Description: Abingdon, Oxon ; New York, NY : Routledge, 2017. | Includes bibliographical references and index.
Identifiers: LCCN 2017015785 | ISBN 9781138743632 (hardback) | ISBN 9781138743656 (pbk.) | ISBN 9781315181684 (ebook)
Subjects: LCSH: Qualitative research—Data processing. | ATLAS.ti (Computer file)
Classification: LCC Q180.55.E4 W56 2017 | DDC 001.4/2028553—dc23
LC record available at https://lccn.loc.gov/2017015785

ISBN: 978-1-138-74363-2 (hbk)
ISBN: 978-1-138-74365-6 (pbk)
ISBN: 978-1-315-18168-4 (ebk)

Typeset in Bembo
by Apex CoVantage, LLC

Visit the companion website: www.routledgetextbooks.com/textbooks/5LQDA

Dedicated to Ben Woolf,
who fearlessly overcame
seemingly insurmountable obstacles
with grace and humor.

1980–2015

CONTENTS

EXTENDED CONTENTS

FIGURES

TABLES

BOXES

ACKNOWLEDGMENTS

This long, long labor of love would have never reached fruition without the enthusiastic support of many people. Jan Morse believed in the project when it was still a germinating seed, and it would not have happened without her encouragement. Trena Paulus stands out for critiquing early drafts, asking if she could test the *Five-Level QDA* method at the University of Georgia, and inviting us to join her and Elizabeth Pope in their research of the use of the method. Trena has a knack for critiquing our writing with an apparently innocuous question that cuts to the core of an issue, and we thank her for the contributions she made to our thinking. We are also indebted to Sarajane Woolf for her relentless editing; we turned over chapters to Sarajane thinking them in excellent shape, but quickly learned otherwise.

Numerous leaders and teachers in the CAQDAS community have provided the encouragement we needed to keep going. As you will soon be reading, the *Five-Level QDA* method is all about making conscious what CAQDAS experts have unconsciously learned to do. We want to thank all the CAQDAS experts who have told us so enthusiastically in their own different ways that the *Five-Level QDA* approach spells out what they have been thinking but haven't been able to articulate. We particularly want to thank Ann Lewins, Kristi Jackson, Michelle Salmona, Sarah L Bulloch, Eli Lieber, Judy Davidson, Daniel Turner, Steve Wright, Pat Bazeley, Susanne Friese, and Thomas Muhr and the ATLAS.ti development team at Scientific Software Development GmbH for their positive encouragement and support over the years. Finally we would like to thank Hannah Shakespeare at Routledge for her efficient and cheerful shepherding of this project through to completion.

We solicited case contributions for the book and for the numerous mini-cases on the companion website (www.routledgetextbooks.com/textbooks/5LQDA). We were delighted to find experienced researchers who recognized that the *Five-Level QDA* method resonated with their work and were eager to take the time to write up their projects for us. We thank them all for the courteous and collaborative manner in which they contributed their work. We particularly thank Trena Paulus, Mary Alice Varga, and Elizabeth Pope for the cases that are printed in Chapters 8 and 9 of this book.

Each of us received invaluable encouragement from so many colleagues, family, and friends through the many years of this project—to all our supporters, a heartfelt thank you. Nick would particularly like to thank Jim Quinn for his never-ending support, expertise, and encouragement, and Sarajane for her standard response to the long hours and late nights on the project: "keep working." Christina would particularly like to thank Ann Lewins for commenting on early drafts with wit and detailed perception, and Sarah L. Bulloch for her accuracy checks and enthusiasm in integrating the *Five-Level QDA* method into her own teaching. In addition Christina's family: Jason, Christopher, Nelleke, Derek, and Deanna for their ceaseless support and encouragement, and Nathanael and Magdalena for illustrating that there is always light at the end of the tunnel.

CASE CONTRIBUTORS

Chapter 8: An Exploratory Literature Review

Elizabeth M. Pope is a doctoral candidate pursuing a degree in Adult Education and a Certificate in Interdisciplinary Qualitative Studies at the University of Georgia, Department of Lifelong Education, Administration, and Policy. With a background in the field of religion, Elizabeth is merging the two disciplines in her dissertation, "This Is a Head, Hearts, and Hands Enterprise: Interfaith Dialogue and Perspective Transformation." Her research interests are in religious studies, adult learning, qualitative research, and transformational learning in interfaith and cross-cultural contexts.

Chapter 9: A Discourse Analysis Study

Trena M. Paulus, PhD, is a Professor of Qualitative Research Methods and Interdisciplinary Qualitative Studies at the University of Georgia. She holds a PhD from Indiana University in Instructional Systems Technology and Computer-Mediated Communication and an MA in Applied Linguistics from Ohio University. Dr. Paulus has published over 50 peer-reviewed journal articles on topics related to online learning, computer-mediated communication, and language-based methodologies for investigating online talk and text. She is a certified professional trainer for ATLAS.ti and co-author of *Digital Tools for Qualitative Research* (Sage Publications, 2014.) She is a founding member of the international Microanalysis of Online Data network and the International Congress of Qualitative Inquiry's special interest group on Digital Tools for Qualitative Research.

Mary Alice Varga, PhD, is an Assistant Professor of Educational Research in the Department of Leadership, Research, and School Improvement at the University of West Georgia. She is also the Director of the School Improvement Doctoral Program. She teaches graduate-level courses on quantitative, qualitative, and mixed-methods research. Her primary research focuses on student grief, online grief support, and ethics in online grief research.

ORIENTATION

Learning to do qualitative analysis with ATLAS.ti does not mean *learning how to operate the program really well*. Instead it means *learning to harness ATLAS.ti powerfully*. These two objectives could not be more different, and this orientation prepares you for what is to come.

Orientation means *finding one's location in an environment*. Orientations are common in the business world to socialize new employees in an organization, with activities to gain their commitment, reduce their anxiety, and let them know what they should expect from the organization. Only then are employees trained for their specific jobs. It is in this sense that we provide this orientation. The purpose is to alleviate your concerns and enlist your patience for what is to come by telling you why this book is written in the way that it is.

Three areas require orientation. The first is what kind of program ATLAS.ti is and what it means to harness it powerfully. The second area is the best way to learn to do this. We have drawn on our combined 40 years of teaching experience to develop an approach to learning that is not what is generally expected in software training. The third area concerns the differences between using ATLAS.ti in solo research projects and in research teams. The orientation ends with a roadmap through the book.

ATLAS.ti Is Not an Analysis Program

Some researchers expect—or hope—that ATLAS.ti will somehow do the analysis and reduce the hard mental work of qualitative analysis. Others are fully aware that this is not the case, yet they unconsciously expect that ATLAS.ti will make at least some contribution to the analysis. Part of the problem is the names for these types of programs—Computer-Assisted Qualitative Data AnalysiS (CAQDAS), or qualitative data analysis software (QDAS), or simply qualitative analysis software. All have *software* and *analysis* in them, which inevitably suggests that the software performs analysis. (See Box 0.1 for more on the history of acronyms for these dedicated software packages).

The idea that the software does some kind of analysis can be hard to overcome. The natural assumption is that ATLAS.ti is a qualitative cousin to statistical software packages like SPSS or SAS. But programs like Scrivener or Microsoft Word that support the writing process offer a more useful comparison. Microsoft Word is never called a computer-assisted writing program—it is not a writing program at all. It just displays characters corresponding to the keys you press, with bells and whistles to move text around and format text to make it look appealing. There are no

---

BOX 0.1 WHY WE USE THE ACRONYM CAQDAS

Several acronyms are used for a group of dedicated software programs that qualitative researchers use to assist them in conducting their analysis. Some writers use QDAS for these programs, which stands for Qualitative Data Analysis Software (e.g., Bazeley & Jackson, 2013; di Gregorio & Davidson, 2008). We prefer not to use this acronym because it can be misunderstood to mean software that performs analysis, which none of the writers who use the acronym intend to mean. Other writers use CAQDAS, which stands for Computer-Assisted Qualitative Data AnalysiS (e.g., Friese, 2014; Paulus, Lester, & Dempster, 2014). We also prefer to use CAQDAS, the original term for this software, because of its historical roots and more general use and acceptance in the field.

The acronym CAQDAS was first coined by Raymond Lee and Nigel Fielding in their 1991 book *Using Computers in Qualitative Research*, which was published following the first conference on qualitative software that they convened in 1989, the *Surrey Research Methods Conference* (Fielding & Lee, 1991). This conference brought together pioneers in the field to discuss the issues for the first time. Their debates revealed that use of computers for qualitative analysis was a thorny issue, and Lee and Fielding wanted to reflect this in the acronym, so they intentionally designed the acronym CAQDAS to evoke a big thorny plant—the cactus. Another reason for the acronym is that at the same time other technology-based methodological innovations, such as CAPI (Computer-Assisted Personal Interviewing) and CATI (Computer-Assisted Telephone Interviewing) were using "computer-assisted" in their acronyms, so Lee and Fielding felt it made sense to follow this trend. In 1994 Fielding and Lee went on to establish the CAQDAS Networking Project (CNP) at the University of Surrey, UK, which became an internationally reputed and independent source for practical support, training, information, and debate in the use of these technologies. The establishment of the CNP had the effect of "fixing" the acronym. Originally the second S stood for "software," but in response to suggestions that it is illogical to have both the term "computer-assisted" and "software" in the same acronym, over time the second S has come to refer to the second S in AnalysiS, and this is now the way the CNP uses the acronym. For more information about CNP and the origins of the CAQDAS acronym, see www.surrey.ac.uk/sociology/research/researchcentres/caqdas/support/choosing/caqdas_definition.htm.

---

buttons or menus for writing tasks like *compose short story*, or *outline critical essay*, or *write novel in Russian*. Similarly, ATLAS.ti has no buttons for *identify themes* or *compare the meaning of a statement in one context rather than another*. There is no menu for *grounded theory* or *discourse analysis*. Where Microsoft Word is essentially a character display program, ATLAS.ti is essentially a program for managing concepts. You provide concepts, and ATLAS.ti provides many bells and whistles to organize, display, and work with them according to your instructions. You as the researcher do 100 percent of the intellectual work.

ATLAS.ti therefore makes no analytical contribution to your research. We hope this does not make you sad. If it does, and you wonder if you have made the right decision to learn to harness ATLAS.ti powerfully, think analogously about Microsoft Word. Just because Microsoft Word can't actually write by itself, would you want to go back to writing by hand, if you have ever done such a thing? We imagine you would agree that time spent learning how to take advantage of Microsoft Word was time well spent. We are confident you will feel the same about ATLAS.ti.

What It Means to Harness ATLAS.ti Powerfully

Since the early 1990s we have taught hundreds of workshops for many thousand novice and highly experienced researchers on using ATLAS.ti to conduct qualitative data analysis. Our experience is that simply learning how to operate ATLAS.ti—learning what happens when each button is clicked and each menu item is selected—does not lead to powerful use of the program. This book is the result of observing how experienced researchers who have become expert users of ATLAS.ti use the program. We saw that they learned for themselves how to take full advantage of the program in every stage of a project while remaining true throughout to the emergent spirit of qualitative research. This is what we call *harnessing ATLAS.ti powerfully*, and learning how to do this is the purpose of this book.

Taking full advantage of ATLAS.ti throughout a project is highly efficient. There is no need to switch back and forth between programs or between software and manual methods, unless there is a compelling reason to do so. However, many researchers do not use ATLAS.ti in every stage of their projects because they are uncertain if the software is unduly influencing the conduct of their analysis. In other words, can you conduct qualitative analysis using software and remain true throughout to the emergent spirit of qualitative research? This leads to the central issue in harnessing ATLAS.ti powerfully: the basic contrast between the nature of qualitative analysis and the nature of computer software. The purpose of the *Five-Level QDA* method is to resolve this contrast. (QDA stands for qualitative data analysis. For brevity we use the term *qualitative analysis*, or simply *analysis*.)

Qualitative analysis is a systematic process, in the dictionary sense of doing something *according to a careful plan and in a thorough way*. At the same time, most styles of qualitative analysis are, to various extents, open ended, organic, and unpredictable in the way they develop. As a shorthand we refer to qualitative analysis as *emergent*. This word comes with a lot of baggage, which we discuss further in Chapter 1. At this point it is enough to say that although qualitative analysis is systematic, it is not intended to proceed in a predetermined, step-by-step manner. Imagine being a painter with a definite idea of what you want to paint. Each brushstroke has an effect, leading to a fresh consideration of the progress of the entire picture. Certainly the next 20 brushstrokes cannot be planned out in advance and applied without modification one by one, regardless of the newly apparent and unpredictable effects of each one. Qualitative analysis is similarly emergent.

Computer software works in the opposite way: it is more like painting-by-numbers. The software features work in a predetermined and predictable way—when we press a button or choose a menu option, something specific always happens because it has been preprogrammed this way. We refer to this as being *cut and dried*. We have observed thousands of researchers—novice and experienced—struggle with using a cut-and-dried software package that appears to bear little resemblance to the emergent practice of qualitative research. Some researchers decide not to use ATLAS.ti after all, or they use it for the first stages of a project, before the more subtle aspects of the analysis emerge. They then continue the project on paper, or with yellow stickies, or on a whiteboard, or in a more generic program like Microsoft Word or Excel, just when ATLAS.ti could be helping the most. Worse is the opposite situation, when less experienced researchers change the character of the analysis to more easily fit the software, thereby suppressing the more emergent aspects of a qualitative analysis.

None of these alternatives is necessary, and by proceeding systematically through this book they can be avoided. The key is to recognize that harnessing ATLAS.ti powerfully is a skill *additional* to the ability to conduct qualitative analysis and to operate the software, one that allows you to transcend the contrast between emergent qualitative analysis and cut-and-dried software. Learning this skill is the focus of this book. We will continue to use the longer phrase *harness ATLAS.ti powerfully* to describe this skill. We don't want to start abbreviating it to *use ATLAS.ti* because that inevitably sounds like *operate the software*, which is the least important of the needed skills.

Is harnessing ATLAS.ti powerfully relevant to your own work? Are you an academic researcher planning to use ATLAS.ti for a particular style of analysis? Or are you doing applied work, such as program evaluation or public-sector consultations? Or are you using ATLAS.ti for a purpose not generally thought of as research, whether you are an author needing to organize a vast and disparate body of source materials, or a student undertaking a literature review, or a physician planning to organize or analyze patient records? There are no typical ATLAS.ti users and no typical ATLAS.ti projects—every kind of project calls for a somewhat different way of using the program. But underlying these disparate projects is a common feature: we all work with unstructured data. The *structure* of data refers to its degree of organization. *Fully structured data* are preorganized in numeric categories, ready for statistical analysis. *Unstructured data* are not preorganized in numeric categories. Unstructured data are often in the form of speech, audio-recorded and then transcribed, or notes or videos taken while observing others, or archival materials of all kinds—audio and video recordings; images like photographs, drawings, or diagrams; websites, blog posts, or social media interactions; and PDF files, which may have a mix of text and graphic data. All these forms of data come with some degree of preorganization or structure—for example, a transcript of free-flowing conversation may be structured according to who is speaking. But we call them all unstructured because they do not cross the line of being organized numerically.

All our approaches to working with such data share the same goal—making sense of or giving meaning to a mass of unstructured data. For some, the approach is prescribed in a research methodology, so the conclusions can be justified and evaluated in a recognized way. Others, who do not see their projects as academic or even as research at all, will simply choose the analytic approach or procedure that fulfills the purpose of collecting the data. All these activities are, to some extent, emergent, even if you do not use that word to describe your work. Harnessing ATLAS.ti powerfully is relevant to all of these projects because they all require making sense of a body of unstructured data.

One caveat: using ATLAS.ti throughout a project may include activities other than data analysis, such as project planning, preliminary or pilot study activities, data collection, or representation of results. This book is focused only on data analysis. But we hope you will draw analogies for using the *Five-Level QDA* method in other phases of your project.

How to Learn to Harness ATLAS.ti Powerfully

Experts in any field have mentally "automatized" what they do so that it has become unconscious. Experts just know what to do in each new circumstance, but they have difficulty describing how or why they do what they do (Sternberg & Frensch, 1992). This describes the skills of expert users of ATLAS.ti. The purpose of this book is to unpack this black box of expert performance. We make the process explicit so that you can learn this skill more easily.

Learning to harness ATLAS.ti powerfully is not like learning the finer skills of Microsoft Word, which are best learned independently of learning how to write—because these skills and writing skills are independent. With ATLAS.ti, however, learning to use the program in a sophisticated way is intricately bound up with the specific analytic task that is being executed in the software. Yet there is a contradiction between the emergent nature of qualitative analysis and the step-by-step nature of computer software. The *Five-Level QDA* method is a way of managing this contradiction.

Over two decades of teaching, we saw that the *Five-Level QDA* approach is most effectively learned when the principles come first and hands-on use of the software comes last. Many of our students say they prefer learning by doing from the outset, but our experience has been that this does not work—beginning with hands-on learning unconsciously establishes a step-by-step software mind-set. We delayed opening the computers for hands-on learning until later and later in the workshops, and our participants quickly realized the benefit of this approach (Silver & Woolf, 2015). And that is what we do in this book.

A natural reason to prefer immediate hands-on learning is the misunderstanding that some ATLAS.ti features are basic and some are advanced, so that it makes sense to first jump into the basic features hands-on and later move on to learning more advanced features if they seem to be needed. We have noticed that qualitative researchers tend to humility and assume that their own projects are "basic" and only call for "basic" software features—only other people's projects are "advanced" and call for "advanced" software features. Distinguishing between basic and advanced features is neither true nor helpful. In reality all the features taken together are like a single palette containing all the colors that a painter has available to use. For any particular painting, some colors would be used and others not. But at the outset you still need *all* the colors to be known and available. And just as there are straightforward and more sophisticated ways to use all the paints on a palette, there are straightforward and sophisticated ways to use *all* the software features.

In summary, we do not begin right away with hands-on learning of "basic" features of the program and move on to the "advanced." We instead adopt a layered approach, moving from abstract to concrete learning, beginning with the principles of the *Five-Level QDA* method in Part 1, moving on to the application of those principles in Part 2, and finally to hands-on learning in Part 3. Each layer is a prerequisite for making sense of the next and takes for granted all that comes before. We therefore appeal to your patience in moving through the chapters in the sequence presented.

Learning to Operate ATLAS.ti

We mentioned earlier that this book is not about learning the basics of operating ATLAS.ti. You may wonder how and when you are supposed to learn to operate the program.

Because the *Five-Level QDA* method sits between research methods and software operations, use of the method requires that you know your research methodology and how to mechanically operate the software. If you already use ATLAS.ti and are familiar with its features, you are ready to learn to use it in a more powerful way. If you are not yet familiar with the program, the best time to gain that skill is immediately after reading Chapter 5 in Part 2 of this book.

Learning to operate ATLAS.ti is best accomplished in two phases. First is understanding how the program has been designed and how it works. We call this the architecture of the program. It is a great advantage to understand this before learning hands-on operation. The second phase is hands-on experience of manipulating or operating the software, including how to manage the computer files, open and use the various windows, locate menus and buttons, enter information, and so on.

The first phase is ideal to present in narrative form in a book. We teach this in Chapter 5. This chapter thoroughly explains the architecture of ATLAS.ti—the design of the program and the intended purpose of each of its features. We also provide short orientation videos on the companion website to make the abstract instruction in Chapter 5 concrete. These videos are only for orientation purposes and do not comprise hands-on instruction in operating the program.

Learning to operate ATLAS.ti is independent of learning the *Five-Level QDA* method. We recommend face-to-face instruction, online webinars, or online videos for learning to operate the program. ATLAS.ti is updated frequently and automatically with bug fixes and new and improved ways to carry out tasks, and so face-to-face or online instruction ensures you will be seeing the exact same, most recently updated version of the software that also appears on your own computer screen. We therefore invite you after reading about the architecture of the program in Chapter 5 to take advantage of the numerous free online resources or fee-based face-to-face workshops offered by the ATLAS.ti developer at www.atlasti.com. This site also provides an up-to-date listing of independent training companies offering their own courses. These learning resources vary in their approach to using ATLAS.ti for qualitative analysis, but all include the basic skills of operating the software, which is all that is needed as a companion to this book.

Working in Teams

Conducting research in teams is very different from researching alone. Team research adds two new tasks: deciding *who does what* and on that basis deciding *how each team members' contributions will be integrated*. These are significant decisions for the successful progress of a project. But they do not affect how each team member harnesses ATLAS.ti powerfully using the *Five-Level QDA* method, because ATLAS.ti is not a multiuser program. Each team member works independently in ATLAS.ti on their own assigned analytic tasks, just as if they were working on a solo research project. Then periodically each team member's work is merged together in ATLAS.ti with the other team members' work. This task is unrelated to *Five-Level QDA* principles, but it does affect how ATLAS.ti is used. We discuss *who does what* in Chapter 4 and the technical aspects of *integrating team members' work* in Chapter 5.

A Roadmap Through the Book

This book has three parts. Each part is a layer of learning that assumes knowledge of what has been covered in the prior layers. Part I covers all the *Five-Level QDA* principles. Part II illustrates the practical mechanics of the method in preparation for hands-on practice. Part III provides full-case and mini-case illustrations of real-world research projects. These cases are demonstrated in videos on the companion website (www.routledgetextbooks.com/textbooks/5LQDA).

Part I—The Principles of the Five-Level QDA *Method*

Part I sets the stage for what is to come with an explanation of the principles behind the *Five-Level QDA* method and a description of each of the five levels. Chapter 1 begins with the core principle, the difference between strategies and tactics. We then explain why there is a contradiction between the nature of the analytic strategies of a qualitative analysis and the nature of the software tactics that we use to accomplish the strategies. There is more than one way to reconcile this contradiction, and we contrast three approaches that we call One-Level QDA (which involves not addressing the contradiction), Three-Level QDA (which involves introducing a compromise), and our own preferred approach, the *Five-Level QDA* method, which involves going beyond, or transcending, the contradiction by keeping the strategies and tactics distinct and separate and "translating" back and forth between them.

Chapter 2 focuses on Levels 1 and 2, which are concerned with the strategies. This means the objectives or research questions of a project and the analytic plan to fulfill the objectives. This is the area of research methods, and this book does not teach research methods. But because clear, coherent strategies are an essential prerequisite to successfully putting the *Five-Level QDA* method into practice, we discuss these areas in some detail so that you know what is needed to write clear, coherent objectives, to select a methodology, and to develop an analytic plan. We also suggest resources for further guidance in these areas.

Chapter 3 focuses on Levels 3, 4, and 5, the mechanics of translating between analytic strategies and software tactics. This leads to operating the software in either a straightforward or a more sophisticated way in order to accomplish each analytic task. Our layered approach to learning requires the complete exposition of all five levels before moving on to describing the architecture of ATLAS.ti in terms of these principles. We therefore illustrate the process of translation at this early stage using an everyday activity rather than an ATLAS.ti research project. This also serves to focus attention on the translation process rather than the specifics of a research project. The situation changes in Parts II and III, and all further illustrations are in terms of real-world research projects.

Part II—The **Five-Level QDA** *Method in Practice*

Part II describes the architecture of ATLAS.ti and provides in-depth instruction in the mechanics of the *Five-Level QDA* translation process.

Chapter 4 is a short orientation to ATLAS.ti. If you have recently upgraded to Version 8 or plan to upgrade soon, we are happy to report that even though Version 8 has been entirely redesigned to conform to a more modern screen design and operation, the basic functions of the program have not changed and do not need to be relearned. This chapter also introduces the other ATLAS.ti products: ATLAS.ti for Mac and ATLAS.ti Mobile.

Chapter 4 also contrasts the use of ATLAS.ti by a sole researcher or by a member of a research team. Chapter 4 discusses the human side of working in a team—*who does what.*

Chapter 5 introduces the design or architecture of ATLAS.ti in terms of *Five-Level QDA* principles. This means focusing on what we call ATLAS.ti's *components* rather than its *features.* Focusing on components is a much simpler way to describe how the program works, and components play a significant role in the *Five-Level QDA* translation process. This chapter takes each component in turn and describes its purpose and how it works. Many users of ATLAS.ti are not aware of much of this information, and it is often the missing link in a researcher's understanding of how best to take advantage of the software. This is more important than learning how to operate the program— what buttons to click and which menu items to use. We provide *Component Orientation* video demonstrations of each component on the companion website, but we do not provide complete training in operating ATLAS.ti in the book. Chapter 5 also deals with the technical issues of working in teams—*integrating team members' work.*

If you are not already familiar with operating ATLAS.ti, we indicate in Chapter 5 that this is the time to learn to operate the program by taking advantage of either the free or fee-based workshops offered by the software developers and independent training companies.

Chapter 6 builds on all the earlier layers of understanding about the translation of strategies into tactics. This chapter describes and illustrates the mechanics of translation in a practical manner in terms of real-world research tasks. Following Chapter 6 you will be ready to learn from the case illustrations and video demonstrations of the translation process in Part III and conduct your own project using *Five-Level QDA* principles.

Part III—Case Illustrations

According to educational researchers, people learn best in the context of doing something personally meaningful, which facilitates the *transfer* of what they have learned in one context to their own, very different context (Merriam & Leahy, 2005). Learning through real-world activities is perhaps the best approach to making learning personally meaningful (Woolf & Quinn, 2009). Because of the great variety of qualitative methodologies, styles of analysis, research contexts, and disciplines, we illustrate a wide variety of case illustrations to serve as analogies to transfer to your own projects. The variety is also intended to emphasize that there is no "correct" way to use ATLAS.ti.

Chapter 7 is an orientation to the case illustrations and how to access the accompanying video demonstrations on the companion website. These are case illustrations, not case studies. A case study is concerned with the *content* of a case. Our case illustrations illustrate the *Five-Level QDA process*, and so we focus on how ATLAS.ti was harnessed rather than on the content or conclusions of the studies. We provide two sets of case illustrations—full cases and mini-cases.

For the full cases we have chosen two research studies. The first is a more straightforward project. This serves as a starting point for those with little or no experience in qualitative research or for those with no experience in using ATLAS.ti. The second is a more sophisticated project. This is intended for those who already have experience in both qualitative research and ATLAS.ti and as a second step of learning for those who have watched the videos of the first full case. Both projects are described in full in Chapters 8 and 9 in a standard *Five-Level QDA* format. Chapter 8 is a literature review for a PhD dissertation, contributed by Elizabeth Pope at the University of Georgia. Chapter 9 is a discourse analysis study contributed by Dr. Trena Paulus, Professor of Qualitative Research Methods and Interdisciplinary Qualitative Studies at the University of Georgia, and Dr. Mary Alice Varga, University of West Georgia. An important feature of the two full cases is that the analysis process is not sanitized to save space, as in a journal article. Rather, they include the detours and messiness that are part and parcel of real-world qualitative analysis. The objective is to illustrate how an ATLAS.ti project actually progresses.

No two projects can illustrate all uses of ATLAS.ti. We have therefore included a variety of mini-cases to illustrate additional or unusual uses of ATLAS.ti not illustrated in the two full cases. The mini-cases are described in an abbreviated *Five-Level QDA* format and are available for download on the companion website.

Both the full cases and the mini-cases have accompanying video demonstrations on the companion website, described in the next section.

The Companion Website

The companion website (www.routledgetextbooks.com/textbooks/5LQDA) contains the three sets of video demonstrations—*Component Orientation* videos, *Case Illustration* videos, and *Harnessing Components* videos.

The *Component Orientation* videos provide a concrete orientation to each component as a supplement to the instruction in Chapter 5. These videos assume that you have read the associated section in Chapter 5 that describes that component, as they are not intended as meaningful standalone instruction. Prompts in the text suggest the most helpful time to view these videos.

The *Case Illustration* videos demonstrate the full-case illustrations in order to show the progress of real-world projects that use ATLAS.ti, and include videos that demonstrate how selected analytic tasks were fulfilled using ATLAS.ti. Videos of the more sophisticated full-case in Chapter 9 include dialogue with the case contributor about the pros and cons of alternative ways in which ATLAS.ti could have been harnessed.

The *Harnessing Components* videos are the culmination of the instruction in this book. They contain a variety of demonstrations of the translation of individual analytic tasks and focus on the contrasting ways that components can be harnessed. These videos assume knowledge of the entire *Five-Level QDA* process contained in Parts I and II, and they assume that the videos for at least one of the two full-case illustrations have been viewed.

To register and log in to the companion website go to www.routledgetextbooks.com/textbooks/5LQDA and follow the on-screen instructions.

We hope you enjoy the book!

References

Bazeley, P., & Jackson, K. (2013). *Qualitative analysis with NVivo* (2nd ed.). Thousand Oaks: Sage.
di Gregorio, S., & Davidson, J. (2008). *Qualitative research design for software users*. Maidenhead, UK: McGraw Hill/Open University Press.
Fielding, N., & Lee, R. M. (Eds.). (1991). *Computing for qualitative research*. London: Sage.
Friese, S. (2014). *Qualitative analysis with ATLAS.ti* (2nd ed.). Thousand Oaks, CA: Sage.

Merriam, S. B., & Leahy, B. (2005). Learning transfer: A review of the research in adult education and training. *PAACE Journal of Lifelong Learning*, 14(1), 1–24.

Paulus, T. M., Lester, J. N., & Dempster, P. G. (2014). *Digital tools for qualitative research*. Thousand Oaks, CA: Sage.

Silver, C., & Lewins, A. (2014). *Using software in qualitative research: A step-by-step guide* (2nd ed.). Thousand Oaks, CA: Sage.

Silver, C., & Woolf, N. H. (2015). From guided instruction to facilitation of learning: The development of *Five-Level QDA* as a CAQDAS pedagogy that explicates the practices of expert users. *International Journal of Social Research Methodology*, 18(5), 527–543.

Sternberg, R. J., & Frensch, P. A. (1992). On being an expert: A cost-benefit analysis. In R. Hoffman (Ed.), *The psychology of expertise* (pp. 191–203). New York: Springer-Verlag.

Woolf, N. H., & Quinn, J. (2009). Learners' perceptions of instructional design practice in a situated learning activity. *Educational Technology Research & Development*, 57(1), 25–43.

PART I

The Principles of the *Five-Level* QDA Method

Mastering the *Five-Level QDA* method means first learning the principles before hands-on use of the software. Part I contains all the principles. Chapter 1 lays the groundwork with the central principle—the contradiction between strategies and tactics when using ATLAS.ti to conduct qualitative analysis and the alternative ways to reconcile the contradiction. Chapters 2 and 3 flesh out each of the five levels. Chapter 2 deals with the first two levels of strategy: the objectives of a research project and the analytic plan to fulfill it. Chapter 3 deals with translating those strategies into the tactics of software operations.

1

STRATEGIES AND TACTICS

This chapter describes the principles behind our approach to harnessing ATLAS.ti powerfully. The central issue is the contradiction between the nature of qualitative analysis and the nature of software used to conduct the analysis. The way these contradictions are reconciled determines the approach to harnessing the software. Experienced researchers have learned to reconcile these contradictions unconsciously, but our intention is to make this transparent in order to facilitate learning. In this chapter we compare three possible approaches to reconciling the contradiction in order to highlight the reasons why this book takes the approach that it does.

A word about the illustrations used in this chapter. Because of the need to discuss the principles before we can demonstrate or provide hands-on instruction in ATLAS.ti, we use analogies in this chapter that have nothing to do with qualitative research but refer to everyday experiences we can all relate to. The variety of qualitative methodologies is so great that a single example of research would risk misleading you if you are using a different approach, and it would be cumbersome to offer multiple illustrations at this early stage. Bear with us—we will soon get on to using illustrations from real-world research projects.

The Contradictions Between Strategies and Tactics

This section describes how the nature of qualitative analysis is contradictory to the nature of software. Recognizing this contradiction is the first step in learning to harness ATLAS.ti powerfully.

Over many years of teaching we have tried to get to the bottom of what holds people up from quickly learning to harness ATLAS.ti powerfully. Our conclusion lies in the difference between strategies and tactics. They are often confused with one another or thought of as two ways to say the same thing. Understanding the relationship between strategies and tactics is the key to harnessing ATLAS.ti powerfully.

In any endeavor, strategies refer to *what you plan to do*, and tactics refer to *how you plan to do it*. It makes sense to *first* be clear about what you plan to do and *then* to be clear about how you plan to do it, but often people start with the tactics and hope for the best. A good example is pruning a fruit tree, which requires finding the right tool and then cutting the branches. If the only tools in the shed are a tree lopper and some shears, you may choose the shears and start cutting, but give up when you reach branches that are too thick near the trunk. Next year the results may be disappointing if you were hoping to encourage healthy growth and maximize the number of large, juicy apples. You then decide to read up on how an apple tree should be pruned—the strategies—rather than just start cutting again—the tactics—and you discover there are very different pruning strategies for apple trees of different varieties, ages, and states of health. Sometimes you might cut back whole branches, trim the length of others, remove shoots, and so on. Once the strategies have been decided, the best tool can be selected for each task, whether saw, shears, or small clippers, and no task is particularly difficult because the tactics fit the strategies. The moral is that strategies and tactics are different in nature, and the tactics are made to fit the strategies, not the other way around.

In qualitative research the strategies—*what you plan to do*—are matters like deciding the purpose of the study, determining what kind of data will be required, and choosing methods for analyzing the data. Each of these areas calls for tactics to be considered and put into effect, but the strategies are largely independent of whether the tactics are going to be highlighter pens, general-purpose software like Microsoft Word or Excel, or special-purpose software like ATLAS.ti. Our contention is that when using software to conduct a qualitative analysis, the underlying nature of the strategies is contradictory to the underlying nature of the tactics used to fulfill them.

The high-stakes area of computer security, such as for online banking, provides an example of contradictory strategies and tactics. Successfully encrypting your password and financial information as it moves around the Internet so that it is safe from prying eyes requires the computer to generate random numbers. This is what needs to happen—the strategy. However, computers are deterministic, meaning that they can only follow rules and procedures, referred to as algorithms, which always give the same answer to the same question. Computers cannot function in a truly random way and cannot generate truly random numbers. They can only generate pseudo-random numbers that have an underlying pattern, even though this is not discernible by the average person or computer program. So, the tactics available do not fit the needs of the strategy.

How do computer security people deal with this contradiction between the nature of what they want to do and the nature of the software with which they want to do it? First, they are consciously aware of the issue and do not ignore it. Second, they have decided that for most uses the encryption provided by even pseudo-random numbers provides adequate security. They do not need to find a way to generate truly random numbers. They have reconciled the contradiction between the need for random numbers and the nonrandom nature of computers with a conscious compromise: pseudo-random numbers are good enough (Rubin, 2011).

A similar situation arises when using software in qualitative research, and we are certainly not the first to wonder how software can be used successfully for such an open-ended process as qualitative analysis (e.g., Gilbert, Jackson, & di Gregorio, 2014; Tesch, 1990). Everything about a computer program has been predetermined by its developers to work in the same standard way, regardless of the purpose a researcher has in mind for using the software. Choosing an option from a menu or clicking on a button always has the same predetermined effect, and it is natural to assume that the features of the software are independent and are intended to be used one at a time for their most apparent purpose: in other words, that there must be a correct way to use the software in every analysis. In fact many researchers who are experienced with ATLAS.ti come to our workshops to ensure that they are using the software "correctly." But most kinds of qualitative analysis do not proceed in a predetermined way, following the same steps in the same sequence, and so ATLAS.ti is not used in remotely the same way in every project, and certainly not in a "correct" way.

Qualitative projects are, to varying degrees, *iterative* and *emergent*, with unique strategies evolving from moment to moment as the analysis unfolds. *Iterative* refers to the continual reconsideration of what is being done in light of what has just been done and what is anticipated to come next so that the individual parts of a qualitative analysis develop together as a whole. In an *emergent* system the whole is more than the sum of the parts, but the qualities of the whole are not predictable from the parts (Kauffman, 1995). The results or findings of a whole qualitative research project therefore

STRATEGIES
what you plan to do

The nature of qualitative data analysis is to varying degrees iterative and emergent

The outcome of any analytic task does not always have a predictable effect on the next step of data analysis

...are different
in nature from...

TACTICS
how you plan to do it

The nature of computer software is cut-and-dried

The outcome of any software operation—such as selecting a menu item or clicking on a button—is fully predictable in advance

FIGURE 1.1   The contradictory nature of qualitative data analysis and computer software

emerge as the parts develop in an iterative manner. Although many qualitative research projects are only somewhat iterative or emergent, many are highly so, and in later chapters the case illustrations of more or less iterative and emergent types of projects will make these qualities come to life.

The contradictions between the predetermined and step-by-step processes of software, which we refer to simply as *cut and dried*, and the iterative and emergent processes of qualitative analysis that we refer to simply as *emergent* are illustrated in Figure 1.1. Box 1.1 provides a deeper look into the relationship between cut-and-dried and emergent processes.

BOX 1.1 A DEEPER LOOK: CUT-AND-DRIED VERSUS EMERGENT PROCESSES

One way to think about the contrast between the cut-and-dried nature of computer software and the emergent nature of qualitative data analysis is by considering the contrast between *well-structured* and *ill-structured* activities more generally. These two kinds of activities are at opposite ends of a spectrum and can be considered contradictory. Taking an intentional approach to reconciling the contradiction is the rationale for the *Five-Level QDA* method.

Well-Structured Activities

A structure is an arrangement of the parts of something. Everything—a building, a problem to be solved, a society, a qualitative analysis—has a structure. One characteristic of structure common to all these examples is the *degree* of structure that something has. Churchman (1971) proposed two main classes of problems or activities: well structured and ill structured. In well-structured activities everything is known: there are clear goals, a single correct outcome or purpose, and clear criteria for knowing when the activity is successful or complete. It is a matter of going through a process or a series of steps to complete the activity. Chess is a good example. It is challenging to play well, but everything about it is well structured: how each piece moves, a single result, and a single way of knowing who has won—by the capture of the opposing king. It is therefore amenable to being represented by algorithms, or step-by-step procedures, which explains why computers do it so well.

Computer software is an example of a well-structured domain. Every aspect about using it is definite and always works in the same way (unless there is a bug in the program, but that is a different matter). For example, if you wish to copy and paste in Microsoft Word, selecting some text and pressing the Copy button will always reliably copy those lines of text. Pressing the Paste button at a different location will always reliably paste in the exact same lines. Operating computer software is a step-by-step activity predetermined by the software developer, like following a recipe. And like chess, it is not necessarily easy to learn or use. But each act of using it is a well-structured activity.

Most important is the mind-set involved in using software. Cognitive psychologists have proposed that we create *schema*—mental templates—whenever we do an activity so that next time we meet a similar set of circumstances we have a preorganized set of expectations and blank mental *slots* already prepared to quickly interpret the new situation in terms of our previous experience of a similar activity (Shank & Abelson, 1977). Most people have been using computer software for quite a while and have what we call a well-developed "software schema." When using software we have expectations that everything we do with the program follows a step-by-step procedure, with each task broken down into a set of clear-cut steps that will work in the same way each time. There is nothing iterative about using software because the outcome of an action is always the same. There is nothing emergent about using software because we know what that outcome will be in advance. The "software schema" or mind-set we have all developed sets up a high expectation for an extremely well-structured activity.

Ill-Structured Activities

Activities that lack structure are quite different. Goals are vague, there is incomplete information available, there are many possible outcomes or problem solutions, and there are many possible criteria for knowing if the activity is complete or the problem solved. They are not called ill structured because there is anything wrong with them, they just lack structure—they are uncertain, and information is incomplete in various ways. For example, "solving for x in an algebraic equation" is a well-structured activity, but "judging the adequacy of a theoretical proposition" is ill structured (King & Kitchener, 2004, p. 11). Reitman (1964) and Simon (1973) conducted the pioneering work on how people deal with the ill-structured activities that make up most of everyday life, and Jonassen (1997) summarized the major characteristics of all ill-structured problems. King and Kitchener (2004) developed a program for assessing how people respond to ill-structured problems, focusing on the cognitive skills necessary to work successfully in ill-structured domains. They described seven levels of development of a skill they call "reflective judgment."

Qualitative analysis is certainly an ill-structured activity according to the descriptions of these scholars. Reitman (1964) described how well-structured and ill-structured problems form a continuum, which is helpful when thinking about the degree of emergence in a qualitative research methodology. Schön (1983) described professional practice in many fields as an ill-structured design skill in which a "reflective practitioner . . . must make sense of an uncertain situation that initially makes no sense . . . we *name* the things to which we will attend and *frame* the context in which we will attend to them (p. 40, italics in original). Schön (1983) was describing professional practice generally, but he could be describing qualitative analysis. In our field no piece of data has a single correct meaning; no research question has a single, correct finding; and there is no single criterion to evaluate findings that have been proposed or an obvious ending point at which the analysis is complete.

The consequences of the ill structure of qualitative analysis are to require varying degrees of iteration and emergence, in contradiction to the step-by-step, recipe-like procedures of well-structured computer software. *Iteration*, with its reconsideration and modification of what we had done previously in the light of new perspectives, leads to an evolving relationship between the developing parts—the individual analytic tasks we undertake and their outcomes—and the whole—the overall picture that emerges with each iterative adjustment of one or more or the parts, a process sometimes called entering the *hermeneutic circle* (Packer & Addison, 1989). This is in contradiction to the relationship of parts and wholes in the well-structured nature of computer software, in which describing the whole adds nothing new to describing the individual parts of the whole. To say "cut-and-paste" is functionally identical to saying "select text, copy, move cursor, paste." *Emergence*, a much-abused term that is often used for anything vaguely qualitative, does have a specific meaning regarding parts and wholes. In general, emergence refers to the properties of any complex system (Kauffman, 1995). A system is a general term for any collection of things that are related to one another in some way—the bones in a body, the members of an organization, the atoms in a molecule, the concepts in a qualitative analysis are all systems. When the number of parts in a system and their interconnections reach a certain point, the system is called complex and has emergent qualities in which the whole has characteristics not predictable for any of the parts. Each qualitative project is emergent to greatly different degrees, from very little to a great deal, depending on the guiding methodology and on practical matters such as the time available to bring a project to conclusion.

In summary, the well-structured features of computer software—predetermined and step-by-step—are at the opposite end of Reitman's (1964) spectrum of ill structure from the iterative and emergent features of qualitative analysis. An iterative process cannot be accomplished in a step-by-step fashion, and a step-by-step process cannot be emergent. It is in this sense that the nature of computer software and the nature of qualitative analysis are contradictory, and when dealing with contradictory circumstances, some resolution has to occur to be able to function effectively. Intentionally deciding what approach to take in the face of these contradictions is the underlying principle of this book.

Contradictory strategies and tactics suggest various possible solutions. Imagine you are an architect with a set of building blocks that come in standard shapes and sizes: perhaps square bricks and rectangular bricks with tongues and grooves that fit together in predetermined ways. Some construction projects in this imaginary world might call for exactly these shaped bricks stacked up in various ways just as the tongues and grooves provide for. But many projects might not. They might include circular designs or call for bricks that stack together differently from how the predetermined tongues and grooves connect. An expert architect would find a way to make the standard bricks work; she would overcome the apparent inconsistency between the angular shape of the bricks and the circular designs. A novice architect is more likely to decide that a circular building is impossible to design with these bricks, or she may refuse to use bricks at all, as they are simply the wrong shape. Remember these architects: we'll come back to them.

In qualitative analysis such contradictions between strategies and tactics are in no way a barrier to harnessing ATLAS.ti powerfully. Most qualitative researchers neither want nor expect the cut-and-dried operations of the program—the tactics—to play a role in the emergent strategies of the analysis or to contribute to the interpretive process. It is commonly said that in qualitative research the instrument of research is the mind of the researcher, in which an entire lifetime of accumulated human experience and learning is brought to bear on the interpretation of data in a systematic and justifiable manner. In the language of the *Five-Level QDA* method, the *strategy* levels of qualitative methods are fundamentally the province of the researcher's mind. In contrast, the mechanical levels of *tactics* are the province of the cut-and-dried software operations. The researcher decides how to harness the tactics in the service of her strategies, and developing this skill is the focus of this book. No software program remotely approximates the sophistication of the human brain in finding meaning in a body of data—at least not yet—and the potential misuse of rudimentary automated features that may be introduced in the future are concerning. But that is not the concern of this book.

Different Ways to Reconcile Contradictions

This section describes three different ways to reconcile the contradiction between the nature of qualitative analysis and the nature of software. Each way leads to a different approach to using software for qualitative analysis.

When two things are contradictory, like darkness and light, each one precludes the other: on the face of it you cannot have both. There is more than one way to deal with such a contradiction: first, by avoiding the contradiction; second, by compromising; or third, by going beyond or transcending the contradiction. We begin with a discussion of the first two ways as a context for describing why we choose the third way.

The first way is simply to avoid the contradiction—for example, by ignoring the darkness and stumbling around, knocking things over in the middle of the night on the way to the bathroom. A second way is to find a compromise between the contradictory things, which partially satisfies each one. Perhaps a door can be opened to let in a sliver of moonlight: not enough light to read or do anything useful, but just enough to avoid knocking things over, yet still dark enough to let others sleep. A workable compromise. In situations of contradictory demands, this might be the best we can hope for, a compromise that works well enough, as it did for the computer security engineers who decided that pseudo-random numbers were good enough for their data encryption process.

A third way is to transcend the contradiction so that you do not have to sacrifice the full integrity of either side. This is generally accomplished by seeing the situation in a larger context so that the contradiction is no longer there. The invention of night-vision goggles allowed night to be day. Before this invention, darkness and light referred only to the frequencies of light visible to humans, which are only a small portion of the electromagnetic spectrum. When this limited perspective is expanded to include the much higher (ultraviolet) and much lower (infrared) frequencies that humans cannot see unaided but which can be seen through the goggles, the contradiction between darkness and light is transcended and no longer exists.

Similarly, these different ways to deal with the contradiction between our strategies and tactics lead to different approaches to using ATLAS.ti. Each of the three ways differs regarding what happens in between the two extremes, in the middle area between the strategies (the emergent qualitative analysis) and the tactics (the cut-and-dried features of the software). The first approach of avoiding the contradiction between qualitative analysis and software does not require anything in the middle, because there is no middle: the situation is treated as a single, unproblematic task of *doing-qualitative-data-analysis-with-software*. We call this One-Level QDA. The second approach recognizes that there is indeed a difference between qualitative analysis methods and the software features, and it addresses the difference by creating an analytic process in the middle that becomes a compromise between the emergent nature of qualitative analysis and the cut-and-dried software features. This leads to three separate processes, and so we call this approach Three-Level QDA. The final approach, which we take in this book, transcends the contradiction in order to see it in a larger context. We call this approach the *Five-Level QDA* method. Before saying why we call it *Five-Level QDA*, it is necessary to describe One-Level QDA and Three-Level QDA a little more fully in order that you can appreciate why it is well worth the effort to learn the principles of the *Five-Level QDA* method.

One-Level QDA

Sadly, many people do not harness ATLAS.ti powerfully. Many experienced researchers never try CAQDAS packages at all, having read the unwarranted concerns in the academic literature. For example, they fear that using these programs will impose a particular style of qualitative analysis, or distance the researcher from the data, or that they are a kind of qualitative equivalent to statistical analysis programs that will take over or do the analysis. These largely theoretical concerns were written about in the 1980s or 1990s when few researchers had gained experience in using these programs. Several authors have convincingly refuted these concerns (e.g., Davidson & di Gregorio, 2011; Gilbert, 2002; Gilbert et al., 2014; Jackson, 2017; Nathan & Jackson, 2006).

Many researchers who do embrace the use of software use it superficially. A common approach is to use CAQDAS packages for the initial straightforward stages of a project, but then switch to another program, often Microsoft Word or Excel, or even back to paper and pencil, to complete the analysis (e.g., Ose, 2016). Another approach is to continue using ATLAS.ti in a simplistic or step-by-step way, which can have the effect of suppressing some of the emergent aspects of the analysis. Using ATLAS.ti in a superficial way may be intentional as part of a larger plan for conducting a research project. But more commonly this superficial use is not intentional but an unconscious avoidance of the contradiction between the emergent nature of qualitative analysis and the cut-and-dried nature of software. Avoiding or denying a contradiction is particularly easy for humans—we have a remarkable ability to maintain contradictory ideas at the same time without feeling the need for any resolution (Fitzgerald, 1945, p. 13; Kurzweil, 2012, p. 197). This is helpful in many situations, especially humor, which relies on seeing contradictory ideas occupying the same space (Koestler, 1964).

It's true that many qualitative researchers have a good sense of humor, but nevertheless, avoiding or leaving unresolved the contradictions surrounding the use of software in qualitative analysis does not lead to harnessing ATLAS.ti powerfully. Avoiding the inherent contradictions amounts to considering qualitative analysis and the operations of software as a single process. That means that the strategies and tactics are thought of as a single activity. We could call that *what-you-plan-to-do-and-how-you-plan-to-do-it*, or as we refer to it, One-Level QDA. Strategies and tactics are not differentiated, and if they do not match in the mind of the researcher, then the process grinds to a halt.

In the world of standardized bricks a circular building is simply impossible to design with the available bricks. If only square and rectangular bricks were available, then square and rectangular buildings could be designed; if a circular building is required, then curved bricks must be provided. This is not the reality of expert architects, who find a way to resolve these differences. We now consider two different approaches to resolving these differences in qualitative analysis.

Three-Level QDA

One approach to handling the incompatibility between cut-and-dried software and the emergent nature of qualitative analysis is to organize the analysis into a more structured set of tasks in order to make them more amenable to executing on a computer, a kind of compromise. This is in some ways the most natural thing to do, so we need to dwell on the consequences of this approach in order to describe why we take the approach that we do.

Everyday life requires compromises of all kinds, and this is generally considered a good thing. Neither side gets everything they want, but enough that both sides can live with it. Compromising allows people with very different outlooks to peacefully live together. But the suitability of a compromise depends on the context.

In the earlier example of a darkened bedroom in the middle of the night, partially satisfying each side of the contradiction by opening the door just a little avoided the need to choose between either extreme, complete darkness or complete light—a good thing in this example, as the compromise in the middle is far better than either extreme pole. But in other contexts a compromise that does not fully satisfy either pole may be *less* desirable than choosing between them, and is thus a bad thing. Here's a very different example about a compromise between darkness and light.

A few minutes into the very funny play *Black Comedy* (Shaffer, 1967), there is an electrical short circuit and the action continues in total darkness for most of the play, until near the end when the electricity is restored and it finishes in normal light. That is the plot of the play. In reality, in the theater, there is a reversed lighting scheme. To the audience, the play opens in total darkness but the actors are performing (invisibly to us) as if they are in normal light. When the short circuit happens in the play, the stage lights come on, so we can finally see what is happening on stage. But the actors are acting as if they have now been plunged into total darkness, and they continue acting as if in the dark, which we see under normal lighting. It's very funny. Then towards the end when the electricity is supposedly restored in the play, the stage lights go off again, while the actors finish up the play as if in normal light, we—and they—can see nothing!

What if the theater director had said that this was too complicated and decided to scrap the reverse lighting? According to such a director, at one extreme the reverse lighting is too challenging for the actors to convincingly pull off, but the other extreme of normal lighting—dark on stage when it is dark in the play and light on stage when it is light in the play—eliminates the humor. Neither extreme is good, so perhaps very dim light throughout would be a workable compromise? The audience would get the general idea that the main part of the play is supposedly taking place in pitch blackness, because the light would be very dim, but the actors would have enough light to be able to see their way around the stage. And when the action was supposedly in full light, rather than the stage being completely dark, there would be at least some light for the audience to watch how the actors were managing to act out in the play in darkness, although it wouldn't be complete darkness but very dim light. Not perfect, but a workable compromise.

Would this be better than either of the poles of full light or full darkness? We hope you'll agree it would not be; the play would never have been the award-winning success it was if staged throughout in very dim light. In this context, a compromised, watered-down strategy of acting in very dim light that gives the idea of darkness to the audience is the worst choice. It leads to the unnecessary outcome that the play ceases to be funny.

Which context is more like using software for qualitative analysis? In the going-to-the-bathroom-at-night context, the compromise was not greatly inferior to either pole. Moving around in a sliver of moonlight is just slightly easier than in darkness—basically the same kind of activity; and if the sleepers are wakened by the sliver of moonlight they would likely get back to sleep pretty quickly in the almost darkness. But in *Black Comedy* the compromise of running the whole play in dim light would eliminate the plot and thus the humor, which is created by the inability to see anything in the dark. We suggest that qualitative analysis is more like *Black Comedy*, in which a compromise is not the best choice.

We refer to the addition of a compromise position between the analytic strategies of a qualitative analysis on one side and the software tactics to fulfill them in ATLAS.ti on the other side as

FIGURE 1.2 Three-Level QDA

Three-Level QDA. This is illustrated in Figure 1.2. What does Three-Level QDA look like in practice? The strategies—*what you plan to do*—are at a more abstract level, expressed in conceptual terms: *identifying kinds of leadership behaviors* in an organizational leadership study, *describing degrees of community support* in a community-based public health initiative, or whatever the project involves. The tactics—*how you plan to do it*—are necessarily at a more concrete level. If ATLAS.ti is used for the tactics, this will involve such things as using different colors on screen to represent different types of leadership that are being considered as possible candidate types of leadership or searching for different keywords to explore for possible examples of a kind of community support that is not yet clearly defined. At the strategy level of deciding *what you plan to do*, tasks such as these vary greatly. They vary in how definite or exploratory their purpose is or how settled or interim the result is expected to be, depending on the research methodology being used. In summary, they vary in how emergent the tasks are. Even if the tasks in your project are very different from the tasks in these examples, they will have a degree of emergence, or your projects would not be qualitative. However, at the tactics level these tasks become extremely cut and dried: select a color, find the instances of a word. At the tactics level there is a cut-and-dried way of thinking that is very different from an emergent way of thinking.

Taking a Three-Level QDA approach means bridging this chasm in ways of thinking with a workable compromise between thinking in a fully emergent manner and thinking in a fully cut-and-dried manner. And just in the same way that the compromise of having very dim light throughout *Black Comedy* would spoil the basic rationale for its humor, a compromise is not the best approach for conducting qualitative analysis using ATLAS.ti. Here's what this Three-Level QDA thinking might look like in the example of *identifying kinds of leadership behaviors*.

First, the emergent way of thinking at the strategy level that you might write about in an analytic memo to yourself might be:

> If I understand my methods text correctly as it applies to my project, at this point in my analysis it wants me to read my interviews again. I'll be looking for signs of those leadership behaviors I have been reflecting on and name them in a conceptual way based on what the respondents actually say. That's the first step of a multistep conceptualizing process. Hmm. I think I'll start by looking for different types of leadership behaviors that are very different from one another and see where that gets me.

Looking ahead, it may well be that many steps down this process, the idea of "types of leadership" turns out to be a dead end. The reason is that you discover that the different so-called "types of leadership" you were naming are actually only subtly different manifestations of one of two main kinds of leadership already well understood—"transactional" rather than "transformational" leadership (e.g., Hartog, Muijen, & Koopman, 1997). Transformational leadership seeks to bring about major change, whereas transactional leadership focuses on promoting adherence to the current organizational goals and procedures. However, the various transactional leadership behaviors you discovered varied greatly depending on the size of the organization that the respondent works at, and so that became a very interesting new way forward. The idea of multiple "types of leadership" was ditched as a new direction emerged.

In contrast, the cut-and-dried way of thinking might go like this:

> I have already named and represented seven types of leadership in ATLAS.ti using seven different colors, which I then took several steps further in the software because certain software features made this easy and natural to do. Cancelling the idea of "types of leadership" is basically too late; they are already built in to the analysis as now represented in the software, and that is the path the analysis is taking, even though it doesn't quite fit what the respondents were saying.

This is very far from the ideal of qualitative research. Is there an alternative?

One alternative is a Three-Level QDA way of thinking—to adopt a compromise between the emergent and the cut-and-dried ways of thinking. For example, rather than adopting the suggested strategy in the methods textbook for the leadership study, it might be replaced with a more simple, general, and concrete approach that can be readily executed in the software: *identify how respondents talk about their leadership behaviors, gather together similar examples, represent each group in the software, and think of a way of working further with these groups of examples in ways the software provides*. This does not fully reflect the intentions of the methods text, and although it is not expressed in software terms, it can be directly executed in the software. It is a compromise. However, it is a compromise of the same kind as the very dim light in *Black Comedy*: it weakens the intentions of the methods text to the point that the analysis is no longer in the emergent spirit of qualitative research.

We are not suggesting that Three-Level QDA is a method of analysis that is proposed by any methods writers. It is rather a way of thinking about doing qualitative analysis with software that in our view should be guarded against. Although it may seem like the natural thing to do, our experience suggests that it leads to an unsatisfactory compromise. Texts that aim to assist qualitative researchers in using CAQDAS packages can be easily misinterpreted in the way described earlier. If a text you are using appears to be suggesting a generic, one-size-fits-all approach for conducting analysis, we suggest that you assume that you are misinterpreting the intentions of the writer and that you look for ways to take advantage of their advice that does not amount to a compromise between the emergent nature of your strategies and the cut-and-dried nature of the software.

Five-Level QDA

The key difference between Three-Level QDA and the *Five-Level QDA* method is what happens at the middle level, in between the strategies and the tactics. In our years of teaching and using ATLAS.ti for different kinds of projects, we became convinced that harnessing ATLAS.ti powerfully involves a process of *translation* between the emergent strategies of a qualitative analysis and the cut-and-dried tactics involved in using the software. When researchers harness ATLAS.ti successfully, translation is put into effect in a different way for every project by going back and forth between strategies and tactics without having to compromise either to match the nature of the other. This translation is a separate skill from research or analytical skills. It is the skill of *harnessing* the software rather than simply operating it. The translation process is in no way a complex skill; it is simply a separate skill that has to be recognized, learned, and put into practice.

The *Five-Level QDA* method amounts to transcending the contradictions between the nature of the strategies and the nature of the tactics by placing both in a larger context so that the contradiction between them is unproblematic. This is a standard way of dealing with contradictions that seek a "both/and" rather than an "either/or" solution. Placing them in a larger context means maintaining, distinguishing, and attending to each of the five levels in their own terms, according to their own nature. As a first introduction to the five levels, there are two levels of strategy and two levels of tactics, with an additional level of translation that comes between them.

The principles of the *Five-Level QDA* method developed gradually over many years of teaching and using CAQDAS packages, but its formulation in five formal and related levels is greatly informed by Edward Luttwak's description of five general levels of military strategy (Luttwak, 2001). Some qualitative researchers find military strategy a distasteful metaphor for qualitative data analysis, yet this is the one field in which the contradictions between strategies and tactics have been thought through in most detail. We do not need to dwell on the similarities between the levels of military strategy and qualitative analysis strategy, but we do wish to acknowledge Edward Luttwak's contribution to our thinking (Box 1.2 provides more information about Edward Luttwak's levels of strategy).

An important aspect of the *Five-Level QDA* method is that it is not something new. It is neither a new research method nor a new way of conducting qualitative analysis. It is our way of describing what expert users of ATLAS.ti already do, but generally unconsciously and automatically when harnessing ATLAS.ti through every phase of a project while remaining true throughout to the emergent spirit of qualitative research. Our aim is to make the process explicit so that the process of becoming an expert user can be sped up.

BOX 1.2 A DEEPER LOOK: EDWARD LUTTWAK'S FIVE LEVELS OF MILITARY STRATEGY

We knew that expert users of ATLAS.ti had learned to unconsciously keep separate their strategies from their tactics and to successfully move between them without having their emergent analytic strategies unduly influenced by their cut-and-dried software tactics. But we did not initially know how to unpack the black box of this expertise in order to help others do the same. Nick searched for guidance in other fields, but was mightily disappointed. Various books and articles encouragingly included strategy and tactics in the title, but then used the terms interchangeably as if synonyms, or discussed them separately without relating them together. He found only one field—military studies—that offered a helpful guide. This is the one field in which the contradictions between strategies and tactics have been thought through in detail, most notably by the military strategist Edward Luttwak.

Most writers on military strategy throughout history have prescribed strategic thinking relevant to the conditions and conflicts of their age (Luttwak, 2001, p. 267). Luttwak (2001) set out to describe universal principles of strategy that applied to any age or kind of conflict. Nick was amazed to find how the details of Luttwak's (2001) model so readily applied outside the domain of warfare. Luttwak (2001) identifies five inter-related levels of strategy, each with a different role and type of activity, that are uncannily analogous to the activities of a research project. At the most general level of military strategy are national goals and values—the level of *grand strategy*. Its various characteristics are closely analogous to the objectives and methodology of research projects, which we call Level 1 of the *Five-Level QDA* method. Luttwak's (2001) next level is *theater strategy*, the implementation of grand strategy in a specific, self-contained territory. The characteristics of theater strategy are highly analogous to the tasks of creating a specific analytic plan, our Level 2. For purposes of exposition it is now easiest to move to the end of the list. The fourth and fifth levels in Luttwak's (2001) model are the *technical* development of individual weapons, vehicles, and other equipment and their combined use in combat in *tactical units*. These are directly analogous to our Levels 4 and 5, the levels of selected and constructed software tools.

However, of greatest significance is the middle level between the two levels of strategy and the two levels of tactics. Luttwak (2001) calls this middle level the *operational level*. This is a coordinating level between strategies and tactics that is not directly involved in the activities of either. It is an abstract layer of activity consisting of adding or removing tactical units within a battle in response to the needs of the theater strategy. This is Luttwak's unique contribution, the identification of the separate "operational level of war" that is now a part of U.S. Army doctrine (Luttwak, n.d.). It is directly analogous to the abstract level of activity that we call translation, the additional skill that experienced qualitative researchers have unconsciously learned to use to manage the contradiction between their analytic strategies into their software tactics.

This overview is intended to give credit where credit is due, as these universal principles of strategy assisted greatly in our unpacking and describing what expert users of ATLAS.ti do. For more detailed information on the characteristics of Luttwak's (2001) five levels of strategy and their close analogy to the levels of the *Five-Level QDA* method, see Woolf (2014).

References

Churchman, C. W. (1971). *The design of inquiring systems: Basic concepts of systems and organization.* New York: Basic Books.

Davidson, J., & di Gregorio, S. (2011). Qualitative research and technology: In the midst of a revolution. In N. K. Denzin & Y. S. Lincoln (Eds.), *The SAGE handbook of qualitative research* (4th ed., pp. 627–643). Thousand Oaks: CA: Sage.

Fitzgerald, F. S. (1945). *The crack-up.* New York: James Laughlin.

Gilbert, L. S. (2002). Going the distance: 'Closeness' in qualitative data analysis software. *International Journal of Social Research Methodology,* 5(3), 215–228.

Gilbert, L. S., Jackson, K., & di Gregorio, S. (2014). Tools for analyzing qualitative data: The history and relevance of qualitative data analysis software. In J. M. Spector, M. D. Merrill, J. Elen, & M. J. Bishop (Eds.), *Handbook of research on educational communications and technology* (pp. 221–236). New York: Springer.

Hartog, D. N., Muijen, J. J., & Koopman, P. L. (1997). Transactional versus transformational leadership: An analysis of the MLQ. *Journal of Occupational and Organizational Psychology,* 70(1), 19–34.

Jackson, K. (2017). Chapter 10: Turning against each other in neoliberal times: The discourses of otherizing and how they threaten our scholarship. In N. K. Denzin & M. D. Giardina (Eds.), *Qualitative Inquiry in Neoliberal Times* (pp. 151-165). New York: Routledge.

Jonassen, D. H. (1997). Instructional design models for well-structured and ill-structured problem-solving learning outcomes. *Educational Technology Research & Development,* 45(1), 65–94.

Kauffman, S. (1995). *At home in the universe: The search for laws of self-organization and complexity.* New York: Oxford University Press.

King, P. M., & Kitchener, K. S. (2004). Reflective judgment: Theory and research on the development of epistemic assumptions through adulthood. *Educational Psychologist,* 39(1), 5–18.

Koestler, A. (1964). *The act of creation*. London: Hutchinson.

Kurzweil, R. (2012). *How to create a mind*. New York: Viking.

Luttwak, E. N. (n.d.). In Wikipedia. Retrieved from https://en.wikipedia.org/wiki/Edward_Luttwak, November 18, 2016.

Luttwak, E. N. (2001). *Strategy: The logic of peace and war* (2nd ed.). Cambridge, MA: Harvard University Press.

Nathan, M. J., & Jackson, K. (2006). Boolean classes and qualitative inquiry (WCER Working Paper No. 2006–3). Madison: University of Wisconsin-Madison, Wisconsin Center for Education Research. Retrieved from www.wcer.wisc.edu/publications/workingPapers/papers.php

Ose, S. O. (2016). Using Excel and Word to structure qualitative data. *Journal of Applied Social Science*, 10(2), 147–162.

Packer, M. J., & Addison, R. B. (1989). *Entering the circle: Hermeneutic investigation in psychology*. Albany, NY: SUNY Press.

Reitman, W. R. (1964). Heuristic decision procedures, open constraints, and the structure of ill-defined problems. In M. W. Shelly & G. L. Bryan (Eds.), *Human judgments and optimality* (pp. 282–315). New York: John Wiley & Sons.

Rubin, J. M. (2011). Can a computer generate a truly random number? *MIT School of Engineering: Ask an engineer*. Retrieved from http://engineering.mit.edu/ask/can-computer-generate-truly-random-number

Schön, D. A. (1983). *The reflective practitioner: How professionals think in action*. San Francisco: Jossey-Bass.

Shaffer, P. (1967). *Black comedy*. New York: Samuel French.

Shank, R. C., & Abelson, R. P. (1977). *Scripts, plans, goals, and understanding*. Hillsdale, NJ: Erlbaum.

Simon, H. A. (1973). The structure of ill-structured problems. *Artificial Intelligence*, 4, 181–201.

Tesch, R. (1990). *Qualitative research: Analysis types and software tools*. London: Falmer Press.

Woolf, N. H. (2014). Analytic strategies and analytic tactics. Keynote address at ATLAS.ti User Conference 2013: Fostering Dialog on Qualitative Methods, Technische Universität Berlin. doi:http://nbn-resolving.de/urn:nbn:de:kobv:83-opus4-44159

2

DEVELOPING OBJECTIVES AND ANALYTIC PLANS (LEVELS 1 AND 2)

This chapter describes the two levels of strategy in the *Five-Level QDA* method: Level 1, the objectives of a research project, and Level 2, the analytic plan for meeting those objectives. This book does not teach how to write objectives or research questions or how to select a methodology or develop an analytic plan. But because these are prerequisites for putting the *Five-Level QDA* method into practice at Level 3, we do go into some depth in this chapter about the principles behind what needs to be done at Levels 1 and 2, and we suggest resources for more practical guidance in these areas.

Dealing with five levels of a qualitative analysis is not as daunting as it might seem. The first two levels are the strategies, the last two levels the tactics, and the middle level translates between them. Translation simply means *transforming* the strategies into tactics. Later we take this further by showing what this transformation means in practice, but in this chapter we begin by introducing the principles behind just the first two levels, the strategy levels. Level 1 concerns the formulation of the objectives of a project, usually expressed as a research question and a research methodology. However, many people who use ATLAS.ti do not come from a formal research background and they express their objectives in a less formal way. But one way or another, expressing the objectives has to be the first step, as it is in any successful endeavor, and Level 2 concerns the development of a plan to fulfill these objectives. These two levels of strategy are the prerequisites for harnessing ATLAS.ti powerfully. In this chapter we introduce you to what is needed for Levels 1 and 2, and then we guide you to further resources that you can consult for accomplishing this, if necessary.

Level 2 results in identifying a series of specific analytic tasks to be accomplished. Looking ahead, in the next chapter we begin discussing Level 3, the level of translation. This means transforming the analytic tasks identified in Level 2 into software operations that can be carried out in ATLAS.ti—Levels 4 and 5.

Figure 2.1 lays out the five levels of activity in an orderly way, and we discuss these levels one by one. However, if the layout of Figure 2.1 gives the impression that a research project proceeds in an orderly, linear, step-by-step way in practice, be assured that this is not the case. Qualitative research is, to varying degrees, an emergent activity. The whole emerges out of a series of developing parts—meaning a series of developing analytic tasks. It does not proceed in a linear, step-by-step manner, but in an iterative, cyclical, unpredictable manner. Inevitably there are detours and a good amount of messiness as a qualitative research project progresses. This messiness is not always apparent when reading qualitative research articles. Space in academic journals is limited, and descriptions of the

Two Levels of Strategy >>>>> Translated To >>>>> Two Levels of Tactics				
Level 1	Level 2	Level 3	Level 4	Level 5
Objectives	Analytic plan	Translation	Selected tools	Constructed tools
The purpose and context of a project, usually expressed as research questions and a methodology	The conceptual framework and resulting analytic tasks	Translating from analytic tasks to software tools and translating the results back again	Straightforward choice of individual software operations	Sophisticated use of software by combining operations or performing them in a custom way

FIGURE 2.1   The five levels of the *Five-Level QDA* method

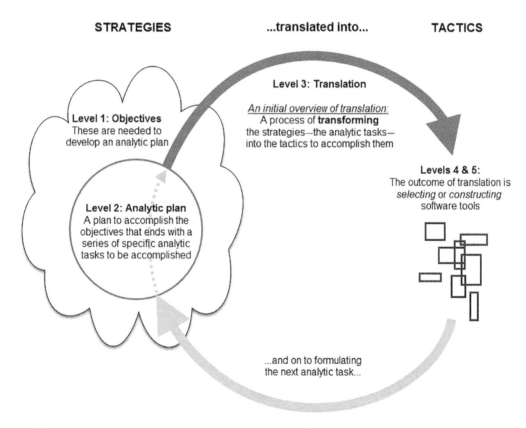

FIGURE 2.2   A first overview of the iterative process of the *Five-Level QDA* method

research process need to be concise and may appear more sanitized and orderly than what actually occurred. The portrayal of the *Five-Level QDA* method in Figure 2.1 should be seen as a convenient way of laying out and explaining each level of the process in an orderly manner. Figure 2.2 offers a more accurate portrayal of the iterative process that better reflects the detours and messiness of real-world projects, which will be on full display in the case illustrations in Part III. Figure 2.2 is a first overview of this iterative process. We will be adding more detail to this circular portrayal as we go more deeply into the process step by step.

But first, we now begin with Level 1—the objectives—and then move on to Level 2—the development of an analytic plan.

Level 1: Objectives

In this section we describe the first level of the *Five-Level QDA* method, the highest level of strategy. This consists of the project objectives, which describe the *purpose* of the project and the *context* in which it occurs and a set of research methods for undertaking the various phases of the project—known as a *methodology*—that guides how the objectives will be fulfilled. Taken together these constitute the boundaries around a universe of interest, and they are the essential starting point of any research project.

It is common for beginning researchers to have vague, partially thought through, or unrealistically broad and ambitious research objectives. However, clear objectives are a prerequisite for harnessing ATLAS.ti powerfully because the objectives that come out of Level 1 lead directly to Level 2—formulating an analytic plan—which leads directly to Level 3—transforming the plan into software operations in ATLAS.ti. If the process begins with vague or inconsistent objectives, these qualities will trickle all the way down to the use of the software.

Learning to formulate clear objectives is not the focus of this book. No single textbook can be a one-stop destination for every phase of qualitative research—the range of activities is too wide and disparate. It would be like having a single book about how to grow your own vegetables in all possible climates integrated with a cookbook for making every kind of dish from all the cuisines of the world. No author could be equally expert in all these topics. Yet the success of the menus in the cookbook depends on the quality of the gardening described in the gardening text.

In a similar way, although our focus is on harnessing ATLAS.ti, it is of great concern to us that your objectives are indeed clear, for otherwise the *Five-Level QDA* method will not accomplish its purpose. We therefore do introduce the subject later to let you know what is needed. The objectives of a project are best thought about in the same way as the *Five-Level QDA* method as a whole—in other words, as having both strategies and tactics. *What* the objectives are comprise the strategies to be accomplished (generally, one or more research questions), and *how* they are to be fulfilled are the tactics (a guiding methodology). First, the strategy.

Clear Objectives

Many ATLAS.ti projects are academic studies in which the objectives are expressed as formal research questions: for example, *How do attitudes and responses to bullying vary across the different schools in a single school district?* But not all ATLAS.ti projects are of this kind. Many users of ATLAS.ti have quite different purposes in mind from answering a research question, such as researchers undertaking a literature review, management consultants studying an organization in order to propose changes to business strategy, authors categorizing or indexing their sources in preparation for writing a book, or physicians organizing and annotating patient records in an electronic system to make it easier to find or communicate information (Fielding & Lee, 2002). All these projects could be accomplished using ATLAS.ti, but they do not have formal research questions. For simplicity, we call all project purposes *objectives*. All these kinds of objectives must be *clear*, whether or not they are research questions, so that the actions inspired by the objectives actually move the project in the desired direction of fulfilling their purpose.

The criteria are the same for all successful objectives: they must be *coherent* (the parts fit together in a logical way and do not contradict one another), *unambiguous* (expressed in a way that makes it clear what is to be accomplished without having to guess what is meant), and *capable of being*

TABLE 2.1 Selected resources for learning to write clear objectives

Miles, M. B., and Huberman, A. M. (1994). Qualitative data analysis: An expanded sourcebook. Thousand Oaks, CA: Sage.	Still the go-to text for a practical approach to qualitative analysis. Includes a helpful section on formulating research questions.
Patton, M. Q. (2015). Qualitative research and evaluation methods: Integrating theory and practice (4th ed.). Thousand Oaks, CA: Sage.	The best general text on qualitative evaluation methods. Includes sections on types of evaluation purposes and developing questions.
Marshall, C., and Rossman, G. B. (2016). Designing qualitative research (6th ed.). Thousand Oaks, CA: Sage.	Now in its sixth edition, this popular text discusses the fundamentals of valid and achievable research objectives and how to write research questions.
Maxwell, J. A. (2013). Qualitative research design: An interactive approach (3rd ed.). Sage. Thousand Oaks, CA: Sage.	Now in its third edition, this is another popular text with an excellent chapter on writing research questions.

answered with the available data or with data that are planned to be collected. It is quick and easy to write incoherent or ambiguous objectives, and usually several drafts are required before they become both clear and fulfillable.

Research studies from different traditions have very different approaches to formulating their research questions, and each has its own texts to offer guidance (Creswell, 2013). But regardless of your approach, research questions are ultimately questions, taking the form of *What. . .*, *How. . .*, or *Why. . .*? If you are not yet familiar with writing research questions and are just considering your approach, one good starting point is the chapter on qualitative research objectives by the anthropologist Harry Wolcott (Wolcott, 1994). The chapter clearly explains the differences between three kinds of objectives that are increasingly abstracted from the data: *describing what is there* (an objective that typically leads to a *What. . .* question); *analyzing how it works* (an objective that typically leads to a *How. . .* question); and *interpreting what it means* (an objective that typically leads to a *Why. . .* question). Wolcott goes on to recommend analytic approaches for beginning, intermediate, and more advanced researchers. Even if your project is not an academic study, you will likely still enjoy reading that chapter. If you do not plan to write formal research questions to express your objectives, you will still likely want to write out your objectives by starting with an action verb that indicates the action to be taken, such as *assess, identify, compare*, and so on.

Many resources are available if more guidance is needed in formulating objectives. If you are not following a prescribed methodology or do not know where to start, Table 2.1 provides an annotated bibliography of some popular authoritative texts that introduce the topic of research objectives.

Adopting a Methodology

Once an objective has been formulated—clearly articulating *what* you plan to do—the next issue is deciding how you will go about fulfilling it, which is the role of methodology. This book does not teach methodology, but we must be sure there are no weak links in the chain from clear objectives down to the use of the software. We therefore introduce several aspects of methodology to sensitize you to the issues to ensure that all the preliminaries are in place for learning to harness ATLAS.ti powerfully.

In the first section, *methodology and methods*, we introduce the idea of methodology in a straightforward and practical way by contrasting it with research methods. The difference between the two is important to understand regardless of whether you conduct theoretical, interpretive, or mixed-methods research or whether you conduct evaluations, policy studies or other applied research, or whether you are harnessing ATLAS.ti for practical projects that you consider nonacademic or not research at all. Methodology applies to all these. In the second section, *different ways of knowing*, we briefly introduce an aspect of methodology that is helpful to be aware of, as it is not completely obvious what it means "to know something." We end with a longer discussion of how researchers *adopt a methodology in practice*.

Methodology and Methods

A *methodology* is not a pretentious way of saying a *method*. A method describes exactly how a particular task should be accomplished, such as how to approach a senior manager in an organization to request an interview or how to write an interpretive rather than a descriptive memo. A methodology describes something much larger than how a particular task is to be performed. A methodology is often called a system of methods, in the sense that a system is something that has a set of interconnected parts. A methodology describes how an entire research project will be conducted and provides guidance for selecting the methods, the specific tasks to be undertaken. Methodology "can only offer general, not specific guidance. But offering guidance is its task" (Hammersley, 2011, p. 39).

For example, a researcher may be hired by an organization to evaluate why a new way of conducting employee performance reviews has been implemented more successfully in some departments than others. The researcher concludes she is being asked to conduct an *implementation evaluation*, and she finds a suitable methodology text to guide her (e.g., Patton, 2008). She chooses one type of implementation evaluation in this text that matches her objectives, the *process evaluation*, which focuses on studying the actual operation of a program, or its process, in order to understand its strengths and weaknesses. The text instructs her to begin by gathering information from people who are "closest to the new program" (p. 325). This methodological guidance then has to be put into practice with a specific course of action, or research method that is relevant to her particular study, which, of course, the methodological textbook knows nothing about. The researcher might decide that for this project, the process of gathering data from those closest to the program should start with interviewing the head of each department because they conduct the reviews in this organization. This in turn requires a method for approaching these individuals that is appropriate to the organization. In small organizations this might simply require an initial email and a follow-up phone call. But her client is a large organization, and she finds an article that describes a suitable method for approaching senior managers that involves first getting in the good graces of the gatekeeper, who might be a personal assistant or secretary (e.g., Bloor & Wood, 2006, pp. 5–9).

This very practical project may not sound anything at all like your own research, but the principles are the same. First a methodology is identified that fits the objectives. This describes the research process in general terms as guidance for choosing specific methods that fit the specific study. This gives confidence that the project is proceeding in a coherent manner, guided by the wisdom of many researchers who have been down a similar path and whose accumulated experience has been set down in a methodology text.

Different Ways of Knowing

There is one further aspect of methodology to be considered. Research of any kind is concerned with finding out something not yet known. This is obvious, but what it means to *know* something is not so obvious. The study of different ways of knowing is referred to as epistemology, a somewhat off-putting term. The methods writer Johnny Saldaña prefers the term "this is where I'm comin' from" (Saldaña, 2014, p. 977). In reality, the issue is not particularly esoteric. For example, does *knowledge* consist of what is known by authorities or experts in the field of study, in which case finding this knowledge is just a matter of asking them? Or is this only a distraction from gaining true or valid knowledge in a field, which can only really be *known* when everyday people describe from their perspective how they interact with the world in that particular context?

Some researchers think long and hard about the appropriateness of the epistemological assumptions underlying the methodology they consider adopting. But many do not, and they are satisfied to go along with whatever epistemological assumptions are built into the methodology they have chosen. Others are not aware that there are alternative assumptions about knowledge and ways of knowing. For a deeper look at alternative ways of knowing, see Box 2.1.

BOX 2.1 A DEEPER LOOK: ALTERNATIVE WAYS OF KNOWING

This deeper look is intended to help you decide whether you want to look further into different ways of knowing, the field of epistemology. It is worth considering this topic because different assumptions about the nature of knowledge lead to different ways of going about gaining knowledge. Every research methodology necessarily has underlying assumptions about what it means to know something, whether the assumptions are explicit or simply implicit. These assumptions about knowledge affect the analytic strategies used to answer research questions, even if you are not really aware of what your "assumptions about knowledge" are. Following we give one practical example that may resonate with your own work and one academic example of two contrasting ways of knowing. Additionally, Carter and Little (2007) provide a concise introduction to epistemology in qualitative research.

A Practical Example

Many qualitative researchers conduct interview research. The way in which researchers conduct their interviews necessarily reflects their assumptions about knowledge, whether recognized or not. For example, one assumption about knowledge may be that you can discover your respondents' true attitudes on a topic by questioning them in an unbiased, depersonalized way, setting aside what you already know about the topic when formulating your follow-up questions. Doing this would ensure that other researchers in a similar context would reach similar conclusions; or in other words, ensure that your conclusions are reliable. Or you may believe the opposite: that a respondent's words alone never give real access to their inner experiences. Therefore, only through interacting with them in a personal way during an interview and reflecting on your role in the interactions and the relationship can you and the respondent jointly create an understanding of the research topic that is valid in that particular context (e.g., Mischler, 1986). Brinkman and Kvale (2015) is also an excellent resource on the interconnectedness of interviewing and theories of knowledge.

An Academic Example

Emile Durkheim's (1951) seminal study of suicide and Jack Douglas's (1967) critique of the study illustrate how researchers' different epistemological positions greatly affect the way research is conducted. Durkheim's (1951) study was part of his effort to establish sociology as a science. His epistemological position, referred to as positivism, was that valid knowledge is only produced by measuring and testing empirical observations of human behavior to uncover what he called the social facts. In this case, the pressures of social structures that accounted for different patterns of suicide in different countries were considered a valid way to understand suicide, rather than studying individuals and what underlay their acts of suicide. In contrast, Douglas's (1967) criticism of Durkheim's conclusions is based on a different epistemological position, social constructivism, which believes that social reality is not a "fact" but is constructed consciously and actively by individuals. Therefore, to understand the social meaning of suicide we must understand how individuals construe their social reality, for example, by talking with individuals who have unsuccessfully attempted suicide, reading the suicide notes of those who succeeded, or studying how coroners record deaths and thereby "create suicide."

Adopting a Methodology in Practice

How do you decide which methodology best fits your objectives? Methodology is more of a "craft [than] an abstractly formulated set of rules or techniques" that can be mechanically matched to objectives (Hammersley, 2011, p. 26). There is no standard list of methodologies with an index of what kinds of objectives are suitable for each. And there is unlikely to be a clear one-to-one match between your research objectives and the guidance of a single methodology text. It is more common that one methodology stands out as best fitting the research objectives generally, but some aspects or phases of a project are better matched to other similar or somewhat different methodologies. In practice, then, the methodology for a project is often put together, or constructed, rather than choosing a single methodology to follow step by step.

How do researchers choose or construct their methodologies in practice? Generally by striking a balance between complete neglect and excessive concern. Clearly there are drawbacks to neglecting methodology altogether, especially for new researchers, as this requires an unnecessarily risky reinventing of the wheel. A lack of fit between the methodology and the objectives may not make itself apparent until well into analysis, when it may be troublesome to go back to choose or construct a more appropriate methodology. On the other hand, an excessive concern with methodology "can be a diversion from real work," as the methods writer Clive Seale suggests, or as Freud put it, "Methodologists remind me of people who clean their glasses so thoroughly that they never have time to look through them" (both cited in Hammersley, 2011, p. 17, 30). So a balance is best. There are three issues when choosing or constructing a methodology in practice: deciding which comes first, the objectives or the methodology; locating candidate methodologies; and finally, considering whether an "implicit methodology" is appropriate.

Regarding which comes first, objectives or methodology, in an ideal world one would formulate research questions and select a methodology as co-constituting activities. In theory, it would not be possible to properly formulate research questions for a project without knowing in advance the philosophical underpinnings of the methodology that would be used to answer them. But at the same time, there is no reason to choose or construct a particular methodology before having a project's specific objectives in mind. In practice, adopting a "co-constituting" approach is rather complicated, and many researchers take a more practical approach. One is to prepare research questions based on the researcher's (or the funder's) interests and then select the most appropriate methodology to answer that question. Another is to select a methodology that appeals or is already familiar and then formulate research questions that make sense for that methodology. A third, perhaps less laudable approach, is to formulate research questions based on your interests or those of the funder and then independently select a methodology because it appeals or because it is familiar or because it is acceptable to the funder and hope for the best.

The next issue is to locate a methodology. Many researchers have already studied certain methodologies and stick to those. If you are new to qualitative research or are looking forward to branching out, think of two broad classes of methodology: generic or specialized. *Generic* has a connotation of inferior or unsophisticated, but it is becoming a more common way to describe qualitative research that focuses on the basic exploratory and inductive purposes of qualitative research without being tied to a particular methodological position. Many researchers using CAQDAS packages describe their methodologies and methods in published articles in quite generic terms, such as a "qualitative design" or a "qualitative, exploratory study" (Woods, Paulus, Atkins, & Macklin, 2016, p. 9). "Generic" refers to all manner of approaches that are in the inductive or emergent spirit of qualitative research. Sharon Merriam is a methods writer who since the 1980s has never shied away from the "generic" label to describe high-quality approaches to methodology (e.g. most recently, Merriam & Tisdell, 2016, p. 23). Other methods writers have now begun to describe generic approaches in more detail (e.g., Kahlke, 2014; Thorne, 2008) or have made proposals for ensuring the quality of generic approaches (e.g., Caelli, Ray, & Mill, 2008; Cooper & Endacott, 2007). If you decide that a generic approach is to your taste, one of the best standard texts for a generic methodological approach is still *Qualitative Data Analysis: An Expanded Sourcebook* by Miles and Huberman (1994).

Of course, much qualitative research is more specialized, and innumerable texts offer guidance in a multitude of approaches. The variety is so great that there is not even a standard scheme for categorizing the range of approaches. One useful resource is Graham Gibbs' helpful webpage at the University of Huddersfield that lists and explains 26 different methodologies, with several textbooks to choose for each (Gibbs, 2011). Another useful text that focuses on the analysis procedures associated with 10 different methodologies is *Analyzing Qualitative Data: Systematic Approaches* by Bernard, Wutich, and Ryan (2017).

Finally, even if no explicit methodology is chosen or constructed to guide a study, there is always an *implicit* methodology at work, the unconscious or taken-for-granted ideas or principles that underlie the process of accomplishing a project's objectives. This could have been absorbed by osmosis from working in an academic institution, or from working in an organization with a community of researchers, or simply as a result of doing what makes sense based on the sum total of your life experiences. Even though (by definition) you are not consciously aware of your implicit methodology, you would not be able to decide what to do next without it. Later in the chapter we describe an implicit methodology to illustrate how it can guide the progress of a project.

At this point you may have your objectives clear and be aware of the guiding principles for how you will go about your analysis, whether from an established methodology described in a textbook, or a methodology you have constructed for your specific objectives, or your implicit methodology that you have now reflected on and decided is appropriate for your project. But if not, it is a good idea to pause until you have settled on these two outcomes of Level 1 before continuing to read the next section, which involves turning objectives into an analytic plan.

If the basic idea of a methodology for fulfilling an objective is still not coming alive, the more concrete everyday illustration that we use for the remainder of Part I may help.

An Everyday Illustration

For the remainder of Part I we use as our primary illustration an everyday activity with clear, achievable objectives and an implicit methodology—the preparation of a gourmet meal. Using an illustration of a meal preparation rather than a qualitative research project ensures that you do not treat an illustrative research project representing one methodology as the "correct way" to do qualitative research. The essence of the *Five-Level QDA* method is the relationship between *tasks* and *tools*. Explaining this process for the first time in terms of an everyday activity focuses attention on the process rather than the content of the illustration. Box 2.2 provides a deeper look into the rationale for using an everyday example.

We will compare the steps of the meal preparation process to the levels of the *Five-Level QDA* method as we go along, but we recommend you do not try to relate the principles you are learning to your own research project. The best approach is to temporarily put aside thoughts of qualitative research and your current project in order to focus on the relationship between tasks and tools.

Now on to the illustration.

BOX 2.2 A DEEPER LOOK: WHY WE USE AN EVERYDAY ILLUSTRATION

There are three reasons we use an everyday activity as an illustration in Part I. First is to overcome the problems with using a single example of a research project. The second is that we have not yet introduced the workings of ATLAS.ti, a consequence of the layered sequence of instruction. Finally, we initially want to focus attention on the underlying process to be learned—the relationship of tasks to tools—rather than the context of the illustration. Using an everyday activity rather than a research project at this early stage facilitates that goal.

The Problem With Single Illustrations

Qualitative research methodologies vary so widely, from positivist to constructivist approaches, that some researchers consider these in opposition to one another. If the methodology represented by the one example was quite different from your own, you might be misled into thinking that the *Five-Level QDA* method is inapplicable to your style of research and read no further.

But at a deeper level, qualitative analysis is an example of an *ill-structured activity*, a kind of activity with incomplete information, no correct conclusion, and no one way to evaluate answers (Jonassen, 1997). Oversimplifying instruction in these ill-structured domains, particularly by using single illustrations, promotes the misunderstanding that they are well structured, which in our case suggests that there is a correct way to conduct qualitative analysis with ATLAS.ti. In order to promote effective learning in ill-structured domains, cognitive flexibility theory proposes "criss-crossing the conceptual landscape" using multiple illustrations (Spiro, Coulson, Feltovich, & Anderson, 1988, p. 6), and in Part III we follow this guidance by using contrasting examples of harnessing each component of ATLAS.ti. In Part I we avoid the pitfalls of single examples by using an everyday activity that cannot be misinterpreted as the one correct way to conduct a qualitative analysis.

The Layered Sequence of Instruction

A second reason for using an everyday activity is a consequence of our layered instruction. This creates a chicken-and-egg quandary for what should be learned first. It is not possible to learn to translate real-world analytic tasks into software operations until understanding the full capabilities of the software that can be harnessed. But conversely, learning to operate the software first without knowing the principles of translation in the *Five-Level QDA* method encourages students to jump in and implement their data analysis in a step-by-step manner, driven by the capabilities of the software. This does not lead to using the software powerfully. We therefore begin with the principles of the *Five-Level QDA* method in Part I without reference to the capabilities of ATLAS.ti. One alternative is to illustrate a qualitative data analysis conducted with a software program that we are all sure to know, such as Microsoft Word or Excel. These are obviously not CAQDAS programs and would not allow us to properly illustrate the principles of the *Five-Level QDA* method. We therefore use an everyday activity to initially illustrate the principles.

Focusing on the Relationship Between Tasks and Tools

The final reason for using an everyday activity is that the subject matter of the book is not research methods, but the relationship between tasks and tools. Initially using an illustration that does not involve qualitative research focuses attention on the process of translation of tasks into tools rather than on the subject matter of the illustration. Using a qualitative research project would inevitably distract from focusing on the relationship between tasks and tools in this initial illustration. After the principles of the *Five-Level QDA* method have been learned in Part I, we focus exclusively on multiple examples of real-world research projects.

Christina is looking for a way to relax after a hard day at the keyboard writing a textbook. First comes Level 1, sufficiently clarifying her objectives so that they can be transformed into a plan at Level 2. As in research projects, this very large goal of *ways to relax* has to be narrowed down to a single purpose or objective, and she narrows it down to *cooking gourmet food*. This objective must now be better specified to be both clear and fulfillable. She decides that her purpose is to cook a meal for the whole family within 90 minutes using ingredients already available in her kitchen, because she does not want to take the time to go shopping. In working through the clarification process with her family, she discovers that they are hungry and they are not prepared to wait a full 90 minutes and 60 minutes is the outside boundary of what they would find acceptable. With the family's agreement Christina settles on a clear objective: *promptly prepare a gourmet family meal with what's already available in the kitchen*. She decided that *promptly* sufficiently clarifies the boundary of the activity's time dimension, and in the present context *promptly* means 60 minutes or less.

For this project the methodology is implicit, based on Christina's prior experience with many informal cooking projects for her family. She gives a name to what she will be doing, *recipe-inspired improvisation*, to remind herself of her approach as she is planning the steps, just as we will later be naming implicit research methodologies when planning the analysis. Her implicit methodology could be summarized as follows: *based on a recipe that stimulates enthusiasm in the chef, adjust every aspect of the recipe in any way desired in order to align the adjusted recipe to the constraints of available time, space, and ingredients*. However, a methodology does not specify the methods of each phase of the project—the particular courses of action—but serves as the framework or guide for selecting and executing methods appropriate to the context.

Christina has now formulated the objectives and the implicit methodology for preparing the meal—a good start.

Level 2: Analytic Plan

This section describes Level 2 of the *Five-Level QDA* method, the second level of strategy (Figure 2.3). This involves converting the objectives of Level 1 into an analytic plan, which includes a conceptual framework and a set of analytic tasks that need to be performed. After explaining this process, we illustrate it by developing a plan of action for Christina's gourmet meal.

Level 1	Level 2	Level 3	Level 4	Level 5
Objectives	Analytic plan	Translation	Selected tools	Constructed tools
The purpose and context of a project, usually expressed as research questions and a methodology	The conceptual framework and resulting analytic tasks	Translating from analytic tasks to software tools and translating the results back again	Straightforward choice of individual software operations	Sophisticated use of software by combining operations or performing them in a custom way

FIGURE 2.3 Level 2 of the *Five-Level QDA* method

Plans of action are referred to in the research literature as *research methods*. This includes how to do all the tasks in a project, including how to gain access to research sites, collect the data, analyze the data, and organize and write the final product of the research, whether a report, an article, book, or a thesis or dissertation. Listing the activities of a research project in this way implies that they are separate and undertaken in sequence. Obviously gaining access to a research site has to come well before a final report can be written, and data have to be collected before they can be analyzed, but there is a surprising amount of overlap between analysis phases and many adjustments to the sequence of activities and tasks in a qualitative research project. For example, the grounded theory methodology calls for an alternation of data collection, analysis, and then further data collection based on the outcome of the first round of analysis (Glaser & Strauss, 1967). Other methodologies, such as qualitative content analysis, require all data to be collected before a systematic analysis of their content can begin. But writing occurs throughout a project, not just in the phase of the final write-up. Analytic writing begins at the very start of a project, as part of the formulation of clear objectives, and continues throughout data collection in order to document the context of the data and to record immediate reflections, whether conducting interviews, visiting research sites, or studying archival data. These informal reflections constitute the first round of analysis, and in this way data collection and analysis overlap.

Qualitative analysis, our primary concern in this book, is not a fixed phase of activity in the middle of a project, between data collection and write-up of findings. It occurs throughout with varying degrees of formality. For example, undertaking a literature review is a form of analysis, and writing up a research report or journal article is also an analytic act. Methods of analysis are often referred to with the general-purpose term *analytic strategies*. To avoid ambiguity with our own terminology, we do not use this general-purpose term. Instead, we call Level 2 the *analytic plan* for the project. Analytic plans consist of a general plan for the whole project and an evolving set of analytic tasks that are the individual action steps.

We refer to the general plan as the *conceptual framework* for the project, which we discuss in detail in the next section. Every qualitative research project has a conceptual framework, whether it is explicit or simply implied. In the *Five-Level QDA* method we make it explicit. The individual analytic tasks, or action steps, that develop out of the conceptual framework are the central building blocks of the *Five-Level QDA* method. They are what are translated into software operations. From this point on ANALYTIC TASK is printed in SMALL CAPS to be clear we are referring to entities with specific characteristics in the *Five-Level QDA* method.

The relationship of the conceptual framework to an ANALYTIC TASK is like the relationship of a map to a journey. A map displays locations, their spatial relationships, and possible routes of traveling. You plan a journey by studying the map to see which route makes the most sense according to the objectives of that journey. For some journeys the most efficient route makes most sense, for others the most scenic route is best, and for others it is the route that passes the most friends with an available spare room: it all depends on the objectives. Remember, though, that once a journey starts there will likely be unexpected circumstances—a road closure, some bad weather, or a friend who gets sick—which may lead to modifications to the travel plan. Such modifications are accomplished by consulting the map, as well as by making sure that the new plan is still consistent with the objectives. This is just what it feels like to be working at Level 2, the level of the analytic plan, when undertaking a qualitative analysis. The conceptual framework—like a map—provides the possibilities for the next ANALYTIC TASK. The ANALYTIC TASK that makes the most sense at any given moment depends on the project's objectives. This also illustrates what we mean when we say that qualitative research projects are both iterative and emergent.

The Conceptual Framework

Nick well remembers the first time he heard the words *conceptual framework* in his first research methods class. The words sounded just right, just what he looked forward to constructing for himself—but how? What would one look like? The professor was so steeped in conceptual frameworks that he had long ago lost all awareness that others did not yet live with them day and night, and it was assumed everyone in the class knew what they were.

For our purposes, a conceptual framework is a set of concepts that are related to one another. Think of concepts in the most general way possible. A concept is the name and meaning of any collection of things, such as seats, or unconscious racial biases, or effective teachers, or positive emotions. To say something is a seat is to say a great deal. It implies membership of a collection of things that has a definition—does it mean it has four legs and some kind of platform to sit on and a back? Or would anything that can be sat on be included, like a rock? It depends on the context. A rock is not generally a seat in a natural history museum, but often is in a campground. In everyday life the meaning of a concept is usually obvious from the context and does not need to be stated. Saying "have a seat" to a visitor in your home does not have to be qualified by adding *that means on one of the chairs, not on that low table or the cabinet ledge please.* But in qualitative research the purpose and meaning of each concept are made explicit. For a good introduction to the creation and use of concepts in qualitative research, see Morse (1995).

A conceptual framework is a set of named concepts that are related to one another. It could take the form of a diagram, a list, a table, or a narrative. We use diagrams in this book as an easy way to communicate concepts. In a research project, using diagrams to illustrate your conceptual framework lets you compare earlier versions as they evolve through the life of the project. Miles and Huberman (1994) discuss and illustrate the use of visual conceptual frameworks in research (pp. 18–22). Also see Maxwell's (2013) excellent chapter on the use of concept maps for visually exploring conceptual frameworks. However, you may prefer writing a narrative to think through the concepts in a project and to represent their relationships as a conceptual framework. How a conceptual framework is represented is a matter of preference.

We now illustrate the narrative development of a conceptual framework, followed by its representation as a diagram, in Christina's planning for her gourmet meal. For her objective to *promptly prepare a gourmet family meal with what's available*, she might identify these concepts as relevant: *60-minute recipes, available ingredients, dietary preferences of family members, complexity of preparation process, degree of relaxation needed*, and *promptly*. In most styles of qualitative research the concepts we create and name are intended to be malleable. Consider *promptly*: as it turned out, despite the family's need for feeding quickly, it became impossible to produce a gourmet meal in 60 minutes. Christina felt confident in justifying that a redefinition of *promptly* up to 75 minutes was quite sufficiently prompt in the context of her need to relax after a long day at the keyboard writing a textbook and the expected excellence of the meal. Similarly, in qualitative research, concepts only have meaning within a certain context (Morse, 2000, p. 335).

Christina decides to draw a diagram of her meal preparation process and put it in a Meal Planning Worksheet along with her objectives, implicit methodology, and the overall plan for what to do next: *review recipe books for suitable recipes*. The worksheet has two purposes—to *manage* the progress of the meal to help it efficiently get completed on deadline and to *document* the process in case it is a great success and she wants a record of what she has done. Figure 2.4 displays the first iteration of the worksheet. This is a simplified version of a similar worksheet, called the ANALYTIC PLANNING WORKSHEET, that we begin illustrating in Part II to manage and document the progress of real-world *Five-Level QDA* projects.

Analytic Tasks

Just as a map is not a journey, but the resource with which to select a journey, a conceptual framework is not an action plan. How the conceptual framework is transformed into a set of ANALYTIC TASKS depends on the dictates of the chosen methodology; or in the case of an implicit methodology, it depends on your intuition or established habits of working that substitute for a chosen methodology.

In qualitative research projects, ANALYTIC TASKS are individual, self-contained steps of action. They are generated by the researcher from the conceptual framework. Rarely can *all* ANALYTIC TASKS be generated in one fell swoop, as qualitative projects are, to some degree, emergent. Initial ANALYTIC TASKS are generated and executed by the researcher, and based on the outcome another set of ANALYTIC TASKS are generated, possibly accompanied by changes to the analytic plan. This is the meaning of iterative. Level 2 is thus traversed in a series of iterative cycles in the light of "what the data are telling us."

In the gourmet meal we will carefully identify each TASK in the process in the same way we do in *Five-Level QDA* research projects, and so we will SMALL CAP the term TASK to be clear we are thinking about these individual activities in an equivalent way. The first TASK can be easily determined now that Christina has a conceptual framework: *find all suitable 60-minutes-or-less recipes*, in which "suitable" means evaluating them against the dietary preferences of the family (which she already knows). Just because the methodology is implicit does not mean that the TASKS cannot be represented formally.

Once Christina has identified the 60-minutes-or-less recipes, she might notice a theme—that many tempting recipes call for fresh ginger. A second and unanticipated TASK might therefore emerge: *check for fresh ginger*. Finding none, she has to decide what to do next. A quick check of the Meal Planning Worksheet reminds her that she already decided to prepare the meal only with what's available to avoid having to go out shopping. Similarly, in qualitative research, referring back to research questions at tricky moments during analysis is a frequent activity that keeps the research on track, and as we will see in Part III, having these written out on the ANALYTIC PLANNING WORKSHEET is a big help in managing the progress of a project.

But back to the need for fresh ginger. Christina could look up the culinary characteristics of fresh ginger in one of her numerous recipe books or Google for an alternative ingredient with the same characteristics and then check if she has any of that. If she unfortunately found none, she could search Google again for related culinary characteristics and then look up ingredients that have those characteristics. This is an iterative process, but time is short, and this degree of iteration is beyond what Christina had in mind for tonight's relaxing activity. So she adjusts her plan by generating a third TASK: *discard recipes requiring fresh ginger*. Figure 2.5 displays the next version of the

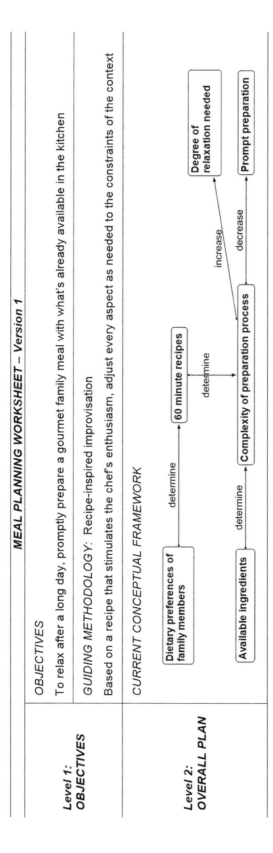

MEAL PLANNING WORKSHEET – Version 1

Level 1: OBJECTIVES	OBJECTIVES To relax after a long day, promptly prepare a gourmet family meal with what's already available in the kitchen GUIDING METHODOLOGY: Recipe-inspired improvisation Based on a recipe that stimulates the chef's enthusiasm, adjust every aspect as needed to the constraints of the context
Level 2: OVERALL PLAN	CURRENT CONCEPTUAL FRAMEWORK Dietary preferences of family members — determine → 60 minute recipes Available ingredients — determine → Complexity of preparation process 60 minute recipes / Complexity of preparation process — determine Complexity of preparation process — increase → Degree of relaxation needed Complexity of preparation process — decrease → Prompt preparation

FIGURE 2.4 Meal Planning Worksheet—Version 1: Objectives and initial plan

MEAL PLANNING WORKSHEET – Version 2

Level 1:
OBJECTIVES

OBJECTIVES
To relax after a long day, promptly prepare a gourmet family meal with what's already available in the kitchen

GUIDING METHODOLOGY: Recipe-inspired improvisation
Based on a recipe that stimulates the chef's enthusiasm, adjust every aspect as needed to the constraints of the context

CURRENT CONCEPTUAL FRAMEWORK

Level 2:
OVERALL PLAN

```
Dietary preferences of        determine
family members    ---------------------------->   75 minute recipes
                                                   Originally 60 minutes, but adjusted to 75 due to
                                                   unsufficient 60 minute recipes and the
                                                   reasonableness of 75 minutes constituting "prompt"
                                                                    |
                                                                    | determine
                                                                    v
Available ingredients   determine    Complexity of preparation process
        --------------------------->
                                                    |        \
                                           increase |         \ decrease
                                                    v          v
                                         Degree of          Prompt preparation
                                         relaxation needed
```

Level 2: TASKS
Find all suitable one hour or less recipes
Check for fresh ginger
Discard recipes requiring fresh ginger

FIGURE 2.5   Meal Planning Worksheet—Version 2: The first three tasks

Meal Planning Worksheet with highlighted updates: the first three TASKS and a new version of the conceptual framework with the 75-minute recipes and the redefinition of "prompt."

This example of suppressing a degree of iteration is quite appropriate for tonight's cooking methodology—one that is guided by *improvisation*. Similarly in qualitative research projects, it is never possible to iterate to the fullest extent possible, or the projects would never end. Some methodologies indicate when enough is enough, such as the idea of *saturation* in grounded theory methodology, which, to put it informally, lets you know that you have done enough to understand a concept when further data collection and analysis are telling you nothing very new (Glaser & Strauss, 1967).

Knowing What You Plan to Do Next

We have not yet discussed the appropriate size for an ANALYTIC TASK, meaning its level of detail. In the gourmet meal a TASK can be more general, such as *prep all the ingredients*, or more detailed, like *open refrigerator door*. In the *Five-Level QDA* method, identifying the level of detail of ANALYTIC TASKS that will most easily TRANSLATE into software operations plays a central role. This is a central skill of the expert qualitative researcher, as it reflects the facility to work at different levels of abstraction of concepts. We elaborate further on this in Chapter 6, and in preparation we consider the underlying principles in more detail at this stage.

Any task can be described with any level of detail. *Prep all the ingredients* is an economical way—a brief way—to start a recipe. But this might not contain enough information for you to know exactly what to do with the ingredients. At a greater level of detail, a recipe could begin with *open the refrigerator door*. This level, however, lies at the other extreme, providing unnecessary information. Something between the two will strike a better balance between economy of expression and informativeness.

Humans have evolved to perceive and describe the world at a middle level, striking a balance between very economical and very informative. For example, everybody says *Is that chair comfortable?* Nobody says *Is that object comfortable?*, which is less informative, but more economical as the speaker could use that question for any number of surfaces a person might sit on. And, in the other direction, nobody says *Is that green, wicker-backed garden seat comfortable?*, which is highly informative but not an economical way of asking generally about the chair's comfort. We naturally organize and describe the world at what psychologists call the *basic level*, a roughly middle level of detail. In this example the basic level is *chair*, the level of detail that is the best balance of economy and informativeness in the context of inquiring about its comfort. The basic level of categorizing things was first proposed by Rosch, Mervis, Gray, Johnson, and Boyes-Braem (1976), and Lakoff (1987) provided a comprehensive discussion of all aspects of basic-level categories.

The basic level of detail comes naturally to the human mind in normal, everyday communication and is almost always the briefest way to describe something. However, deciding on the best level of detail to describe something also depends on the context. Whereas you might respond to a four-legged animal in the street that barks continuously by saying I *wonder what's the matter with that dog?*, a vet in her office surgery surrounded by animals is more likely to say I *wonder what's wrong with that terrier?* Your basic level of description and the vet's basic level of description are different in these two contexts. The situation is similar with ANALYTIC TASKS. There is no "correct" level of detail for every ANALYTIC TASK: it depends on the context. Instead there is a principle that determines the best level of detail. It is the golden rule of decision making in the *Five-Level QDA* method that will come up over and over again: *what you plan to do next*. A TASK is too large if it does not easily refer to the next TASK. For example, in the gourmet meal the very large TASK of *prep all the ingredients* does not have a natural next step that sufficiently assists in the cooking process. There are several types of ingredients, and so matching the next step at the same level of detail, like *cook all the ingredients*, would be lamentably uninformative. So expressing that very large TASK as a set of somewhat smaller TASKS is better, like *chop salad ingredients evenly*, *cut up fish*, and *wash vegetables*, because each has a natural next step. For example, if a later TASK requires placing each person's portion of fish in a parchment pouch, then it is clear how to accomplish the earlier TASK of *cut up fish*—it is not a matter of just cutting the fish into generic pieces, but rather of allocating it in advance for each of the pouches, knowing the appetites of the various family members. Similarly, at the other end of the spectrum, a tiny and self-evident TASK like *retrieve the largest cutting board* is also not helpful as an individual TASK, as it does not have a natural next step by itself—the next TASK will involve using the cutting board for something, and so will require other prior tiny TASKS to also have been completed—perhaps finding a certain kind of knife, certain ingredients, and so on. The TASKS *chop salad ingredients evenly*, *cut up fish*, and *wash vegetables* seem to be at a helpful level of detail because each conveniently leads on to the next TASK.

Determining the best level of detail of an ANALYTIC TASK in a research project comes with experience; it cannot be turned into a neat and tidy procedure. Our purpose in this chapter is to highlight the principle to help create a mind-set that hastens gaining this experience once we are using ATLAS.ti to fulfill ANALYTIC TASKS in Part III. The principle is that we generate ANALYTIC TASKS from conceptual frameworks based on *what we plan to do next* rather than simply at the basic or middle level of detail that comes naturally, because we want the outcome of fulfilling an ANALYTIC TASK in the software to easily refer to the next ANALYTIC TASK that can also be performed in the software. It is true that *what you plan to do next* is never known with certainty, as the process is, to varying degrees, emergent. The best we can do as qualitative researchers is to plan the current ANALYTIC TASK with an eye to the likely next ANALYTIC TASK. Using the ANALYTIC PLANNING WORKSHEET when learning these skills allows us to see the whole picture when planning the next course of action—including the objectives and methodology. This process will become clear in the ANALYTIC PLANNING WORKSHEETS that accompany the illustrations in Parts II and III.

We have now introduced what is needed at Levels 1 and 2 as preparation for harnessing ATLAS.ti powerfully. We can now move on from these strategy preparations to where the detailed instruction in this book begins: Level 3 of the *Five-Level QDA* method, the translation of ANALYTIC TASKS into the tactics for fulfilling them by using ATLAS.ti.

References

Bernard, H. R., Wutich, A. Y., & Ryan, G. W. (2017). *Analyzing qualitative data: Systematic approaches* (2nd ed.). Thousand Oaks, CA: Sage.

Bloor, M., & Wood, F. (2006). *Keywords in qualitative methods: A vocabulary of research concepts.* Newbury Park, CA: Sage.

Brinkman, S., & Kvale, S. (2015). *Interviews: Learning the craft of qualitative research interviewing* (3rd ed., pp. 55–82). Thousand Oaks, CA: Sage.

Caelli, K., Ray, L., & Mill, J. (2008). 'Clear as mud': Toward greater clarity in generic qualitative research. *International Journal of Qualitative Methods*, 2(2), 1–13.

Carter, S. M., & Little, M. (2007). Justifying knowledge, justifying method, taking action: Epistemologies, methodologies, and methods in qualitative research. *Qualitative Health Research*, 17(10), 1316–1328.

Cooper, S., & Endacott, R. (2007). Generic qualitative research: A design for qualitative research in emergency care? *Emergency Medicine Journal*, 24(12), 816–819.

Creswell, J. W. (2013). *Qualitative inquiry and research design: Choosing among five approaches.* Thousand Oaks, CA: Sage.

Douglas, J. D. (1967). *The social meaning of suicide.* Princeton: Princeton University Press.

Durkheim, E. (1951). *Suicide: A study in sociology* (J. A. Spaulding & G. Simpson, Trans.). Glencoe, IL: Free Press. (Original work published in 1897).

Fielding, N., & Lee, R. M. (2002). New patterns in the adoption and use of qualitative software. *Field methods*, 14(2), 197–216.

Gibbs, G. (2011). University of Huddersfield, UK. Retrieved from http://onlineqda.hud.ac.uk/methodologies.php

Glaser, B. G., & Strauss, A. L. (1967). *Discovery of grounded theory.* Chicago: Aldine.

Hammersley, M. (2011). *Methodology: Who needs it.* Thousand Oaks, CA: Sage.

Jonassen, D. H. (1997). Instructional design models for well-structured and ill-structured problem-solving learning outcomes. *Educational Technology Research & Development*, 45(1), 65–94.

Kahlke, R. M. (2014). Generic qualitative approaches: Pitfalls and benefits of methodological mixology. *International Journal of Qualitative Methods*, 13, 37–52.

Lakoff, G. (1987). *Women, fire, and dangerous things.* Chicago: University of Chicago Press.

Maxwell, J. A. (2013). *Qualitative research design: An interactive approach* (3rd ed.). Los Angeles: Sage.

Merriam, S. B., & Tisdell, E. J. (2016). *Qualitative research: A guide to design and implementation* (4th ed.). San Francisco: John wiley.

Miles, M. B., & Huberman, A. M. (1994). *Qualitative data analysis: An expanded sourcebook.* Thousand Oaks, CA: Sage.

Mischler, E. G. (1986). *Research interviewing: Context and narrative* (pp. 52–65). Cambridge, MA: Harvard University Press.

Morse, J. M. (1995). Exploring the theoretical basis of nursing using advanced techniques of concept analysis. *Advances in Nursing Science*, 17(3), 31–46.

Morse, J. M. (2000). Exploring pragmatic utility: Concept analysis by critically appraising the literature. In B. L. Rodgers & K. A. Knafl (Eds.), *Concept development in nursing: Foundations, techniques, and applications* (2nd ed., pp. 333–352). Philadelphia: W. B. Saunders.

Patton, M. Q. (2008). *Utilization-focused evaluation* (4th ed.). Los Angeles, CA: Sage.

Rosch, E., Mervis, C. B., Gray, W. D., Johnson, D. M., & Boyes-Braem, P. (1976). Basic objects in natural categories. *Cognitive Psychology*, 8, 382–439.

Saldaña, J. (2014). Blue-collar qualitative research: A rant. *Qualitative Inquiry*, 20(8), 976–980.

Spiro, R. J., Coulson, R. L., Feltovich, P. J., & Anderson, D. (1988). *Cognitive flexibility theory: Advanced knowledge acquisition in ill-structured domains.* Paper presented at the Proceedings of the 10th Annual Conference of the Cognitive Science Society. Montreal, Quebec, Canada.

Thorne, S. (2008). *Interpretive description.* Walnut Creek, CA: Left Coast Press.

Wolcott, H. F. (1994). *Transforming qualitative data: Description, analysis, and interpretation.* Thousand Oaks, CA: Sage.

Woods, M., Paulus, T., Atkins, D. P., & Macklin, R. (2016). Advancing qualitative research using qualitative data analysis software (QDAS)? Reviewing potential versus practice in published studies using ATLAS.ti and NVivo 1994–2013. *Social Science Computer Review*, 34(5), 597–617.

3

TRANSLATING ANALYTIC TASKS INTO SOFTWARE TOOLS (LEVELS 3, 4, AND 5)

This chapter focuses on the principles of translating analytic strategies into software operations of ATLAS.ti. In Chapter 1 we said that translation means *transforming* strategies into tactics. Now we will describe the process in more detail as the *matching* of ANALYTIC TASKS to software operations. This requires *framing* ANALYTIC TASKS and features of the software in a way that facilitates matching one to the other. The outcome of this matching is to either *select* an existing software tool or *construct* a custom tool for oneself.

This chapter completes Part I—the principles of the *Five-Level QDA* method. Parts II and III of the book build on these principles by demonstrating the practice of translation in the context of real-world research projects.

Level 3: Translation

This section describes how to frame ANALYTIC TASKS and how to frame the features of the software in order to match one to the other.

Translation between analytic strategies and software tactics is required in order to go beyond, or transcend, their contradictory natures. Rather than trying to make the strategies more cut and dried than they really are or trying to think of the software features as more emergent than they really are, we view the strategies and tactics as entirely separate and contrasting elements in the larger *Five-Level QDA* process and translate between them (see Figure 3.1).

We express this contrast between strategies and tactics in how each of them is *framed*. A frame is a way of focusing on some aspects rather than others. For example, organizations can be framed in different ways that lead to different ways of understanding how they work, how they should

Level 1	Level 2	Level 3	Level 4	Level 5
Objectives	Analytic plan	Translation	Selected tools	Constructed tools
The purpose and context of a project, usually expressed as research questions and a methodology	The conceptual framework and resulting analytic tasks	Translating from analytic tasks to software tools and translating the results back again	Straightforward choice of individual software operations	Sophisticated use of software by combining operations or performing them in a custom way

FIGURE 3.1 Level 3 of the *Five-Level QDA* method

be managed, or how they can be changed (Morgan, 2006). An organization can be framed as a machine with clearly defined parts that are intended to work together, such as divisions or departments. Alternatively, the same organization could be framed as a political system, to help understand how and why people in the organization attempt to advance their different interests or agendas. Framing things in different ways leads to entirely different ways of thinking about them.

We must now consider how ANALYTIC TASKS and the features of ATLAS.ti are framed in the *Five-Level QDA* method. Sometimes the two contrasting frames happen to match, and the translation process is simple and obvious. But sometimes they do not, and there has to be a reframing or transformation between them in order to use the software features powerfully. Reframing means seeing something in a different way (Bolman & Deal, 1997).

The Framing of Analytic Tasks

There could be innumerable ways to frame ANALYTIC TASKS. One way could be to express them in terms of the *purpose* of each task in relation to the objectives of the project; another could be in terms of their *complexity*, such as how well defined or ill defined a particular task is. For purposes of the *Five-Level QDA* method we frame ANALYTIC TASKS in terms of their building blocks. These are generally referred to as their units of analysis, or simply units.

The idea of a unit is central to research. Some of the more interpretive styles of qualitative research do not use the word "unit," as it has a reductionist connotation of breaking the whole into separate pieces. Yet units *are* central to the process of all styles of research, even if described in a different way, and we do need to identify units when harnessing ATLAS.ti powerfully.

A unit describes the types of things that you are interested in, the kinds of things that are being analyzed. They could be individual people, or particular groups of people, or factors that are perceived as barriers or facilitators to the accomplishment of something, or as one textbook says, they may be "newspapers, folk tales, countries, or cities" (Bernard, Wutich, & Ryan, 2017). All parts of the analysis are expressed in units which are unique to each project. Much of qualitative analysis is about finding instances in the data of these units.

A project as a whole may be thought of as having a major unit, such as *school*, if the project's primary objective is to compare attitudes and responses to bullying in different schools of a school district. There may be additional units that reflect additional or secondary objectives. For example, if a secondary objective of the study is to explore how different attitudes or responses to bullying found in different schools reflect the socioeconomic characteristics of the neighborhood, an additional unit may be *location*.

It is not likely that you will identify all relevant units at the start of your study. The first reason is that most styles of qualitative research are "grounded" to a greater or lesser degree. "Grounded" means, in general, that the concepts of the study and the units they are expressed in are found in the data as part of the process of analyzing it, rather than being predetermined and brought into the study at the outset. However, even for grounded styles of analysis there will be a research question that is necessarily expressed in units, that is, in terms of the kinds of things that are being studied, so there will be at least one major unit at the outset.

Regardless of how grounded the study is, new units will likely emerge as the analysis continues and new ANALYTIC TASKS are undertaken. In the bullying study you may notice that an unexpected response to bullying seems to be coming up more frequently in teachers who teach a particular subject area. You decide to follow up this surprising observation with an ANALYTIC TASK that looks for examples of this response across all schools in the study, but separating the examples by the teachers' subject area in order to interrogate the data for these differences. Later a new unit might be *teacher* if another objective emerges to understand different responses to bullying by, say, male and female teachers.

It is not standard practice in qualitative research to explicitly identify and name the units of each ANALYTIC TASK. But for purposes of understanding what experienced qualitative researchers who use

ATLAS.ti have come to do intuitively and unconsciously, thinking more consciously about units is essential. For example, an ANALYTIC TASK in our bullying example may be *identify and name types of responses by male teachers to provoked and unprovoked bullying behaviors.* Here there are two units: *teacher response* and *bullying behavior.* If there had been an intention at the outset to distinguish the responses of male and female teachers, perhaps to follow up a finding from earlier research, then the ANALYTIC TASK might have been larger: *identify and name types of responses by male and female teachers to provoked and unprovoked bullying behaviors.* Now we need to capture differences in behavior of male and female teachers, and there would be three units in a single ANALYTIC TASK: *teacher response, bullying behavior,* and *teachers.* That is fine. Identifying an ANALYTIC TASK to work on at any moment is driven by the needs of the analysis at the strategy levels, as we have just described. It is never driven by the convenience or ease of working in ATLAS.ti on an ANALYTIC TASK with more or fewer units.

The Framing of Software Features

What corresponds in ATLAS.ti to these units of the ANALYTIC TASK? Recall that a *frame* is a way of seeing something that focuses on some aspects rather than others. Framing ANALYTIC TASKS in terms of their units is not in any way unusual to researchers. However, the way we frame software features is not the standard way to think about software. We need to go into this in detail as it is central to the translation process.

A "software feature" is not a technical term. The Institute of Electrical and Electronics Engineers defines a "feature" very generally as "a distinguishing characteristic of a software item" (Feature, n.d.). The idea of a software feature can therefore be framed in many ways: in terms of how simple or complex the feature is, or how useful, or how unique compared with other programs, and so on. But the default or automatic way for a user of computer software to unconsciously frame its features is through its *affordances.* We therefore drop the term feature, which doesn't have a specific meaning, and focus on affordances, which does.

One meaning of *afford* is to *make available*, as in *a large tree affords plenty of shade.* The psychologist James Gibson invented the word *affordance* to refer to things that you would automatically know how to do because information about them is directly available in the environment (Gibson, 1979). The standard example is the handle on a door. A thin vertical bar as a door handle affords opening the door toward you because your hand and arm are configured for pulling when you grasp the bar, whereas a flat horizontal plate on a door affords pushing the door away from you (Norman, 1988).

Psychologists and industrial designers have applied this principle of affordances to computer software (e.g., Gaver, 1991; Hartson, 2003; Norman, 1999). Software developers now try to present information on the screen so that the affordances of their programs are correctly perceived, so that users intuitively and effortlessly use the program based on how the developers believe we want to use the software. In the case of CAQDAS packages the variety of ANALYTIC TASKS is so great that it is impossible to predict everyone in advance and provide affordances for each—that is, visible and obvious ways to use the software for each detailed ANALYTIC TASK. The developers therefore create affordances for more general categories of task than the detailed project-specific ANALYTIC TASKS we identify in the *Five-Level QDA* method.

In our experience the affordances of ATLAS.ti—the intuitively obvious things to do based only on information on the screen—are sometimes exactly what we want to do and sometimes mask what we want to do or would like to do in a different way. This has not prevented us or any of the numerous expert users of ATLAS.ti from happily accomplishing what we need to accomplish with the program. Our explanation is that experts have learned unconsciously not to frame the software in terms of its affordances—the directly perceivable information on the screen about the program's action possibilities. Instead they unconsciously frame ATLAS.ti in terms of its "components", the *things* in the program that can be acted on. Separating the "components" of the program from the actions that can be taken on them is a different way of thinking about software. It is not difficult or complicated—quite the opposite. It is just different.

In Part II we provide a list of ATLAS.ti's 14 components. As we have not yet introduced the architecture of ATLAS.ti, we cannot use it to provide a meaningful example of the difference between framing software in terms of its components rather than its affordances. Instead we give an example from a program we all know and use: Microsoft Word. The principle is the same.

A less experienced user of Microsoft Word can produce unexpected and unwanted effects when just relying on the program's *affordances*, whereas a more experienced user who is aware of the software's *components* does not. One affordance of Microsoft Word is to be able to "drag" a section of text with the mouse button held down. When you let go of the mouse button, the text moves to wherever you "drop it." However, if you drag text that is formatted in one way to a location that is formatted in another way, sometimes the result may not be what you want. Figure 3.2 illustrates this situation.

An alternative way to think about Microsoft Word is not in terms of its affordances—the apparently correct way to accomplish something—but in terms of its components. Experienced users of Microsoft Word know—perhaps without thinking of it in this way—that the affordance to drag and drop text involves two components. One component is *text*, and a second component is the *hidden paragraph mark* that comes at the end of each paragraph. They also know that the hidden paragraph mark contains the formatting instructions for that paragraph. If the hidden paragraph mark is unintentionally selected and dragged along with the text, which is what inadvertently happened in Figure 3.2, the formatting gets copied as well, changing the appearance of

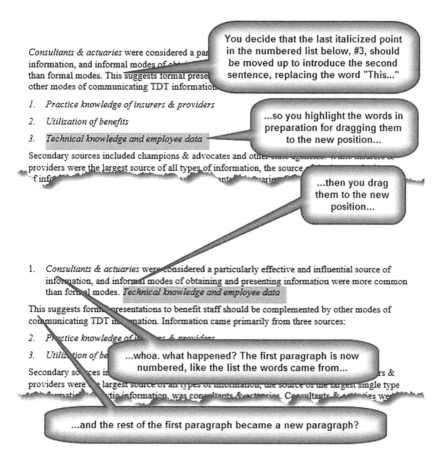

FIGURE 3.2 Thinking with affordances: Drag and drop with unwanted change in formatting

FIGURE 3.3 Thinking with components: Drag and drop with the desired effect

the whole paragraph it is dropped into. In Figure 3.2 the formatting that inadvertently got copied was automatic list numbering. One easy way around this is to select and the drag only the *text*— one component—without including the *hidden paragraph mark*—the second component. Then the drag-and-drop operation does not change the formatting in the new location, and we get the outcome we wanted. This is illustrated in Figure 3.3. (If you are unfamiliar with Microsoft Word and would like a demonstration of this example, see the video on the companion website *Illustration of components in Microsoft Word*).

Thinking in terms of components of Microsoft Word allows a more powerful use of the program, and the principle is exactly the same when thinking in terms of components of ATLAS.ti.

The Process of Translation

As we have now seen, we frame ANALYTIC TASKS in terms of their units, and we frame ATLAS.ti in terms of its components. We now put the term COMPONENT in SMALL CAPS as we are giving it a special meaning. In Chapter 2 we described translation rather generally as the *transformation* of strategies into tactics. We can now describe the mechanics of translation more specifically as *matching* the units of an ANALYTIC TASK to a COMPONENT of the software. See Figure 3.4 for this updated depiction.

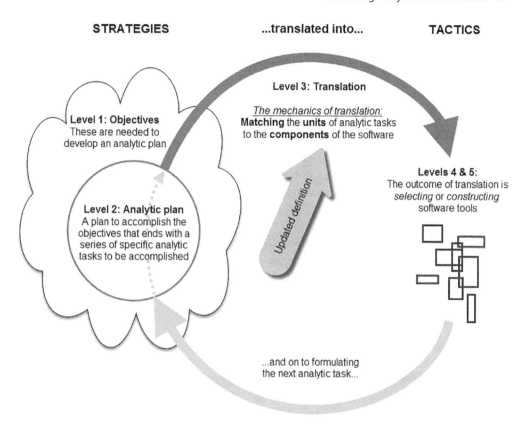

STRATEGIES   **...translated into...**   **TACTICS**

Level 3: Translation

The mechanics of translation:
Matching the **units** of analytic tasks
to the **components** of the software

Level 1: Objectives
These are needed to
develop an analytic plan

Levels 4 & 5:
The outcome of translation is
selecting or *constructing*
software tools

Updated definition

Level 2: Analytic plan
A plan to accomplish the
objectives that ends with a
series of specific analytic
tasks to be accomplished

...and on to formulating
the next analytic task...

FIGURE 3.4   The mechanics of TRANSLATION

First, to avoid confusion we print the word translation in regular type when referring to translation in general, but use SMALL CAPS when referring specifically to TRANSLATION of units of ANALYTIC TASKS to COMPONENTS of ATLAS.ti.

Consider the translation of books from one language to another. This highlights two major ways that a process of translation can occur. If you read a translated book you expect the translated version to be in some way *equivalent* to the original. *Formal equivalence* means a word-by-word translation from one language to the other, regardless of the idioms and natural sound of the second language. *Dynamic equivalence* is quite different. It is not a word-by-word translation, but a translation that sounds to native speakers of the second language as if it had been written in that second language in the first place, so that both the original and the translated versions have roughly the same effect on their respective readers. Clearly there can be many different versions of a translation, and no single translation can be considered right or wrong (Nida & Taber, 1969).

In the same way, TRANSLATION means first looking for a straightforward match—a *formal equivalence*—between the units of an ANALYTIC TASK and a COMPONENT of the software. If there is one, we use the program to act on that COMPONENT in the obvious way. If there is not a workable match, then rather than change the ANALYTIC TASK so that it matches the software, we reframe the process: we look for *dynamic equivalence*, using COMPONENTS of the program in combination or in an unusual way, as if trying to find *just the right word* in a language translation. Just as there is no single correct dynamically equivalent translation of a book, there is often more than one way to do something more sophisticated in ATLAS.ti. The important issue is that different ways to do something more sophisticated may lend themselves to *different next steps*. Therefore, when deciding on which way to do something more sophisticated, the best criterion for deciding will be *what you plan to do next*.

We now move on to the different outcomes of TRANSLATION when there is a straightforward match between the units of an ANALYTIC TASK and a software COMPONENT, or when there needs to be a more sophisticated match.

Level 4: Selected-Tools

This section describes the situation when there is a straightforward match between the units of an ANALYTIC TASK and a COMPONENT of the software, resulting in what we call a SELECTED-TOOL.

The outcome of any translation process is something new. In our case of TRANSLATING units to COMPONENTS, the outcome is a software tool. In general, the nature of software tools is different from other kinds of tools. We are all familiar with physical tools and learning to use them, but software tools are different. According to the educational researcher John Seely Brown, software tools can only be described and learned through their use (Brown, Collins, & Duguid, 1989).

A tool in everyday language is a physical thing like a knife, or a process like a checklist. It is easy to describe how to use these kinds of tools. But thinking of software as a set of tools is different. John Seely Brown studies the use of computers as tools. He emphasizes that the use of software as a tool cannot be explicitly described. Learning to use them can only arise out of their use and is a process of enculturation into the community of those who use the tools—learning is "situated" in the context in which it occurs. This resonates well with our experience of ATLAS.ti. This is because the affordances of ATLAS.ti—the visible and obvious ways to use the program as designed by the developers—do not explicitly describe how researchers use software in their varied and idiosyncratic research projects. Each researcher seems to use the software differently, even for similar tasks, and passes on these ways of using the programs to their colleagues and students.

We refer to a TOOL as a way of acting on COMPONENTS of the program, by clicking buttons, selecting menu items, and so on. A TOOL, as we are using the term, is therefore a combination of a COMPONENT and an action. We print TOOL in SMALL CAPS when referring to this specialized use of the term, and in regular type when talking generally about tools.

There is a comprehensive list of COMPONENTS—the *things* in the program to be acted on—but it makes no sense to have a comprehensive list of TOOLS to pick from, because TOOLS come into being in the course of using the software when the TRANSLATION process has determined a set of action steps that is specific to an ANALYTIC TASK. There would be many hundreds of TOOLS if we tried to create such a list, and it would serve no purpose. Think of the affordances of the program as frozen—they come fully formed, designed as the software developer thought best. In contrast, think of TOOLS as emergent—we create them, and they only exist in the context of use.

It is most helpful to think of a TOOL as a way of thinking about how to fulfill an ANALYTIC TASK, rather than as an established course of action that resides in the software. TOOLS are driven by and are specific to ANALYTIC TASKS. They come into being in the course of use, as John Seely Brown describes (Brown et al., 1989).

When an ANALYTIC TASK has a single unit, and the unit directly matches a COMPONENT of the software, so that acting on the COMPONENT accomplishes the task, then this results in what we call a SELECTED-TOOL, the most straightforward way of using the software. This is Level 4 (see Figure 3.5).

It is not yet practical to illustrate Level 4 with real-world ANALYTIC TASKS to be accomplished in ATLAS.ti. because we have not yet introduced the architecture of the program. We also do not want to use a single research project or methodology to exemplify this process, for the reasons we provided in Chapter 2. We therefore continue with the gourmet meal, in which TRANSLATION to a SELECTED-TOOL can be easily illustrated in concrete, everyday terms. The only change required is to replace the term

Level 1	Level 2	Level 3	Level 4	Level 5
Objectives	Analytic plan	Translation	Selected tools	Constructed tools
The purpose and context of a project, usually expressed as research questions and a methodology	The conceptual framework and resulting analytic tasks	Translating from analytic tasks to software tools and translating the results back again	Straightforward choice of individual software operations	Sophisticated use of software by combining operations or performing them in a custom way

FIGURE 3.5 Level 4 of the *Five-Level QDA* method

ANALYTIC TASK with the word TASK to represent in an equivalent way the meal preparation activities at a level of detail that Christina identifies as most convenient based on what she plans to do next.

You recall from the Meal Planning Worksheet in Chapter 2 (p. 40) that we listed Christina's first three TASKS of the meal preparation process. The first task is to *find all suitable 75 minutes or less recipes* by finding all possibilities and evaluating them against the dietary preferences of the family. The second task, *check for fresh ginger,* was prompted by the fact that many of these recipes happened to call for fresh ginger. After finding none and referring to the objectives on the Meal Planning Worksheet, which reminded her of the decision to prepare the meal only with what is available, she generates a third TASK: *discard recipes requiring fresh ginger.*

In Chapter 2 we had not yet discussed the mechanics of TRANSLATION and so had not fully completed the Meal Planning Worksheet. We will now go back and complete the Meal Planning Worksheet in the same way that we will in the *Five-Level QDA* method. Figure 3.6 illustrates the completion of the first two TASKS, with the TRANSLATION process highlighted. The TRANSLATION column identifies the unit of the TASK, then the kitchen COMPONENT that could potentially match the unit, and finally a summary of the TRANSLATION that describes the matching process. The final column describes the SELECTED-TOOL, in other words, the action that will be taken on an available kitchen COMPONENT to fulfill the task. That is always what we mean by a TOOL—a particular action taken on a COMPONENT. It may not be completely realistic to think that Christina would fill out this Meal Planning Worksheet when preparing a gourmet meal, TASK by TASK. But it is worth studying the highlighted area of Figure 3.6 in this simple example, which identifies the UNITS and COMPONENTS, because this is exactly what we learn how to do in Parts II and III in more complicated research examples.

Figure 3.6 illustrates both of the first two tasks completed, but remember that in reality this is an iterative process carried out TASK by TASK. Only when the outcome of the first TASK is known—in this case, discovering that many recipes called for fresh ginger—does the second TASK become apparent—in this case, *check for fresh ginger.* So in reality the first highlighted line for the first TASK would have been completed and its outcome known before the second TASK had even been identified.

Having completed the second task and determined there is no fresh ginger available, and having reminded herself that the objectives call for only using what is already available in the kitchen, Christina identifies the third task as *discard all the recipes calling for fresh ginger.* She must now find an accurate and—she hopes—efficient way to accomplish this. Unfortunately there is no kitchen COMPONENT on which an action could be taken to accomplish this, such as recipe books that already exclude recipes with fresh ginger. She has to somehow construct a TOOL from what is available in the kitchen.

MEAL PLANNING WORKSHEET – Version 3

Level 1: OBJECTIVES	OBJECTIVES To relax after a long day, promptly prepare a gourmet family meal with what's already available in the kitchen GUIDING METHODOLOGY: Recipe-inspired improvisation Based on a recipe that stimulates the chef's enthusiasm, adjust every aspect as needed to the constraints of the context

CURRENT CONCEPTUAL FRAMEWORK

Level 2: OVERALL PLAN	

Dietary preferences of family members → determine → **75 minute recipes** *Originally 60 minutes, but adjusted to 75 due to unsufficient 60 minute recipes and the reasonableness of 75 minutes constituting "prompt"*

75 minute recipes → determine → Complexity of preparation process

Available ingredients → determine → Complexity of preparation process

Complexity of preparation process → increase → **Degree of relaxation needed**

Complexity of preparation process → decrease → **Prompt preparation**

Level 3: TRANSLATION of TASKS into TOOLS	Levels 4 & 5: SELECTED or CONSTRUCTED TOOLS
UNITS Individual recipes COMPONENTS Pages of recipe books EXPLANATION The recipe books are already organized sequentially by recipes, so there is a direct match between the unit and the component	SELECTED-TOOL Read through each recipe on each recipe book to identify one hour or less recipes
UNITS Pieces of ginger COMPONENTS All containers in every location of kitchen EXPLANATION Each container either does or does not contain a piece of ginger, so there is a direct match	SELECTED-TOOL Inspect every container on every surface and in every draw or shelf for pieces of ginger

Level 2: TASKS	
Find all suitable one hour or less recipes	
Check for fresh ginger	

FIGURE 3.6 Meal Planning Worksheet—Version 3: SELECTED-TOOLS

Level 5: Constructed-Tools

This section describes the outcome of TRANSLATION when there is no direct match between the units of an ANALYTIC TASK and a COMPONENT of the software, resulting in what we call a CONSTRUCTED-TOOL.

Sometimes there is a direct match between a unit of an ANALYTIC TASK and an affordance of ATLAS.ti such that the ANALYTIC TASK can be fulfilled with a single operation of the software, in other words, a SELECTED-TOOL. But it is more common to either require a sequence of software operations or to use the software in a customized way, which requires creating a CONSTRUCTED-TOOL. The skill of harnessing ATLAS.ti powerfully could be described as a facility in using CONSTRUCTED-TOOLS. This is Level 5 (see Figure 3.7). When limited to SELECTED-TOOLS the software is not used powerfully, missing the opportunities for undertaking tasks that may be unrealistically cumbersome without ATLAS.ti.

Coming back to the gourmet meal, Christina is working on her third TASK, to find an accurate and efficient way to *discard recipes requiring fresh ginger*. There is no available COMPONENT in the kitchen for automatically hiding or eliminating some recipes in a physical recipe book, so she has to construct a way to do this.

Looking around the kitchen, Christina seeks TOOLS she could harness for this purpose. She could use a marker to cross out the unneeded recipes, use scissors to cut them out of the recipe book, use paper clips to temporarily indicate where they are, or prepare a list of them on a separate piece of paper, noting the recipe book and page number. All would work, but which TOOL best matches the task? The criterion for choosing, as always, is *what you plan to do next*. In an emergent activity like recipe-inspired meal improvisation—not to mention qualitative analysis—this can never be known in advance, and therefore requires reflection. Christina reflects on two issues: the need to continue reviewing and choosing among suitable recipes for tonight's meal, but also not to ruin the recipe book for future meals. This requires thinking more about what it means to *discard* in the context of tonight's TASK. (Stopping to investigate the meaning of a concept in a particular context is also a common activity in qualitative analysis.) One of the many dimensions of *discard* is *how long lasting* the discarding should be, which could vary a lot. Christina only needs to discard recipes in order to more easily focus on those that are feasible within her objectives. The discarding is therefore not intended to be long lasting, let alone permanent, and so she does not want to cut the unwanted recipes out of the book with scissors and make them unavailable in the future.

Another dimension of *discard* is how *abstract or concrete* the discarding needs to be in order to be effective in the context. The most abstract way to discard recipes would be to remember which ones had been discarded while flipping back and forth among them; more concrete would be a visual indication that lets Christina see the ones previously discarded; and the most concrete would be the physical removal of the pages with discarded recipes, an option already rejected. Because

Level 1	Level 2	Level 3	Level 4	Level 5
Objectives	Analytic plan	Translation	Selected tools	Constructed tools
The purpose and context of a project, usually expressed as research questions and a methodology	The conceptual framework and resulting analytic tasks	Translating from analytic tasks to software tools and translating the results back again	Straightforward choice of individual software operations	Sophisticated use of software by combining operations or performing them in a custom way

FIGURE 3.7   Level 5 of the *Five-Level QDA* method

what Christina *plans to do next* is to revisit the ginger-less recipes many times back and forth while focusing on other aspects of the recipes besides ginger, a visual indication for the duration of the meal preparation seems to best serve the purpose. It looks like using paper clips to visually signify the temporarily feasible ginger-less recipes is the best way to go, reminding Christina which ones are suitable candidates as she flips back and forth through the recipe books without having to remember them all. This is a *custom* use of the kitchen COMPONENT paper clip. Everyone knows that paper clips are designed to secure together a number of sheets of paper, the number depending on the size of the clip. The paper clips in the junk drawer in Christina's kitchen are medium-sized and offer the affordance *attach together up to about 20 sheets of paper*. However, that means that attaching a paper clip to a single piece of paper is also afforded, but there wouldn't be much point unless you were using the paper clip for a different purpose—not for *attaching together* but for *visually marking a single piece of paper*. This use is perfect in the recipe-selection context to serve as a temporary indicator. This unusual or at least less common use of the paper clip becomes a CONSTRUCTED-TOOL. The highlighted area of Figure 3.8 illustrates this translation of the third TASK.

Clearly this laboriously elaborated thinking process would be entirely unconscious and experienced as a single quick task in the case of deciding how to *discard recipes requiring fresh ginger*. But it is a realistic model of the thinking that occurs for complicated ANALYTIC TASKS in real-world qualitative research studies using ATLAS.ti. Expert ATLAS.ti users perform this thinking process quickly and unconsciously, just like Christina would do in the kitchen with her paper clips. But when initially learning to harness ATLAS.ti powerfully, this needs to be thought through consciously in order to shortcut the long process of trial and error, and this is what we will be doing in Parts II and III.

The Sequence of Tasks

We have now completed the principles of the *Five-Level QDA* method and introduced each of its levels. Figure 3.9 displays the five levels of the process. A final point to dwell on is the one-way circular path of action depicted in Figure 3.9, and the question of where one starts on this circular path. It is important to recognize the difference between a fixed sequence of activities—which is *not* the nature of qualitative research and not intended in the *Five-Level QDA* method—and a one-way direction around the five levels—which is intended.

Unlike quantitative or statistical research, qualitative research does not have a fixed sequence of activities. The logic of quantitative or statistical research calls for a predetermined sequence: developing a hypothesis, then gathering data to test it, and finally performing the statistical analysis of the data. After the results are in there is no revisiting and modifying the hypothesis or collecting more data in order to fine-tune the results. But qualitative research has a different logic based on iteration and emergence, and so emergence does not have such a fixed sequence of activities. The specifics depend on the guiding methodology, but as a general principle if you recognize partway through a qualitative study that the data are *telling you* something different from what you thought you were investigating, it would not violate the underlying logic of qualitative research to modify the research question appropriately, provided it still meets the needs of the study objectives or the funders.

The *Five-Level QDA* method is no different—there is no predetermined sequence of activities that is the same in every project. But there *is* a one-way-only direction around the circular path of five levels that serves the iterative and emergent spirit of qualitative research. This is because the iterative process of qualitative research all takes place at the strategy levels—Levels 1 and 2—inside the cloud-like area of Figure 3.9 in which there is no set sequence of activities other than what the guiding methodology suggests. But once an ANALYTIC TASK has been identified, it emerges from the cloud and is on its way, first to Level 3, to be TRANSLATED to either a Level 4 SELECTED-TOOL or a Level 5 CONSTRUCTED-TOOL. When the outcome of those software operations is known, the activity

MEAL PLANNING WORKSHEET – Version 4

Level 1: OBJECTIVES		
OBJECTIVES		
To relax after a long day, promptly prepare a gourmet family meal with what's already available in the kitchen		
GUIDING METHODOLOGY: Recipe-inspired improvisation		
Based on a recipe that stimulates the chef's enthusiasm, adjust every aspect as needed to the constraints of the context		

Level 2: OVERALL PLAN
CURRENT CONCEPTUAL FRAMEWORK

Dietary preferences of family members —determine→ **75 minute recipes** (*Originally 60 minutes, but adjusted to 75 due to unsufficient 60 minute recipes and the reasonableness of 75 minutes constituting "prompt"*)

75 minute recipes —determine→ **Complexity of preparation process**

Available ingredients —determine→ **Complexity of preparation process**

Complexity of preparation process —increase→ **Degree of relaxation needed**

Complexity of preparation process —decrease→ **Prompt preparation**

Level 3: TRANSLATION of TASKS into TOOLS	Levels 4 & 5: SELECTED or CONSTRUCTED TOOLS
Find all suitable one hour or less recipes	
UNITS Individual recipes	SELECTED-TOOL
COMPONENTS Pages of recipe books	Read through each recipe on each recipe book to identify one hour or less recipes
EXPLANATION The recipe books are already organized sequentially by recipes, so there is a direct match between the unit and the component	
Check for fresh ginger	
UNITS Pieces of ginger	SELECTED-TOOL
COMPONENTS All containers in every location of kitchen	Inspect every container on every surface and in every draw or shelf for pieces of ginger
EXPLANATION Each container either does or does not contain a piece of ginger, so there is a direct match	
Discard recipes requiring fresh ginger	
UNITS Individual recipes	CONSTRUCTED-TOOL
COMPONENTS *Paperclips and pages of recipe books*	1. Identify a recipe not requiring ginger
EXPLANATION Use paper clips in custom way by marking a single page rather than attach multiple pages together	2. Attach a paper clip to the first page of the recipe

FIGURE 3.8 Meal Planning Worksheet—Version 4: CONSTRUCTED-TOOLS

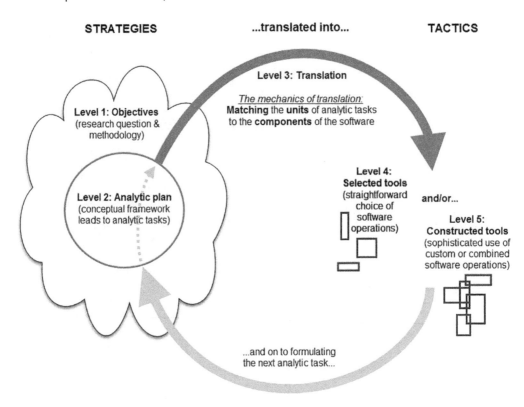

FIGURE 3.9 The five levels of the *Five-Level QDA* method

journeys back to the ANALYTIC PLAN at Level 2 until the next ANALYTIC TASK is produced *in terms of the conceptual framework* of the project, not in terms of the COMPONENTS of the software.

In contrast, the first sign of using ATLAS.ti superficially is the use of an abbreviated process in the opposite direction: first learning how to operate the software in the most straightforward way at Level 4 and then looking around for ways to make use of it in the analysis, at Level 2. This is intuitive, not unreasonable, and a common way of engaging with ATLAS.ti, but it means letting the tactics determine the strategy. This often leads to dead ends because the ANALYTIC TASKS grow out of the software's capabilities rather than the conceptual framework that has been honed from the objectives of the project.

In summary, qualitative analysis means working at the strategy levels, Levels 1 and 2. Once an ANALYTIC TASK has been identified, expressed in its own units, *then* it begins its cyclic one-way-only journey around the *Five-Level QDA* process. This is the essence of harnessing ATLAS.ti powerfully.

References

Bernard, H. R., Wutich, A. Y., & Ryan, G. W. (2017). *Analyzing qualitative data: Systematic approaches* (2nd ed.). Thousand Oaks, CA: Sage.

Bolman, L. G., & Deal, T. E. (1997). *Reframing organizations*. San Francisco: Jossey-Bass.

Brown, J. S., Collins, A., & Duguid, P. (1989). Situated cognition and the culture of learning. *Educational Researcher*, 18(1), 32–42.

Feature. (n.d.). In Wikipedia. Retrieved from https://en.wikipedia.org/wiki/Software_feature, November 4, 2016.

Gaver, W. W. (1991). Technology affordances. In S. P. Robertson, G. M. Olson, & J. S. Olson (Eds.), *Proceedings of the SIGCHI conference on Human Factors in Computing Systems* (pp. 79-84). NY: ACM.

Gibson, J. J. (1979). *The ecological approach to visual perception.* Boston: Houghton Mifflin.

Hartson, R. (2003). Cognitive, physical, sensory, and functional affordances in interaction design. *Behaviour & Information Technology*, 22(5), 315–338.

Morgan, G. (2006). *Images of organization* (Updated ed.). Thousands Oaks, CA: Sage.

Nida, E. A., & Taber, C. R. (1969). *The theory and practice of translation.* Leiden: E. J. Brill.

Norman, D. A. (1988). *The psychology of everyday things.* New York: Basic Books.

Norman, D. A. (1999). Affordance, conventions, and design. *Interactions*, 6(3), 38–43.

PART II

The *Five-Level QDA* Method in Practice

Part II applies the principles of Part I in describing how ATLAS.ti works and how translation is accomplished in practice. Chapter 4 provides an orientation to ATLAS.ti for those upgrading to Version 8 of the program and for those who work in research teams. Chapter 5 describes in depth how ATLAS.ti works in terms of *Five-Level QDA* principles, meaning in terms of its components rather than its features. Chapter 5 is accompanied by videos on the companion website (www.routledgetextbooks.com/textbooks/5LQDA) for each component. Chapter 6 describes in depth the five steps of the translation process, with examples from a variety of research projects.

4

ORIENTATION TO ATLAS.ti

If you are upgrading to ATLAS.ti 8 from an earlier version of the program, or if you work in teams, this chapter provides orientation to ATLAS.ti in these areas. We also discuss the other ATLAS.ti products currently available—ATLAS.ti for the Mac and ATLAS.ti Mobile.

Upgrading to ATLAS.ti 8

If you have been working with ATLAS.ti 7 and plan to upgrade to ATLAS.ti 8, which was released at the end of 2016, this section tells you what has changed and what new features have been added.

The tried-and-true architecture of ATLAS.ti, including its 14 COMPONENTS and how they work, has not changed at all, other than a significant simplification of the document management system. This means that the *Five-Level QDA* method can be adopted in exactly the same way in either ATLAS.ti 7 or ATLAS.ti 8. However, in ATLAS.ti 8 the screens, interface, and look and feel have been completely redesigned so it appears to be a completely different program. Whereas ATLAS.ti 7 is somewhat quirky and idiosyncratic, ATLAS.ti 8 is modern and streamlined. ATLAS.ti 8 uses ribbons organized around functions rather than menus organized around COMPONENTS, as in ATLAS.ti 7, so one finds things in different places. In ATLAS.ti 7 all the moveable windows float free, whereas in ATLAS.ti 8 all windows can be either docked in a tabbed central area or they can float free. All actions taken in ATLAS.ti 8 are almost completely consistent from window to window, as are the icon designs for each action taken. The new design is intended to make some tasks easier to understand and operate by making them visual, particularly when building queries in the Query Tool by dragging items and operators into a "visual query." New features include more powerful search features; the ability to undo and redo; and the ability to import new forms of data from Twitter, Evernote, Endnote, and geo-data, which are worked with in the same way as other forms of data. From the perspective of the *Five-Level QDA* method, none of these changes affect the process of TRANSLATION or how a researcher harnesses ATLAS.ti powerfully. However, one small difference you will find in ATLAS.ti 8 is that a few of the COMPONENTS have new names, displayed in Table 4.1.

TABLE 4.1 Changes to component names in ATLAS.ti 8

Name in *ATLAS.ti* 7	Name in *ATLAS.ti* 8
HU (Hermeneutic unit)	Project
Primary document (PD)	Document
Supercode	Smart code
Family	Group
Superfamily	Smart group

Working in Teams

Conducting research in teams is very different from researching alone. In a solo project every role and task are conducted by the same person. Team projects are different and involve two additional issues: *who does what* and *integrating each team member's contribution*. These are, respectively, the human aspect and the technical aspect of working in teams. This chapter describes the human aspect of *who does what*, which is a necessary preparation for learning about the technical aspect of *integrating each team member's contribution* in Chapter 5.

ATLAS.ti is not a multiuser program. Team members work independently in ATLAS.ti on their own assigned analytic activities, just as they would if each were working on a solo research project. Then periodically each team member's work is merged in ATLAS.ti with the other team members' work.

Once a team member has an assigned task, she harnesses the program powerfully using the *Five-Level QDA* method in the same way as if working alone. There are therefore no separate or different *Five-Level QDA* principles when working in a team and no separate chapter in this book. However, there are important issues to be considered in determining *who does what*. Even though this has nothing directly to do with the *Five-Level QDA* method, we discuss some important aspects *of who does what* before going on to discuss how ATLAS.ti has been designed to *integrate team members' work*.

Deciding *who does what* raises a number of questions, and the answers vary greatly from team to team. Here we discuss four questions: Can some tasks be delegated to less experienced team members? Is the style of leadership more democratic or centralized? Are constraints needed on team members' freedom of action? And finally, how frequently should team members' work be integrated?

Delegation

Does the style of analysis lend itself to delegating some tasks to less experienced researchers? Some leaders of qualitative research projects have had an earlier career in quantitative research and are accustomed to delegating tasks, such as running experiments or the data entry of a large number of survey responses, to less experienced research assistants or clerical staff. Qualitative research has few, if any, comparable tasks, and managing a qualitative project similarly to a quantitative study can lead to anomalous situations if a critical part of a study—for example, the initial reading of texts and the generation of data-driven codes or categories—is considered to be humdrum work and assigned to the least experienced research assistant. Some methodologies do include phases of less interpretive activities—such as a period of use of predetermined and well-defined codes or categories to accumulate examples in the data for subsequent interpretation—and these methodologies accommodate delegation of these tasks to less experienced team members. But other methodologies do not, particularly those in which interpretation is to the fore. For these projects it is difficult to escape the conclusion that there are no lesser or more junior analytic activities, and to a large extent every team member has the same analytic status in the team. The underlying issue is whether the inevitable compromises in any research project with limited time and funding have to extend to delegating core or critical analytic activities to less experienced team members.

Leadership Style

Is the team more of a democratic venture, with each researcher's contribution having similar weight, or more centralized, with one or more Principal Investigators serving as decision makers in a group of contributing researchers? Our experience is that qualitative researchers are generally democratic, but they sometimes underestimate the significant increase in time required to incorporate and integrate the conceptual contributions of multiple researchers. Centralized projects involve a Principal Investigator receiving the contributions of each team member in each round of analysis, making all decisions about what to accept and how it is to be integrated, and then providing explanations of her decisions to inform the next round of analysis. This is a much faster and more streamlined process. Before deciding on a leadership style, consider the purpose of conducting the research in a team. In some projects the rationale is to investigate a phenomenon from the perspective of different disciplines, and so the contributions of each discipline's representative need to have equal or at least significant weight. In this case, the data analysis must proceed in a more democratic fashion. In other projects the purpose of having a team is to meet a tight completion deadline that a single researcher could not accomplish. Time constraints lend themselves to a more centralized approach. In other teams personalities play an undeniable role. But we are surprised that many teams are unclear about why their project is being conducted with multiple researchers in the first place. When planning *who does what* in a team project, the best question to ask first may be: *Why are we conducting this project in a team?*

Constraints

Are constraints needed on team members' freedom of action? When working alone, each ANALYTIC TASK is individually TRANSLATED into a SELECTED- or CONSTRUCTED-TOOL with reference to what is coming next—no predetermined constraints are needed. But when working in a team the actions taken by a team member can have unexpected outcomes when merged with other team members' work. At the most general level there are only three possible actions when merging team members' work: to *add* something, to *modify* something, or to *delete* something.

In principle, *adding* something is no problem. This, in fact, what we want team members to do, whether identifying new meaning units of data, adding new codes, adding new analytic writing, adding new visual representations, or adding something to another team member's work. Certainly policies are needed so that each team member knows what is expected of them. This is all part of designing their assigned tasks. But there is nothing technically problematic about a team member adding something in ATLAS.ti.

Deleting something intuitively feels like something we need to control. If an inexperienced team member deletes something important, such as a code or a piece of analytic writing, this might be expected to cause a problem. Unexpectedly, it does not. If at least one other team member has not also deleted that same thing, it will automatically reappear when every team member's work is merged together. However, we do not want to encourage team members to feel free to delete things willy-nilly. Deleting has an indirect effect because the team member who deletes something—for example, a code—will continue her work under the mistaken assumption that the code no longer exists, but her subsequent coding will then be subtly different from everyone else's. A policy is therefore needed for deleting things. This could be flagging something with a comment suggesting it be deleted, rather than actually deleting it, or simply bringing it to the team's attention at the next team meeting. Appropriate policies will vary depending on the stage of the project and the relationships, status, or physical proximity of the various team members.

In contrast to *adding* things—which is not problematic in general—and *deleting* things—which is to some extent an impotent act—*modifying* or changing things is almost always problematic. For example, if we have a code named *hard and invigorating*, a team member decides that a better code name would be *stressful*, so that it could also apply to respondents' experiences that had a tinge of stress. This effectively broadens the meaning of the code. Consider what happens on merging each team member's project file, which in ATLAS.ti is called a PROJECT. The original code *hard and invigorating* still exists on everyone else's PROJECTS, so it appears in the merged PROJECT. But the new code *stressful* also appears in the merged PROJECT. This new code contains all this team member's newly coded segments of data to his newly renamed code, but it also contains all the segments originally coded to *hard and invigorating* in all earlier rounds of work coded by all team members. These segments are therefore now attached to both codes in the merged PROJECT. There is now overlap and a degree of incoherence in the coding scheme, particularly if other team members have been coding respondents' stressful experiences to an entirely different code. What happens next depends on the policies for dealing with newly appearing codes. In the best case, all new codes are routinely brought to the team's attention and discussed. This would lead to a decision about whether or not to integrate the new code *stressful* into the conceptual framework and perhaps remove the earlier *hard and invigorating* codings now mistakenly double-coded to the new code *stressful*. In the worst case, teams do not establish a policy for making modifications or they allow team members free rein.

In summary, the cause of conceptual coherence in the emerging analysis is best served if policies are thought through for *adding*, *deleting*, and *modifying* and appropriate constraints put on the freedom of action of each team member. In our consulting practice we give team members free rein to *add* things, but we prohibit *deleting* and *modifying*. We instead decide on a workable method for team members to communicate their proposed deletions and modifications and for these to be put into effect immediately following the next merge of all PROJECTS.

Frequency of Integration

How frequently should you merge team members' work? ATLAS.ti is unconcerned about this because each merge operation is independent. But from the human point of view an intentional plan is best. Think in terms of merge cycles. After each cycle of work all team members must stop work while their PROJECTS are collected and merged, and so they must not continue until the merged PROJECT is redistributed to each team for the next round of work. How often should this occur? There is no typical or recommended plan. We have worked with team projects in which each team member analyzes all the data separately from their disciplinary perspective, followed by a single integration or merge of all members' contributions at the end. And we have worked with a multinational team at the opposite end of the spectrum, in which researchers in vastly different time zones merged all their work nightly so that everyone could see the next day what everyone else had done the previous day. This was unusual and challenging to accomplish on the human side but unproblematic on the technical side regarding ATLAS.ti procedures. In practice most projects fall somewhere in the middle, with smaller projects merging their work on an ad hoc basis at turning points in the analysis or whenever the currently assigned tasks are completed. Larger or longer-term projects with many researchers conducting different parts of the analysis on different schedules often have a more structured plan, such as merging every Friday afternoon.

Chapter 5 discusses the technical aspects of combining team members' work.

ATLAS.ti for Mac, iPad, iPhone, and Android

ATLAS.ti has been a Windows program since the early 1990s. In 2016 a Mac version was released with the same COMPONENTS but not all of the features of the Windows version. We understand that an updated version called ATLAS.ti for Mac 1.5 will be released after this book has gone to press and that this Mac version will be similar, but not identical, to ATLAS.ti 8 for Windows. We anticipate that the *Five-Level QDA* method described in this book will be easily adopted by users of the Mac version of the program, although there will be some differences in screen and interface design. We recommend learning about the capabilities of ATLAS.ti for Mac 1.5 from the developer's website: www.atlasti.com.

In 2013 ATLAS.ti Mobile for iOS and Android was released. These mobile applications are designed to facilitate data collection and initial analysis and integrate with both the Windows and Mac versions of ATLAS.ti. ATLAS.ti Mobile allows data to be collected, edited, and coded while in the field; to be tagged with a geographical location; and to be written about using memos and comments. ATLAS.ti Mobile supports text, graphic, and audio and video documents. ATLAS.ti Mobile projects are exported via Dropbox or iTunes and then imported into ATLAS.ti to continue working on. More information about ATLAS.ti Mobile can be found on the ATLAS.ti website: http://atlasti.com/product/.

5

THE ARCHITECTURE OF ATLAS.ti

This chapter describes the architecture of ATLAS.ti, focusing on the design and purpose of each COMPONENT rather than the nuts-and-bolts of operating the software. The purpose is to provide a comprehensive understanding of the program. If you are not already familiar with operating ATLAS.ti 8, then immediately after reading this chapter is the time to take advantage of the free online resources or fee-based workshops offered by the software developers at www.atlasti.com. This site also provides an up-to-date listing of independent training companies offering their own courses.

Component Orientation Videos

After reading about each COMPONENT in this chapter we invite you to view a short orientation video of that COMPONENT at the companion website. These videos make the abstract learning about each component concrete, but are not hands-on instruction in operating the program. We recommend that you read about a component and watch the corresponding video before moving on to the next one. To register and log in to the companion website go to www.routledgetextbooks.com/textbooks/5LQDA and follow the on-screen instructions.

The Organization of the Program

There are many ways to describe how ATLAS.ti is organized. As discussed in Chapter 3 we do not focus on the features of the software. "Feature" is a common term to describe generally what a program can do. Developers try to make the features visible on the screen so that it is as obvious as possible how to operate the program according to their assumptions about how the software will be used. In our experience it is not helpful to focus on features when learning ATLAS.ti, because simply knowing what the program can do does not result in harnessing the software powerfully. We therefore do not go through ATLAS.ti feature by feature. Instead we think separately about ATLAS.ti's COMPONENTS and the actions that can be taken on those COMPONENTS in order to select and construct TOOLS. Explicit awareness of COMPONENTS facilitates powerful harnessing of the program.

Regarding terminology, for terms with specific ATLAS.ti meanings, such as Project Library, we capitalize them to indicate these are terms you will see on the screen. When we use terms that have a specific *Five-Level QDA* meaning, we continue to present them in SMALL CAPS. If a term is both a *Five-Level QDA* term and an ATLAS.ti term, SMALL CAPS wins, as in CODE. We do this because we are teaching the *Five-Level QDA* method, not the fine details of operating ATLAS.ti.

Components

For convenience we discuss the COMPONENTS in this chapter in five clusters. There is no significance to the clusters themselves—this is simply a way to divide the information so that it's easier to digest. The five clusters are listed in Table 5.1, and the COMPONENTS are listed and defined in Table 5.2.

TABLE 5.1 The five clusters of components

Providing data	Providing the data to ATLAS.ti and everything to do with organizing, managing, and using data files.
Segmenting data	Creating and working with defined segments of data, called quotations. These have primacy in ATLAS.ti as the main building block in a qualitative analysis.
Conceptualizing data	Most commonly accomplished by using codes to represent the concepts in a study, by linking them to quotations, or by grouping them to represent more general concepts. Other components may be harnessed for these conceptualizing purposes, and codes may be harnessed for purposes other than conceptualizing data.
Writing	Writing can be captured in comments (annotations of other components), in standalone memos, and by directly editing documents inside ATLAS.ti.
Visualizing	Any components can be displayed and worked with visually in an ATLAS.ti display called a network.

TABLE 5.2 The 14 components of ATLAS.ti

Components		*Definition*
Providing data	DOCUMENT	A data file displayed in the ATLAS.ti-PROJECT
	DOCUMENT-GROUPS AND SMART-GROUPS	A DOCUMENT-GROUP is a collection of DOCUMENTS, and a DOCUMENT-SMART-GROUP is a collection of DOCUMENT-GROUPS
Segmenting data	QUOTATION	A defined segment of data that is not linked to anything else in the ATLAS.ti-PROJECT
	HYPERLINKED-QUOTATION	A pair of QUOTATIONS that have been linked with a named "relation"
Conceptualizing data	CODE	A named concept that can be linked to other COMPONENTS for either analytic or housekeeping purposes
	CODED-QUOTATION	A QUOTATION linked to one or more CODES
	CODE-GROUPS AND SMART-GROUPS	A CODE-GROUP is a collection of CODES, and a CODE-SMART-GROUP is a collection of CODE-GROUPS
	SMART-CODE	A special kind of CODE that consists of a saved query of other CODES
	SMART-CODE-SNAPSHOT	A frozen SMART-CODE automatically linked by ATLAS.ti to all the QUOTATIONS retrieved by a SMART-CODE at a moment in time
Writing	COMMENT	An annotation of any length written on any COMPONENT
	MEMO	A piece of writing that can be stand-alone or linked to other COMPONENTS
	MEMO-GROUPS AND SMART-GROUPS	A MEMO-GROUP is a collection of MEMOS, and a MEMO-SMART-GROUP is a collection of MEMO-GROUPS
Visualizing	NETWORK	Graphical windows to display and work visually with any set of COMPONENTS
	NETWORK-GROUPS AND SMART-GROUPS	A NETWORK-GROUP is a collection of NETWORKS, and a NETWORK-SMART-GROUP is a collection of NETWORK-GROUPS

Actions

The *Five-Level QDA* method describes ATLAS.ti in terms of these COMPONENTS—the things that can be acted on. This chapter describes the COMPONENTS and how they work. The next chapter focuses on the TRANSLATION process—taking the UNITS of ANALYTIC TASKS and matching them to these COMPONENTS of the software. At that point we have to know what actions we can take on each COMPONENT. In the next chapter we therefore list these actions—one set of actions common to all COMPONENTS, and one set specific to each COMPONENT. Focusing on how the COMPONENTS work first and listing the actions that can be taken on them later is the easiest way to master the *Five-Level QDA* process.

Tools

In the *Five-Level QDA* method, a TOOL is the combination of a COMPONENT and an action appropriate for a specific ANALYTIC TASK. There is no definitive list of TOOLS, because there are so many ways of acting on each COMPONENT and so many possible ANALYTIC TASKS and contexts. No benefit would be served by attempting to list hundreds of TOOLS, even if such a list were possible.

The ATLAS.ti Interface

We begin with the program interface as a whole. The ATLAS.ti screen has four main elements.

1. *Navigators.* These are lists of COMPONENTS that can be opened and docked in tabbed navigator panels on the right or left side of the screen, or both.
2. *Workspace.* The central area of the screen that contains tabbed windows.
3. *Menu Tabs and Associated Ribbons.* The ribbon displays the relevant toolbar for whichever menu tab at the top of the screen is selected. Additional menu tabs appear for the area of the program that is currently the "live" window.
4. *Floating Windows.* Each COMPONENT can be opened as a floating window to be moved around the screen as convenient, as an alternative to "docking" them in the navigator panels to the left or right or in the central workspace. These floating windows are called Managers. They contain a listing of their COMPONENT, like the Navigators, but they also include many more actions to take on the COMPONENTS

There is enormous flexibility in arranging the screen to suit your preferences and the needs of any project, and it is simple and intuitive to open and arrange the screen elements. In general there are two main ways to take actions: first, by clicking on a main menu tab to reveal its ribbon and then choosing an option; second, by right-clicking on a particular area or object on the screen. If a context menu comes up, options will be available to take actions relevant to whatever you right-clicked on.

Figure 5.1 illustrates the four main elements of the screen. Now that we have introduced you to ATLAS.ti, we invite you to go to the companion website to view the first *Component Orientation* videos, *The ATLAS.ti Windows interface* and *The ATLAS.ti Mac interface.* These videos demonstrates how to work with the four main elements and navigate around the screen.

The ATLAS.ti Project

All your work for all your ATLAS.ti projects appears inside ATLAS.ti. There are no external files of any kind that you deal with directly—unless you are working with large video or audio files

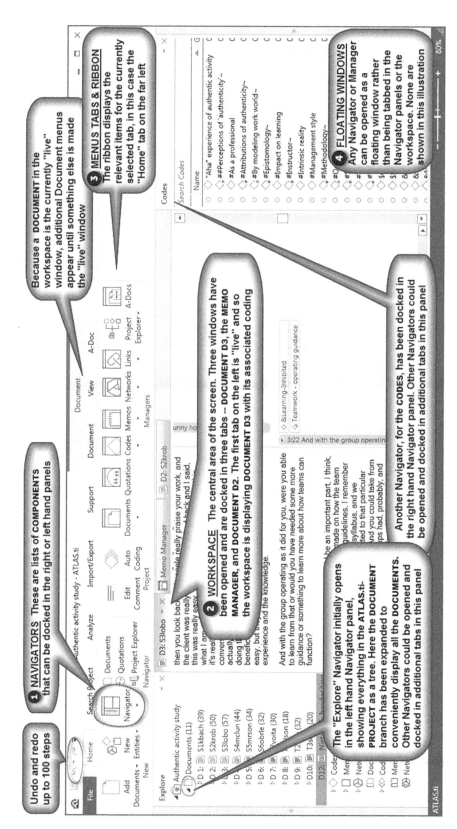

FIGURE 5.1 The ATLAS.ti interface

that you store in a location of your choice outside the program and which ATLAS.ti accesses separately. But other than that exception, ATLAS.ti takes care of managing all files from within the program.

You begin by opening ATLAS.ti, and on the opening screen you see all the projects you have been working on. From this screen you have the opportunity to do several things:

- Create a new project.
- Open, rename, or delete a project you created earlier.
- Import a previously backed up or "bundled" project.
- Import a project from Version 5, 6, or 7 of ATLAS.ti, which then becomes a version 8 project.

Once you open a project or create a new one, you enter the ATLAS.ti main screen to view your project, as illustrated in Figure 5.1. Throughout the book we use the term "project" for your research study, which means your project at the strategy levels. ATLAS.ti also uses the term "project" for your ATLAS.ti project at the tactics levels, which you can only locate and work on within the program. We therefore call this the ATLAS.ti-PROJECT. There is no separate computer file for the ATLAS.ti-PROJECT; it is only accessed through the program screen, as illustrated in Figure 5.1. ATLAS.ti stores all the information about each ATLAS.ti-PROJECT on our hard drives in a Project Library that you do not need to visit or know how to access.

The next sections describe several other aspects of an ATLAS.ti-PROJECT. The ATLAS.ti-PROJECT is not a COMPONENT in its own right, but the container for all the other COMPONENTS. There is therefore no *Component Orientation* video for this topic on the companion website.

Adding Data to an ATLAS.ti-Project

When you add data such as a Microsoft Word or PDF file to your ATLAS.ti-PROJECT, ATLAS.ti makes a copy of it in a particular database format and stores this file in its hidden Project Library on your hard drive. We do not have—or need—direct access to these versions of our data files stored in the ATLAS.ti Project Library. Your original copy of the data file is unaffected by all this—it was only read by ATLAS.ti, and it remains where it is, unchanged, no longer needed by ATLAS.ti once ATLAS.ti has made its version for the Project Library.

One exception to the usual practice of adding data is asking ATLAS.ti to *link* to any large multimedia files stored on your hard drive, rather than *copy* enormous files into the Project Library. If you do link multimedia documents to an ATLAS.ti-PROJECT, you must be sure not to move these files or edit them outside ATLAS.ti; otherwise, the program will no longer be able to find and display them correctly in its workspace. This is the same commonsense principle that applies to other external links within your data files, such as to webpages and to geo-locations through direct integration with Google Earth. If the link is changed or broken, naturally ATLAS.ti cannot access it. Further details about preparing data files and adding them to the ATLAS.ti-PROJECT are discussed later in the section on providing data.

Backing Up an ATLAS.ti-Project

You may be concerned with backing up your ATLAS.ti-PROJECT. How would you do this if there is no separate project file to back up? ATLAS.ti has a feature to export a Project Bundle of an entire ATLAS.ti-PROJECT into a file that you can save anywhere you wish. This file includes everything needed, including all the data, to later import the Project Bundle back into the program as a working ATLAS.ti-PROJECT. You cannot open or make use of the Project Bundle file other than by importing it back into ATLAS.ti. It therefore serves as a confidential backup of the project. Further details about backing up and moving ATLAS.ti-PROJECTS appear in the section on the ATLAS.ti-PROJECT as a whole.

One ATLAS.ti-Project per Research Project

Each ATLAS.ti-PROJECT is self-contained and does not "communicate" with any other ATLAS.ti-PROJECT. It is therefore not possible to conduct any analytic activities across different ATLAS.ti-PROJECTS. The usual way to proceed is to have one ATLAS.ti-PROJECT for each research project, no matter how large it is or how many different people are working on the project. If a research project has several separate parts, there are many ways inside ATLAS.ti to focus on just a part of the project or temporarily hide parts. It rarely makes sense to divide a project into parts and create a separate ATLAS.ti-PROJECT for each part. Very little would be gained and potentially a lot of opportunity to review other parts of the project while working on a different part would be lost. Likewise, the opportunity to later compare or cross-analyze between parts of the project, something you might not have anticipated at the beginning, would be lost.

ATLAS.ti is a single-user program. This means that in team projects each team member has their own copy of the ATLAS.ti-PROJECT to work on in their own copy of the program and that these copies are periodically merged. Each team member will be assigned certain tasks, which we discussed in Chapter 4 as the human aspect of working in teams—*who does what.* Even though it is likely that each team member will be analyzing only part of the data, it still makes sense in almost all circumstances to have a single ATLAS.ti-PROJECT for the entire research project. This is because ATLAS.ti makes it easy to focus on just some parts of an ATLAS.ti-PROJECT, and there is no reason to sacrifice a view of the whole project in a single ATLAS.ti-PROJECT just because each team member is working on only a part. The technical aspects of working in teams—*integrating each team member's contribution*—are discussed in detail in the final section of this chapter, "Working in Teams."

Providing Data

When some or all of the data are available to be analyzed, it is time to provide them to the ATLAS.ti-PROJECT. Two of the 14 COMPONENTS are most closely associated with this activity, displayed in Table 5.3.

Documents

DOCUMENTS are the data that you work with inside an ATLAS.ti-PROJECT. Because ATLAS.ti uses the term DOCUMENT, to avoid confusion we no longer use the term document (in regular type) for the data files you have created and saved on your computer, network, memory stick, etc. Instead

TABLE 5.3 Components most associated with providing data to an ATLAS.ti-PROJECT

Components	Definition
DOCUMENT	A data file displayed in the ATLAS.ti-PROJECT.
DOCUMENT-GROUPS and SMART-GROUPS	DOCUMENTS can be organized into DOCUMENT-GROUPS. DOCUMENT-GROUPS can themselves be organized into DOCUMENT-SMART-GROUPS.

we use terms that refer to the type of data file we are discussing, such as Microsoft Word files, digital photographs, video files, or Microsoft Excel spreadsheets. When talking generically we refer to the computer files containing your data simply as *data files*, or just *data* or just *files*.

Ways to Provide Data

ATLAS.ti offers four ways to provide data to an ATLAS.ti-PROJECT: *adding* files, *importing* files, *linking* files, and directly *creating* DOCUMENTS. You can provide as many data files as you want—there is no limit. And you can do so at any time—all at once at the beginning or some initially and others later.

- *Adding a file.* ATLAS.ti simply creates a new DOCUMENT for a file that is added inside the ATLAS.ti-PROJECT, ready to work with. ATLAS.ti does this by creating and storing a copy of the file in ATLAS.ti's Project Library. ATLAS.ti manages all this for us in the background. All that we see is the new DOCUMENT inside the ATLAS.ti-PROJECT, and the original data files stay wherever they are, untouched and no longer needed by the program. ATLAS.ti is happy to accept files in a wide variety of formats—all the commonly used formats for Microsoft Word and other text files, PDF files, graphic files, audio files, or video files.

Importing a file works in a different way for other kinds of files that cannot be directly added. ATLAS.ti extracts data from these files and puts them into different places within the ATLAS.ti-PROJECT. The way in which data are imported depends on the source. ATLAS.ti can currently import data from Microsoft Excel, Twitter, Endnote, and Evernote. Additional types may be added by the software developers in future updates.

- *Importing Microsoft Excel data.* Microsoft Excel files cannot themselves be added to an ATLAS.ti-PROJECT, but all the items of data contained within them can be imported. This is typically used when survey data have been collected in the cells of a spreadsheet, with a row for each respondent and columns for different kinds of responses, ranging from yes/no responses to extensive amounts of text. The imported data are turned into a set of DOCUMENTS, coded and organized according to the kinds of data in each column. Among other uses, this can facilitate mixed-methods analysis.
- *Importing Twitter data.* This requires authorizing ATLAS.ti to access your Twitter account. Tweets are imported and created as a set of DOCUMENTS CODED to their hashtags.
- *Importing Endnote data.* For Endnote records that have a file attached, that file can be imported as a DOCUMENT. In this case other fields in the Endnote record are created as DOCUMENT-GROUPS for all other Endnote DOCUMENTS imported with the same values in those fields.
- *Importing Evernote data.* This requires authorizing ATLAS.ti to access your Evernote account. Each note is imported as a DOCUMENT, and DOCUMENT-GROUPS are created for each Evernote notebook.

In addition to adding or importing data, some files can be *linked* to the ATLAS.ti-PROJECT.

- *Linking audio or video files.* If you work with large audio or video files, you can link the files to the ATLAS.ti-PROJECT rather than add them. This avoids ATLAS.ti creating a copy of very large files in the Project Library. ATLAS.ti will access the linked files from wherever the files are stored on your computer hard drive and display them in the ATLAS.ti-PROJECT. Once a file is linked, you must not move or edit the files outside ATLAS.ti or they can no longer be located by the program or worked with inside the ATLAS.ti-PROJECT.

- **Audio or video files synchronized with their transcripts.** Transcripts of audio or video files and the audio or video itself are all created as DOCUMENTS. The transcripts can be associated with their corresponding media file by inserting time-based anchors in the transcript DOCUMENT. As you move through either the text or the media DOCUMENT, the associated DOCUMENT follows in sync, highlighting the parts of the transcript that correspond to the portion of the media file being played.

Finally, DOCUMENTS can be directly created within the ATLAS.ti-PROJECT.

- **Creating empty DOCUMENTS within ATLAS.ti.** A new empty DOCUMENT can be created inside the ATLAS.ti-PROJECT and data typed or pasted in.
- **Geo-documents.** Links can be created from within an ATLAS.ti-PROJECT to Goggle Earth locations.
- **Convert a MEMO into a DOCUMENT.** Any memo can be converted into a DOCUMENT so that actions relating to documents can be undertaken on your own writing, such as coding. The memo remains as both a memo and a document, unless you delete one version.

Organizing Data into Documents

There are many possible ways to organize the information in your data files before adding them to the ATLAS.ti-PROJECT. For example, if you were interviewing 10 participants three times each, once before a new training program was to start, once during the training, and once three months later, you could make one Microsoft Word file for the transcript of each interview, leading to 30 DOCUMENTS in all. This would be the most straightforward way to organize the data. Or you could have one Microsoft Word file for each participant and put each participant's three interview transcripts all in one file, leading to 10 documents in all, one per person. The way you organize the data into files before adding them to the ATLAS.ti-PROJECT affects whether or not you can SELECT or CONSTRUCT TOOLS that act on DOCUMENTS to fulfill a particular ANALYTIC TASK. For example, if the purpose is to compare each participant's first interview with their last, and each participant's first, second, and third interview are all in one DOCUMENT, you could not use DOCUMENT-level TOOLS for this purpose. However, there will always be other ways to accomplish the same task, albeit less conveniently, and so the organization of the data is never critical, but more a matter of convenience. Nevertheless, to allow the most efficient use of the program, it makes sense to think about your research objectives when organizing data files before you add them to the ATLAS.ti-PROJECT. Once you have finished studying this chapter and have the broad overview of the whole program, it will be possible to make informed decisions about the most efficient way to organize data into DOCUMENTS.

In general you only have one opportunity to organize the data before adding files to the ATLAS.ti-PROJECT and they become set as DOCUMENTS. This is the only area of ATLAS.ti that is fixed—everything else can be changed easily at will. There is one exception that is discussed in the next section—text DOCUMENTS are editable within ATLAS.ti and so can be changed after they have been added to the ATLAS.ti-PROJECT. All other kinds of DOCUMENTS, including PDF DOCUMENTS, cannot be edited or changed within ATLAS.ti.

Editing Text Documents

If you later realize after adding text files to an ATLAS.ti-PROJECT that there would have been a more convenient way to organize the data into DOCUMENTS, it is possible to edit the text. Therefore in theory it is possible to reorganize a whole set of DOCUMENTS by cutting and pasting text from one DOCUMENT to another. In practice this is not a common solution, and it is almost always easier to SELECT or CONSTRUCT alternative TOOLS to fulfill a task in a different way, and editing DOCUMENTS is usually adopted for smaller tasks than reorganizing the data.

Many researchers are uncomfortable with changing data in any way. But there are many legitimate purposes for DOCUMENT editing, such as removing inadvertent identifying information from transcripts, correcting transcription errors, adding annotations directly into the text, or appending new data to a DOCUMENT, such as additional posts in an online discussion forum.

Exploring Documents

Once files have been added to an ATLAS.ti-PROJECT, a common first step is to explore the DOCU-MENTS. In the most general sense this means looking for what is in the data before identifying and conceptualizing data segments, but exploration is also undertaken throughout a project. Exploring is different from interrogating, discussed later, which is asking questions about what has already been done in order to move to the next step.

At the strategy levels *exploring data* has different meanings depending on the methodology. Some methodologies seek clear-cut, descriptive accounts of content, and the resulting ANALYTIC TASKS may include careful reading of the data, as well as various counts of the content. For methodologies that are more concerned with the interpretation of lived experience, exploration is an interpretive process of sense-making before segmenting or conceptualizing the data. And other methodologies are between these extremes. In Chapter 6 we discuss a variety of ANALYTIC TASKS whose purpose is exploration. In this chapter we are concerned with the mechanisms of exploring DOCUMENTS that will be useful in a variety of ANALYTIC TASKS. ATLAS.ti offers the following features for finding, searching, and counting the content of DOCUMENTS:

- **Searching a DOCUMENT.** A DOCUMENT that is displayed in the live window can be searched for any contiguous sequence of characters, whether a whole word or part of a word. Clicking on any "hit" in the list of results takes you to its location in the DOCUMENT.
- **Searching the whole ATLAS.ti-PROJECT.** A feature called Search Project also searches for a contiguous sequence of characters, not only in DOCUMENTS but also in any COMPONENT or combination of COMPONENTS.
- **Auto-coding.** Finds any sequence of characters, whether a whole word, part of a word, a phrase, or a selection of words, and automatically turns each example into CODED-QUOTATIONS, which can then be accessed later to work on. Auto-coding is discussed further in the section on conceptualizing data.
- **Counting words.** The Word List counts the number and percentage of each word in a DOCU-MENT and offers a variety of options for outputting.
- **Visualizing words.** The Word Cloud counts the words in one or more DOCUMENTS and displays the cloud in a "spiral" or "typewriter" format.

Figure 5.2 illustrates how DOCUMENTS appear in ATLAS.ti. We now invite you to go to the companion website to view the *Component Orientation* video for this COMPONENT.

Document-Groups and Document-Smart-Groups

DOCUMENTS can be grouped for a variety of purposes. ATLAS.ti allows you to put DOCUMENTS into simple GROUPS or to combine groups into SMART-GROUPS. Once created, both GROUPS and SMART-GROUPS serve the same variety of purposes.

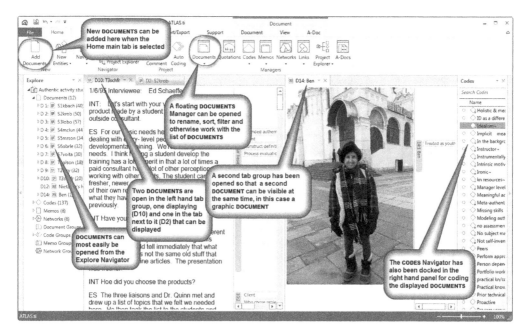

FIGURE 5.2   DOCUMENTS

Groups

DOCUMENTS can be put into DOCUMENT-GROUPS. Any DOCUMENT can be a member of any number of DOCUMENT-GROUPS. There are varied and innumerable reasons for doing this, some obvious and some subtle, depending on the purpose of the ANALYTIC TASK, and many different uses will be illustrated in the video demonstrations. All these uses fall into the following general categories:

- ***Acting on many*** *DOCUMENTS*. Putting documents into DOCUMENT-GROUPS or DOCUMENT-SMART-GROUPS enables actions to be taken on all those DOCUMENTS at once. For example, in the study described earlier, if each participant's three interviews were in separate DOCUMENTS, and an ANALYTIC TASK required interrogating all of one participant's interviews, then the three DOCUMENTS could be put in a DOCUMENT-GROUP, allowing all three interviews to be interrogated with a single action.
- ***Filtering.*** DOCUMENT-GROUPS are used to filter lists of DOCUMENTS. This means seeing only a subset of all the DOCUMENTS—the ones that are in the DOCUMENT-GROUP—with all the others temporarily hidden.

Smart-Groups

DOCUMENT-GROUPS can themselves be put into groups, called DOCUMENT-SMART-GROUPS. They are "smart" because there is a logical criterion for a DOCUMENT-GROUP to be a member of a SMART-GROUP. DOCUMENT-SMART-GROUPS allow much more sophisticated grouping of documents. Once either kind is created, they both function in the same way and serve the same innumerable purposes.

DOCUMENT-SMART-GROUPS are formed by combining DOCUMENT-GROUPS using operators—*OR, AND,* and *NOT.* For example, we could use one DOCUMENT-GROUP for male interviews and another

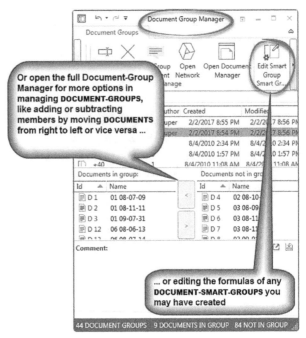

FIGURE 5.3 DOCUMENT–GROUPS AND DOCUMENT–SMART–GROUPS

for female interviews, and also DOCUMENT-GROUPS for the different sets of interviews—one for the first interviews, one for the second interviews, and one for the third interviews. Then we could use the *AND* operator to combine the DOCUMENT-GROUPS for the male interviews *AND* the first interviews into a new DOCUMENT-SMART-GROUP containing only the first interviews with men. Alternatively we could use the *OR* operator to combine the second and third interviews DOCUMENT-GROUPS. This would create a new DOCUMENT-SMART-GROUP containing all the second and third interviews, whether with men or women, but none of the first set of interviews.

One advantage of creating DOCUMENT-SMART-GROUPS is that they update automatically. If a new female participant is added to the study, her DOCUMENTS can be added to the appropriate DOCUMENT-GROUPS, and any associated DOCUMENT-SMART-GROUP will automatically include this new DOCUMENT the next time it is used.

Figure 5.3 illustrates how DOCUMENT-GROUPS and DOCUMENT-SMART-GROUPS appear in ATLAS.ti. We now invite you to go to the companion website to view the *Component Orientation* video for this COMPONENT.

Segmenting Data

Much of the activity in a qualitative analysis is accomplished by identifying meaningful segments of data within DOCUMENTS and working with those segments. Two of the 14 COMPONENTS most closely associated with segmenting data are QUOTATIONS and HYPERLINKED-QUOTATIONS, displayed in Table 5.4.

A primary activity of many qualitative methodologies is to first explore the data and then identify and mark segments that are considered meaningful. In ATLAS.ti *segmenting data* always means *creating* QUOTATIONS, which then become COMPONENTS that can be acted on. An important aspect of the design of ATLAS.ti is the primacy of QUOTATIONS over other COMPONENTS.

TABLE 5.4 Components most associated with segmenting data

Components	Definition
QUOTATION	A defined segment of data that is not linked to anything else in the ATLAS.ti-PROJECT
HYPERLINKED–QUOTATION	A pair of QUOTATIONS that have been linked with a named "relation"

Quotations

A QUOTATION is ATLAS.ti's name for a segment of data that has been identified as meaningful. Creating a QUOTATION marks it in the DOCUMENT and makes it available to later be retrieved or linked to other COMPONENTS. QUOTATIONS can be created in any type of DOCUMENT, but how they are created and what they consist of differ according to the type of data. For example, QUOTATIONS in text DOCUMENTS consist of stretches of text of any length, but in graphic DOCUMENTS such as photographs or drawings, they consist of rectangular selections of parts of the image. The same applies to the text and embedded graphical parts of PDF documents and Twitter, Endnote, and Evernote data. In audio and video files QUOTATIONS consist of a number of milliseconds of audio or frames of video. If you have synchronized a written transcript with the media file, QUOTATIONS can be created in the transcript and read when listening to the audio or viewing the video.

The principles that apply to working with QUOTATIONS are the same whatever the form of the data. The only differences between using text, graphic, audio, or video QUOTATIONS are how they are presented on the screen, with slight differences in the mechanics of operating the software and the way QUOTATIONS are outputted.

Quotations Can Be of Any Size

There are no restrictions on the size of QUOTATIONS. They can be as small as one character of text, or even a single space, or at the other extreme as long as the entire DOCUMENT, which is useful for several specialized purposes. Almost all QUOTATIONS fall somewhere between these extremes. For example, when working with text data, QUOTATIONS may consist of a sentence or a few sentences, a short paragraph or a few paragraphs, but there are no rules: it depends on the nature of the data, the dictates of the methodology, and the purpose of the particular ANALYTIC TASK being undertaken.

Quotations Can Overlap

There are no restrictions on the location of QUOTATIONS in a DOCUMENT, meaning that QUOTATIONS can overlap one another in any way. One QUOTATION might comprise a large paragraph of text, and another QUOTATION might comprise just one sentence in the middle of the same paragraph. This second QUOTATION is an independent COMPONENT that, technically, is completely unrelated to the first, even though the same lines of text appear in both the embedded and the enclosing QUOTATION. The smaller QUOTATION comprises a different and independent unit of meaning that serves a different analytic purpose than the QUOTATION comprising the entire paragraph.

A Quotation Can Be Redefined at Any Time

A QUOTATION can be made larger or smaller at any time, in other words, resized to have different segments of data associated with it. When working with text data, for example, it is common to reread a QUOTATION on screen and decide to extend its range in order to include the additional context in the following two or three sentences, or perhaps include the interview question that helps make sense of the response.

Viewing Quotations

There are unlimited reasons for viewing and reading QUOTATIONS. A common reason is to view all QUOTATIONS coded to a CODE in order to read together all the different pieces of evidence for the concept reflected by the CODE. The purpose may be to assess the quality or validity of the coding or to assess the meaning or validity of the evolving concept reflected by the CODE.

There are three ways to view QUOTATIONS:

- **View QUOTATIONS *on screen*.** QUOTATIONS can be viewed on screen in context as a highlighted segment within the DOCUMENT, with their surrounding data visible above and below. This is useful for quick reviews of the data associated with a CODE or when reading data in context is important.

- **Extract and export.** QUOTATIONS can be extracted from their context for review outside of ATLAS.ti, for example, in a Microsoft Word or PDF file. This is useful for reading and reflecting on a larger number of QUOTATIONS associated with a CODE, or perhaps a group of CODES. In addition to text, graphical QUOTATIONS appear in outputted files. Audio or video QUOTATIONS cannot be extracted or exported outside of ATLAS.ti.

- **View QUOTATIONS *visually within ATLAS.ti*.** QUOTATIONS can be extracted from their context and viewed with other QUOTATIONS in a visual window called a NETWORK, within the ATLAS.ti-PROJECT. These displays can be copied into a slide or a report, or they can be used as a different way of working with groups of QUOTATIONS. For example, QUOTATIONS can be linked or unlinked from CODES while displayed in the NETWORK, or they can simply be displayed in order to read and compare them. We discuss NETWORKS in detail in the section on visualizing data.

Figure 5.4 illustrates how QUOTATIONS appear in ATLAS.ti. We now invite you to go to the companion website to view the *Component Orientation* video for this COMPONENT.

FIGURE 5.4 QUOTATIONS

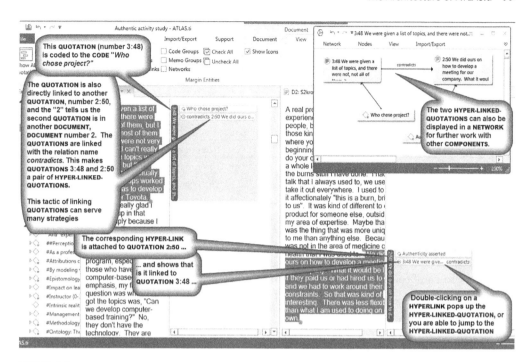

FIGURE 5.5   HYPERLINKED QUOTATIONS

Hyperlinked-Quotations

Any pair of QUOTATIONS can be linked together, and the pair are then called HYPERLINKED-QUOTATIONS. Linking QUOTATIONS can be useful in many circumstances, for example, when two segments that are physically separated in the data comprise a single segment of meaning when linked, such as when the beginning and the end of a single story are recounted at different times in an interview. Linking them together produces a single segment of meaning represented by a single COMPONENT, a pair of HYPERLINKED-QUOTATIONS. Linking QUOTATIONS may also serve the purpose of tracking a process, a contradiction, or other meaningful associations among pairs of QUOTATIONS. When linking two QUOTATIONS, a name is given to the link to indicate the kind of relationship between the two. Linking QUOTATIONS is not an alternative to coding but is instead a separate task with different purposes.

Figure 5.5 illustrates how HYPERLINKED-QUOTATIONS appear in ATLAS.ti. We now invite you to go to the companion website to view the *Component Orientation* video for this COMPONENT.

Conceptualizing Data

Conceptualizing data is the most general way of describing what occurs in all kinds of qualitative analysis, regardless of the methodology. Five of the 14 COMPONENTS most closely associated with this activity are CODES, CODED-QUOTATIONS, CODE-GROUPS AND CODE-SMART-GROUPS, SMART-CODES, and SMART-CODE-SNAPSHOTS, displayed in Table 5.5

Codes

The term *code* in ATLAS.ti refers to any named concept that represents what is identified in the data as meaningful in relation to the project objectives. CODES can be linked to other COMPONENTS

TABLE 5.5 Components most associated with conceptualizing data

Components	Definition
CODE	A named concept that can be linked to other COMPONENTS for either analytic or housekeeping purposes.
CODED–QUOTATION	A QUOTATION linked to one or more CODES.
CODE–GROUPS AND SMART–GROUPS	CODES can be organized into CODE–GROUPS. CODE–GROUPS can themselves be organized into CODE–SMART–GROUPS.
SMART–CODE	A special kind of CODE that consists of a saved query of other CODES.
SMART–CODE–SNAPSHOT	A frozen SMART–CODE is a regular CODE automatically linked by ATLAS.ti to all the QUOTATIONS retrieved by a SMART–CODE at a moment in time.

for various purposes, but before we describe these, we need to discuss codes and concepts and the difference between "codes" at the strategies levels and CODES at the tactics levels.

Codes and Concepts

We use the term *concept* for the name and meaning of any collection of things (for a fuller discussion see p. 37). In qualitative research, concepts are created and named to represent collections of data segments. This is part of the general process of reducing a large volume of unstructured data to a small and digestible number of related concepts that communicate the researcher's account of a whole body of data. The meaning of a concept is not fixed, but is emergent to varying degrees—its meaning evolves as more data are explored and associated with the concept. Most methodologies do not describe qualitative analysis as a basic conceptualizing process in this way, but rather they give different kinds of concepts specific names to communicate their purpose. Saldaña (2015) suggests that in "traditional approaches" to qualitative analysis there are four increasingly general kinds of concepts: *code, pattern, category*, and *theme*. A code is a word or short phrase that evokes an attribute of an item of data. Coding gives rise to recurring patterns, which are grouped and transformed into categories, and in turn grouped into themes that represent larger "implicit topics" (Saldaña, 2015, p. 11–13). Saldaña (2015) notes that coding is definitely not the only way to conduct a qualitative analysis, but it is "one of the most frequently used methods, particularly for those undertaking grounded theory studies" (p. 12). Coding is also the basis for conceptualizing in other methodologies, such as qualitative content analysis. But coding either plays a smaller role or comes into play much later in the process in the more interpretive styles of qualitative research such as discourse analysis and the various forms of phenomenology.

This does not even scratch the surface of the range of opinions on codes and coding as the basis of conceptualizing qualitative data. And every methodological text that does prescribe coding defines the nature and purpose of codes specifically for their methods of analysis. For those interested in coding as a method in itself, Saldaña (2016)'s *Coding Manual for Qualitative Researchers* provides a resource of 32 distinct coding methods.

Codes Are Different at the Strategy and Tactics Levels

This discussion of codes and coding refers to the strategy levels of the *Five-Level QDA* method. At the strategy levels a "code" refers to something different from one methodology to the next, with different types of codes serving different purposes. For example, in one style of grounded theory there are *open codes*, *axial codes*, and *selective codes* (Corbin & Strauss, 2014), and in another *open codes*, *focused codes*, and *theoretical codes* (Charmaz, 2014).

At the tactics levels, any of these types of code could be represented by several different COMPONENTS in the software. It is true that one COMPONENT in ATLAS.ti—CODE—is most commonly used to represent codes at the strategy levels. But in some situations a code at the strategy levels is best represented by a different COMPONENT, such as a MEMO or a QUOTATION at the tactics levels. Conversely, the COMPONENT in ATLAS.ti called a CODE can be used for housekeeping purposes unrelated to any conceptualizing activity involving codes and coding. It is inconvenient that a code at the strategy levels (and therefore intentionally printed in regular type) shares the same name as a CODE at the tactics levels (and therefore intentionally printed in SMALL CAPS). The shared name makes it easy to assume they are one and the same, leading to One-Level QDA thinking, which conflates strategies and tactics into a single process of *what-you-plan-to-do-and-how-you-plan-to-do-it*. Researchers whose methods are not centered around codes and coding then become concerned that ATLAS.ti is an unsuitable program for their projects. This is not the case, because with methodologies that are not centered around codes and coding, researchers can TRANSLATE their ANALYTIC TASKS into other COMPONENTS of the software for their purposes and do not have to use CODES in the software at all.

The conclusion is to note the typeface: a code is a concept at the strategy levels of a project; a CODE is COMPONENT at the tactics levels. Although it is common for a CODE to represent a code, it is most helpful to think of the two as separate and independent.

The Multiple Roles of Codes at the Tactics Levels

Although there is only one kind of CODE in the software at the tactics levels, there are many different purposes for which these CODES are harnessed. Even though CODES are mechanical and always work in the same way, creating CODES must be a thoughtful and cautious process to ensure that they best serve the purpose of the project objectives. But because it is so effortless to create CODES, a common problem is uncontrolled CODE creation and the unfortunate question asked of research consultants: "I've created 300 codes and coded my data. That was easy. What's next?" In *Five-Level QDA* terms this means the researcher has remained at the tactics levels rather than alternating back and forth between strategies and tactics and TRANSLATING between them. Often there isn't anything next other than recognizing that although a lot has been learned about the data from this uncontrolled coding, the resulting multiplicity of CODES has not been focused on fulfilling the needs of particular ANALYTIC TASKS, and the only practical way forward is either to start again or to engage in significant restructuring, grouping, and merging of codes to mold them into what is required at the strategy levels. To avoid this issue and keep the CODE-creation process intentional, it helps to think about four main purposes of CODES that are harnessed during TRANSLATION:

- *CODES used for concepts.* This is a very common use. CODES directly represent concepts in the data, and they are typically linked to segments of data—QUOTATIONS—that are examples of the concept.
- *CODES used for counting.* CODES can be created specifically to count instances of meaning in data whenever there is a need to quantify. For example, in a video project studying nonverbal interaction, each use of a particular hand gesture would be coded with a CODE for that gesture in order to quantify its frequency. These CODES would be used for different purposes than other CODES used to conceptualize the types or other characteristics of gestures.
- *CODES used for evaluation.* A separate set of evaluative CODES can supplement concept CODES. This avoids having a single CODE serve two purposes and thereby reduce the power of later

interrogations. If our bullying study is concerned with exploring the impact of bullying on aspects of self-esteem, we might create evaluative CODES: evaluative CODES named *low, medium,* or *high impact* (to code for the degree of impact) and various self-esteem concept CODES.

- **CODES used for housekeeping.** CODES can serve administrative or organizational purposes. For example, at the end of a working day you may link a CODE named *where I am* to the last QUOTATION worked on—this allows you to jump straight there the next morning. Or a CODE named *good quote* might be linked to QUOTATIONS that are candidates for illustrating a concept in a report.

Codes Must Be Organized

In ATLAS.ti all CODES appear together in one long alphabetical list. Yet because there are several different uses of CODES—the four outlined earlier and maybe other uses that emerge in a particular project—it helps to distinguish and organize CODES rather than only having them available as a single alphabetic list.

There is no set way to organize the list of CODES in ATLAS.ti. This is good, because everybody develops their own ideas about what it means to organize CODES based on how they like to work and the nature of their projects. Five increasingly sophisticated ways of bringing organization to the CODES are listed next. However, sophisticated doesn't mean better. Each way of organizing CODES has advantages and disadvantages and is appropriate for different purposes.

- **Using colors.** CODES can be given a color to draw attention to their purpose or particular features they might have, or to indicate which team member uses which CODES, yet they can still all sort together alphabetically. At the time of writing, the list of CODES can be filtered to only see the colored CODES, but cannot sort the list by color. The colors therefore primarily serve as visual cues.
- **Using prefixes.** The names of certain CODES can begin with a symbol, for example *#Low,* *#Medium,* and *#High.* This draws attention to the specialized purpose or features of this group of CODES and causes them to sort together as a group in the Code Manager. Many groups of CODES serving different purposes can have names starting with their own symbol.
- **Using GROUPS.** CODES can be grouped into CODE-FAMILIES, and CODE-FAMILIES can be grouped into CODE-SMART-FAMILIES. These COMPONENTS are described further later.
- **Using links** CODES can be linked together with named relationships in order to display and work with them visually in NETWORKS or to create hierarchies of CODES.

Manual Coding and Auto-Coding

Creating CODES and linking them to QUOTATIONS is generally a manual process accomplished one QUOTATION at a time with a great deal of thought. But there can also be a role for auto-coding in which you instruct ATLAS.ti to find a string (for example, part of a word, a whole word, or a phrase) and automatically create a QUOTATION and link it to a specified CODE. A helpful feature allows you to look for more than one word if you consider them synonyms in the data. In the bullying study you could ask the auto-coder to look for *bull* (to find *bullying, bullied,* etc.), but also *shov* (to find *shoved, shoving,* etc.) and *push* (to find *pushed, pushing,* etc.). Phrases can be used, such as *big bully,* if there is confidence the phrase would always appear exactly in that form.

Auto-coding is not a substitute for manual coding. One reason is that possible transcribing or spelling mistakes make searching for a specific sequence of characters unreliable. A more significant reason is that a particular sequence of characters will rarely identify a concept reliably. Although *bull* will find sentences containing *bullying* and *bullied*, it will also find *the teacher's ebullience made for a happy classroom*—not what we had in mind. Auto-coding is therefore most helpful for special purposes, such as the following examples:

- **Technical terms.** Often not much is learned just because a particular word is used in the data. But if technical or highly specific words do reliably indicate a meaningful response, then auto-coding is a useful timesaver.
- **First cut through data.** As we discussed in the section on exploring documents (p. 74), the use of certain words may point to an area of the data that merits further consideration. In these cases auto-coding based on this group of words can be used as a first cut through the data, followed by a second round of manual coding.
- **Earlier examples of a new CODE.** If a new CODE is created part way through a project, a choice has to be made about whether to go back to explore the already-coded data for what the CODE represents. Depending on methodology, the new CODE could be ignored in the earlier data, or the earlier data could be entirely reread to find examples of the new CODE. Between these two extremes could be auto-coding the already-coded DOCUMENTS for all words considered synonymous with the new concept, with the hope that this locates most of the missed examples.
- **Exploring structure in the data.** In data with repeated structures—for example, multiple speakers in a focus group transcript—each individual's responses can be transcribed with identifiers to allow auto-coding for later interrogation of, for example, responses about certain issues by particular individuals, or just the females, etc. Any repeated structure in the data can be explored and captured with the auto-coder in this way, provided the data have been transcribed consistently.

Figure 5.6 illustrates how CODES appear in ATLAS.ti. We now invite you to go to the companion website to view the *Component Orientation* video for this COMPONENT.

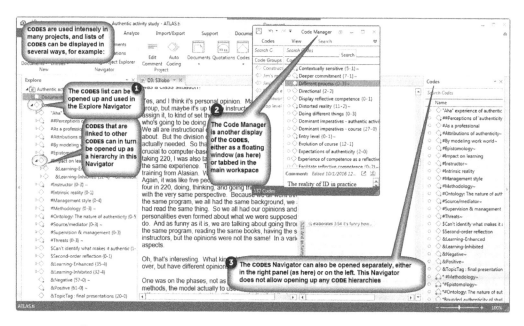

FIGURE 5.6   CODES

Coded-Quotations

A CODED-QUOTATION is a QUOTATION that has been linked to a CODE. The same QUOTATION can be linked to any number of CODES. QUOTATIONS are a primary building-block of the analysis in ATLAS.ti because a set of QUOTATIONS is always the final outcome of any interrogating activities, meaning the many kinds of additional work that are carried on when revisiting what has already been done. However, interrogating the data most commonly involves CODED-QUOTATIONS, rather than "free" QUOTATIONS not linked to CODES. For example, the purpose of interrogation is often to seek a focused set of QUOTATIONS based on some combination of the CODES linked to QUOTATIONS. This provides a snapshot of your current thinking about a concept, or finds evidence for a concept, or helps understand the substance of a concept. Other interrogations of CODED-QUOTATIONS serve different purposes. For example, we mentioned earlier the "housekeeping" use of a CODE named *good quote* to code QUOTATIONS for potential inclusion in a report. The CODED-QUOTATIONS can be interrogated at any time for all examples of QUOTATIONS coded both to, say, *verbal bullying* and also to *good quote*, and a list of the QUOTATIONS that qualify would be found.

Interrogating the ATLAS.ti-PROJECT to produce CODED-QUOTATIONS can involve two general kinds of activities. The first is finding or getting a focused set of QUOTATIONS that meet a coding criterion in order to read the set of QUOTATIONS together, which is generally referred to as *retrieval*. The second is *counting* the number of CODED-QUOTATIONS that meet a criterion, which we discuss further later.

Simple and Complex Retrieval

ATLAS.ti retrievals can be either simple or complex. The simplest possible criterion by which QUOTATIONS can be retrieved is to get all the QUOTATIONS that have been linked to a single CODE. This software operation is performed extremely frequently in order to read and review the QUOTATIONS currently linked to a CODE. Once retrieved the QUOTATIONS can be viewed in a variety of ways—as a list in a pop-up window to be browsed through and read in context one by one, or saved in a file, or printed, or viewed visually within a NETWORK to be further worked on in that mode.

Complex retrievals also produce a set of QUOTATIONS that meet a coding criterion, but they go beyond retrieving QUOTATIONS linked to a single CODE. Complex retrievals therefore play a major role in fulfilling the purposes of more sophisticated ANALYTIC TASKS. ATLAS.ti's Query Tool allows CODED-QUOTATIONS to be retrieved based on their coding to more than one CODE. This works by combining two or more CODES into a formula, referred to as a *query*, using operators. We earlier described the three operators *OR*, *AND*, and *NOT* for combining GROUPS into SMART-GROUPS. The Query Tool goes beyond this when combining CODES, as it has 14 operators that allow a wide variety of queries to be created. The 14 operators are organized in the Query Tool in three groups:

- **Boolean operators.** These are the straightforward logical operators, *OR*, *AND*, and *NOT*. *OR* is the most expansive, retrieving all QUOTATIONS coded to *either* one CODE *or* another CODE *or* both. *AND* is the most restrictive, even though it sounds expansive. This operator retrieves QUOTATIONS coded to *both* one CODE *and also* another CODE. *NOT* excludes QUOTATIONS coded to a CODE. One further Boolean operator—*EXCLUSIVE OR*—retrieves QUOTATIONS coded to *either* one CODE *or* another CODE *but not* both, for more specialized uses.
- **Hierarchical operators.** Three operators, called *semantic operators* by ATLAS.ti, retrieve QUOTATIONS up and down hierarchies of CODES that you have constructed. One retrieves QUOTATIONS coded to either a CODE or the CODE's "parent" CODES above it in a hierarchical tree. Another retrieves QUOTATIONS down the tree to include the CODE's "child" CODES, and a third retrieves all QUOTATIONS at the same level in a hierarchy of CODES.

- *Proximity operators.* Seven operators retrieve QUOTATIONS based on the proximity of one CODED-QUOTATION to another. There are three kinds of proximity—where a QUOTATION coded to one CODE *ENCLOSES* a QUOTATION coded to a second CODE, where a QUOTATION coded to one CODE *OVERLAPS* a QUOTATION coded to a second CODE, and where a QUOTATION coded to one CODE *FOLLOWS* by a certain number of paragraphs a QUOTATION coded to a second CODE. These operators come in pairs, for example, to allow you to retrieve either the enclosing or the enclosed QUOTATIONS. The final operator, *CO-OCCUR*, is a less restrictive combination of other operators.

Straightforward queries combine two CODES with one operator, whereas sophisticated queries can be built up layer by layer. The list of 14 operators may seem exciting or daunting, but in practice four operators are most commonly used: *OR, AND, NOT*, and *CO-OCCUR*. *CO-OCCUR* has a particularly important role in many researchers' work as a general-purpose retrieval tool that is useful in both highly structured and less structured coding schemes. *CO-OCCUR* is discussed in more detail in the next section.

The Query Tool retrieves a set of QUOTATIONS based on the CODES they are coded to. Once QUOTATIONS have been retrieved in the Query Tool, they can be further limited to those coming from any combination of DOCUMENTS. This is a valuable use of DOCUMENT-GROUPS and DOCUMENT-SMART-GROUPS, which can be set up to allow the Query Tool to limit the retrieved QUOTATIONS from a query to any set of DOCUMENTS with a single operation. The ability of the Query Tool to retrieve QUOTATIONS based on both coding criteria and on DOCUMENT selection greatly increases the range of analytic possibilities. A demonstration of the Query Tool is included in the *Component Orientation* video for CODED-QUOTATIONS.

Co-occur

In everyday language a *co-occurrence* means *when two things are found together.* At the tactics levels of a qualitative analysis, a common meaning for a co-occurrence is that two or more CODES have been used together in some way that is analogous to a correlation. What this signifies at the strategy levels of the analysis depends on the methodology and the intentions of the researcher in looking for co-occurrences. In ATLAS.ti *co-occur* has a specific, mechanical meaning and refers to overlapping QUOTATIONS. Two CODES are co-occurring if a QUOTATION coded to the first CODE overlaps to any degree with a QUOTATION coded to the second CODE. For example, if coding has captured descriptions of different kinds of bullying—such as *verbal bullying, social bullying, physical bullying*—and also indicators of different degrees of impact—*high, medium,* or *low*—the *CO-OCCUR* operator of the Query Tool can retrieve the co-occurring QUOTATIONS—that is, the overlapping QUOTATIONS—coded to any pair of these CODES. What this co-occurrence or correlation between the two CODES means is then a concern addressed at the strategy levels of the analysis.

A Co-occurrence Table displays the co-occurring QUOTATIONS for any pair of CODES in each cell of the table, and these QUOTATIONS can be browsed and read in context. The table can also be exported to a Microsoft Excel spreadsheet for further analysis, but only of the numbers of co-occurring QUOTATIONS in each cell, as there is no direct access to the underlying QUOTATIONS once you are working in Microsoft Excel.

Counting

Counting things is a major part of many projects and valued by many qualitative researchers, but it is of less value or even contentious to others. For some methodologies the *frequency* with which certain words are used may be an indicator of meaning, or the *amount* of data associated with a

CODE may indicate the salience or validity of a concept. For example, the count of the number of QUOTATIONS coded to each CODE might be used to identify CODES with fewer than, say, three QUOTATIONS in order to assess the salience of these infrequently expressed concepts. Conversely, this count may be used to identify and investigate all CODES coded to a single QUOTATION in order to seek out potentially discrepant cases if this analytic activity is prescribed by the methodology. However, for other methodologies it is the *content* of the retrieved data that tells the researcher what is important rather than the *frequency* or *amount* of data having significance.

- ***Counts of each COMPONENT.*** All components have their own Manager or list of items, with the total number of items always displayed. If the Manager has been filtered, then the filtered number or subset of items is displayed.
- ***Counts of COMPONENT characteristics.*** Each component's Manager has columns displaying the counts of its various characteristics. For example, the Code Manager has a column displaying the number of other CODES linked to each CODE.
- ***Counts of CODED-QUOTATIONS.*** Wherever a CODE or SMART-CODE is displayed anywhere in the ATLAS.ti-PROJECT, the number of QUOTATIONS linked to it is always available, either in brackets or in a box or separate column, depending on the context.
- ***Code-Document Table.*** This table displays the number of CODED-QUOTATIONS for each chosen CODE, CODE-GROUP, or CODE-SMART-GROUP (as the rows or columns) in each chosen DOCUMENT, DOCUMENT-GROUP, or DOCUMENT-SMART-GROUP (as the columns or rows). The table can also be exported out of ATLAS.ti as a Microsoft Excel spreadsheet.
- ***Code Co-occurrence Table.*** This table displays the number of co-occurring QUOTATIONS for any pair of CODES. The table can also be exported to a Microsoft Excel spreadsheet for further review or quantitative analysis of the frequency of co-occurring QUOTATIONS in each cell, without access to the underlying CODED-QUOTATIONS.
- ***SPSS runnable job.*** For researchers conducting statistical analysis, often as part of a mixed-methods study, the entire ATLAS.ti-PROJECT can be exported as an SPSS runnable job. In SPSS language, each QUOTATION becomes a case, and each CODE, SMART-CODE, or CODE-GROUP becomes a variable.

Figure 5.7 illustrates the Query Tool, which is used for complex retrieval of CODED-QUOTATIONS in ATLAS.ti. We now invite you to go to the companion website to view the *Component Orientation* video for all aspects of this COMPONENT.

Code-Groups and Code-Smart-Groups

CODES can be put into CODE-GROUPS, and CODE-GROUPS combined into CODE-SMART-GROUPS in exactly the same way and for the same overall purposes as DOCUMENTS can be put into DOCUMENT-GROUPS, and DOCUMENT-GROUPS combined into DOCUMENT-SMART-GROUPS, as described on pp. 74–76. In summary:

- Any CODE can be a member of any number of CODE-GROUPS. CODE-GROUPS in turn can be combined with operators into any number of CODE-SMART-GROUPS.
- The only difference between a CODE-GROUP and a CODE-SMART-GROUP is the method by which CODES become members. Once created, they both function in the same way.
- An advantage of creating CODE-SMART-GROUPS is that they update automatically when CODES are added to or removed from the underlying CODE-GROUPS.

- One purpose of putting CODES into a CODE-GROUP is to be able to take an action on all the CODES at once.
- Another purpose is to filter all the CODES by CODE-GROUP in order to see or work with a subset of the CODES.

For example, all the CODES created and used in the first stage of a team project could be put into a new CODE-GROUP called, for example, *first stage*. The second stage of analysis may have an additional focus based on the team's conclusions about the first stage. In the second stage, team members will create new CODES that reflect this new focus, as well as continuing to use the first-stage CODES. There may occasionally be a need to reflect on just the codes created since stage two began. A CODE-SMART-GROUP can be created for this purpose called, for example, *second stage*, by applying the *NOT* operator to the *first-stage* CODE-GROUP. This CODE-SMART-GROUP is updated automatically to reflect both newly created CODES (because these are not in the *first-stage* CODE-GROUP) as well as the addition or removal of CODES from the *first-stage* CODE-GROUP.

Figure 5.8 illustrates how CODE-GROUPS AND CODE-SMART-GROUPS appear in ATLAS.ti. We now invite you to go to the companion website to view the *Component Orientation* video for this COMPONENT.

Smart-Codes

A SMART-CODE is a saved query created in the Query Tool. Sometimes complex retrievals are done once to produce a desired focused set of QUOTATIONS, and then the task is complete. But sometimes a query of CODES will be useful again, for example to retrieve QUOTATIONS meeting this coding criterion after additional coding has been undertaken. In this case the query can be saved for future

FIGURE 5.7   CODED–QUOTATIONS

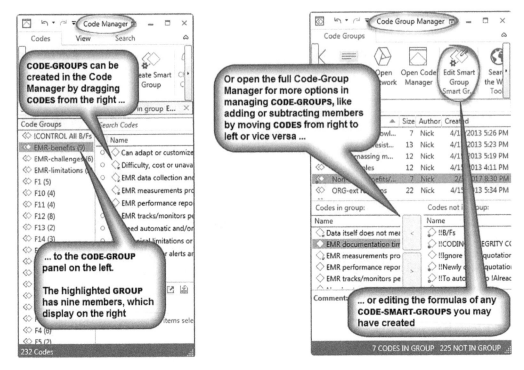

FIGURE 5.8 Codes-Groups and Code-Smart-Groups

use as a SMART-CODE. It will appear in the list of CODES along with all the other CODES. SMART-CODES behave just like all other CODES, with one difference: a SMART-CODE cannot be directly linked to a QUOTATION. SMART-CODES are, as it were, *indirectly* linked to QUOTATIONS through the CODES that comprise their query.

A SMART-CODE consists of the query, *not* the resulting set of retrieved QUOTATIONS. A SMART-CODE is therefore *dynamic*, as the QUOTATIONS retrieved will change as coding continues and more of those CODES meet the coding criteria in the query. This is particularly helpful when you know early on what some of the useful queries will be. You can create the SMART-CODES for these QUERIES and as you progress with coding keep running them to check whether patterns you expect are indeed present.

Figure 5.9 illustrates how SMART-CODES appear in ATLAS.ti. We now invite you to go to the companion website to view the *Component Orientation* video for this COMPONENT.

Smart-Code-Snapshot

There is a simple way to freeze a snapshot of the QUOTATIONS that result from a SMART-CODE retrieval. Doing this creates a SMART-CODE-SNAPSHOT, which is a regular CODE linked to the set of QUOTATIONS that were retrieved at that moment, just as if you had coded them manually to this CODE. A SMART-CODE-SNAPSHOT is therefore *static*—a frozen version of a SMART-CODE. This is helpful when you need to compare the status of coding at different points in an analysis—for example, if you conduct a longitudinal project and want to compare situations at the end of separate phases. The *dynamic* SMART-CODES and the *static* SMART-CODE-SNAPSHOTS offer great flexibility for conducting and saving complex retrievals with a variety of purposes.

Figure 5.10 illustrates how SMART-CODE-SNAPSHOTS appear in ATLAS.ti. The demonstration of SMART-CODE-SNAPSHOTS is included in the *Component Orientation* video for SMART-CODES.

FIGURE 5.9 Smart–Codes

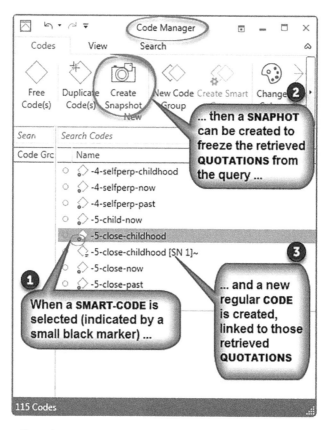

FIGURE 5.10 Smart–Code–Snapshots

TABLE 5.6 Components most associated with writing

Components	Definition
COMMENT	An annotation of any length written on any COMPONENT.
MEMO	A piece of writing that can be standalone or linked to other COMPONENTS.
MEMO–GROUPS AND SMART–GROUPS	MEMOS can be organized into MEMO-GROUPS. MEMO-GROUPS can themselves be organized into MEMO-SMART-GROUPS.

Writing

Writing is central to qualitative research. ATLAS.ti makes it easy to capture all thoughts and insights in their appropriate context as they occur. Three of the 14 COMPONENTS most closely associated with this activity are COMMENTS, MEMOS, and MEMO-GROUPS and MEMO-SMART-GROUPS, displayed in Table 5.6.

All analytic activities in a qualitative project lead to the central activity of writing. Writing is best done at every step, not just at the end, in order to capture every thought, insight, interpretation, or new questions about what is going on in the data analysis. Every methodology has its own recommendations about what, how, and when to write. Our philosophy is to think like an economist, from a purely cost/benefit point of view, and capture every stray thought that might bear on the data analysis. The greatest cost in qualitative analysis—meaning effort and time expended—is engaging your mind in making sense of a segment of data. What did the person mean by that statement? What does that image convey, and what does it hide? How does this unit of meaning support or contrast with the meaning of other parts of the data? Which ways of looking at this segment of data are most helpful to answering the research question? These significant mental acts bring to bear the researcher's entire lifetime of accumulated sense-making experience onto a single segment of data, what an artificial intelligence cannot (currently) do as well. At the moment of sense-making, valuable thoughts emerge that may contribute to the progress of the qualitative data analysis, and they should be captured then and there. The cost of writing down a thought already experienced is quite small, but the benefit of capturing it as soon as it is experienced is truly great— weeks later the thought will not be easily remembered, especially if subtle, and certainly not its location in the data. Real-time writing capitalizes on the significant mental investment we make in the sense-making process.

In addition to all this analytic writing, other kinds of writing are needed—writing about the methods you are using and the processes you are going through, summarizing or appraising previous literature about your topic, describing a respondent or case or situation, or keeping notes about discussions with supervisors or team members.

ATLAS.ti offers great flexibility in capturing all these kinds of writing in different writing spaces. ATLAS.ti offers three spaces in which to write: COMMENTS, MEMOS, and by direct editing of text DOCUMENTS. Each has advantages and disadvantages in different contexts. We have already discussed editing text DOCUMENTS as one way to write, in the section on DOCUMENTS on p. 73. The following two sections compare COMMENTS and MEMOS as writing spaces. Also see Woolf (2015) for an extended discussion of alternative ways to use COMMENTS and MEMOS in ATLAS.ti.

Comments

COMMENTS are not independent writing spaces, but an inseparable annotation of another COMPO-NENT. Every COMPONENT has its own COMMENT area to write in. A COMMENT is not an independent

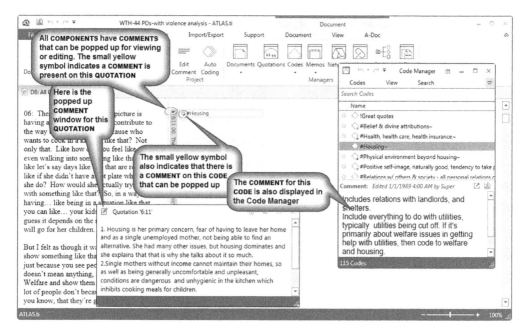

FIGURE 5.11 COMMENTS

COMPONENT with its own Manager window—COMMENTS cannot be listed or retrieved or outputted separately from the COMPONENT they annotate. But whenever another COMPONENT is retrieved or outputted, its COMMENT comes along with it.

At the start of a project, decide on a strategy for what types of writing go in the COMMENTS of which COMPONENTS. One approach is to write about the meaning, definition, or intended use of CODES in the CODE comments rather than, say, the COMMENT of one QUOTATION linked to that CODE, and it makes sense to write commentary about the meaning of particular data segments in their QUOTATION comments rather than in the COMMENT of the whole DOCUMENT. A more specialized strategy may make sense for locating COMMENTS, particularly in team projects. But a consistent strategy for where to capture COMMENT writing in a project allows orderly location and reading of this material later.

Figure 5.11 illustrates how COMMENTS appear in ATLAS.ti. We now invite you to go to the companion website to view the *Component Orientation* video for this COMPONENT.

Memos

Most textbooks use the term *memo* to refer to all the kinds of writing we have been discussing. But ATLAS.ti uses this term for just one of the writing spaces in the program. To avoid confusion and to clearly distinguish strategies from tactics, we do not use the term *memo* at all at the strategy levels; instead we use *writing* with an appropriate adjective: *analytic writing, process writing*, and so on. At the tactics levels we use the term MEMO to refer to the ATLAS.ti writing space.

In contrast to COMMENTS, MEMOS are independent pieces of writing, separate from the COMPONENTS you may be writing about. Think of them as a set of independent Microsoft Word files, except that they are named spaces inside the ATLAS.ti-PROJECT. A MEMO can contain text, images, or embedded tables, and a MEMO can be linked to any existing QUOTATION, CODE, or another MEMO. MEMOS are organized by type—the program comes with four basic types of MEMOS, and other types

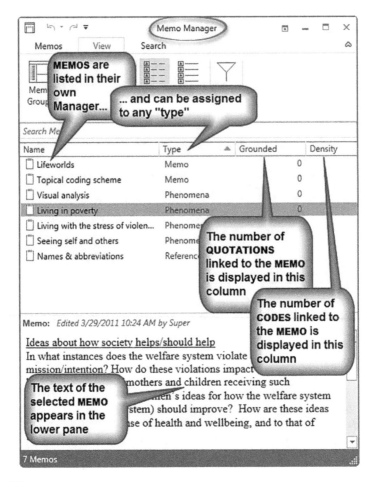

FIGURE 5.12 MEMOS

can be added. MEMOS can also be turned into a DOCUMENT. In this case its content is duplicated—it still exists as a MEMO and now also as a DOCUMENT.

Figure 5.12 illustrates how MEMOS appear in ATLAS.ti. We now invite you to go to the companion website to view the *Component Orientation* video for this COMPONENT.

Memo-Groups and Memo-Smart-Groups

MEMOS can be put into MEMO-GROUPS, and MEMO-GROUPS combined into MEMO-SMART-GROUPS in the same way as DOCUMENTS and CODES are combined into GROUPS and SMART-GROUPS, as described on pp. 74–76. In summary:

- Any MEMO can be a member of any number of MEMO-GROUPS. MEMO-GROUPS in turn can be combined with operators into any number of MEMO-SMART-GROUPS.
- The difference between a MEMO-GROUP and a MEMO-SMART-GROUP is the method by which CODES become members. Once created, they both function in the same way.
- An advantage of creating MEMO-SMART-GROUPS is that they update automatically when CODES are added to or removed from the underlying MEMO-GROUPS.

MEMO-GROUPS and MEMO-SMART-GROUPS can be used to organize different pieces of writing for filtering purposes so that a focused listing of the MEMOS is always available. For example, preliminary pieces of writing about different kinds of literature in a literature review could be organized into MEMO-GROUPS called *theoretical literature, substantive literature,* and *methodological literature,* which could be combined with the *OR* operator into a MEMO-SMART-GROUP called *Writing about literature.* Focused listings of MEMOS are then always available for each individual kind of literature or for all the MEMOS about literature.

The mechanisms for creating and managing MEMO-GROUPS AND MEMO-SMART-GROUPS are the same as for DOCUMENT-GROUPS AND DOCUMENT-SMART-GROUPS, illustrated in Figure 5.3, and for CODE-GROUPS AND CODE-SMART-GROUPS, illustrated in Figure 5.8. We now invite you to go to the companion website to view the *Component Orientation* video for this COMPONENT.

Visualizing

Visualizing means working visually with any COMPONENTS by displaying them graphically. The two COMPONENTS most closely associated with this activity are NETWORKS and NETWORK-GROUPS AND NETWORK-SMART-GROUPS, displayed in Table 5.7.

Networks

ATLAS.ti's NETWORKS can be used for many kinds of visual interrogation. NETWORKS are a working tool, integrated with the rest of the ATLAS.ti-PROJECT, not an after-the-fact drawing feature to simply represent part of a completed project in graphical form, although NETWORKS can certainly be used in that way. Any number of separate NETWORKS can be saved to display parts of the project in different ways.

One use of NETWORKS is to explore groups of linked CODES that represent new or evolving ways of thinking about the related concepts in a project. CODES are displayed in a NETWORK as individual boxes that can be physically placed to represent their inter-relationships. An advantage of working with CODES in NETWORKS is that the associated CODED-QUOTATIONS for any CODE can always be accessed from within the NETWORK and browsed to in context. This allows you to remain close to the data while working conceptually with the CODES. There are many uses of NETWORKS of CODES, including:

- Displaying a typology of CODES to communicate the results of a content analysis.
- Building a model of a social process.
- Displaying an existing theory to visually contrast and link to CODES that represent emerging concepts identified in the data.
- Developing an ongoing, freeform, organic concept map to represent an emerging set of findings as they become apparent.
- Constructing a hierarchy of CODES which can also be viewed as a CODE tree in the Navigator window and used for CODING.

TABLE 5.7 Components most associated with visualizing

Components	Definition
NETWORK	Graphical windows to display and work visually with any set of COMPONENTS.
NETWORK-GROUPS AND SMART-GROUPS	NETWORKS can be organized into NETWORK-GROUPS. NETWORK-GROUPS can themselves be organized into NETWORK-SMART-GROUPS.

To facilitate this visual working style CODES can be linked to one another with a named relationship, which ATLAS.ti calls a *relation*. ATLAS.ti comes with a small starter set of relations, and any number can be easily created. A relation consists of its name, such as *part of* or *contrasts with*, and its type. There are three types of relations. One type is nondirectional and displays visually as a simple line that links two CODES. The other two types are directional, with an arrow at one end of the line. One of these directional types is hierarchical, and it must be used if you wish to see and use the list of CODES as a hierarchical tree.

Because NETWORKS are just a different way of viewing and working with COMPONENTS, and because any COMPONENT, not just CODES, can be displayed, NETWORKS serve as a full-fledged general-purpose working tool. For example, there may be a number of QUOTATIONS within many different DOCUMENTS that are linked to a single CODE, which is now recognized to be insufficiently detailed. The QUOTATIONS can be recoded to several more detailed CODES by linking and unlinking the CODES and QUOTATIONS visually within a NETWORK.

Everything that can be done to a COMPONENT when displayed in a Manager listing or in the main workspace can be carried out visually in a NETWORK. Your choice will depend on which way of working is more convenient at a given moment. Common tasks include adding, deleting, renaming, or merging COMPONENTS; changing their color; adding to a COMMENT; etc.

Figure 5.13 illustrates how NETWORKS appear in ATLAS.ti. We now invite you to go to the companion website to view the *Component Orientation* video for this COMPONENT.

Network-Groups and Network-Smart-Groups

NETWORKS can be put into NETWORK-GROUPS, and these NETWORK-GROUPS combined into NETWORK-SMART-GROUPS in the same way as for DOCUMENTS, CODES, and MEMOS, described in detail on pp. 74–76, summarized on p. 86, and illustrated in Figures 5.3 and 5.8. These GROUPS and SMART-GROUPS can be used to organize NETWORKS for filtering purposes so that many focused listings of the NETWORKS based on these groupings are always available. We now invite you to go to the companion website to view the *Component Orientation* video for this component.

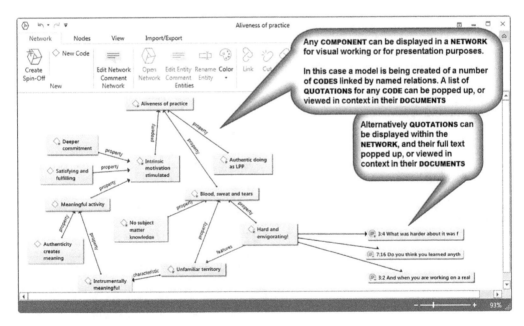

FIGURE 5.13 NETWORKS

The ATLAS.ti-Project as a Whole

This section covers various tasks and housekeeping features not related to specific COMPONENTS of the program: *interrogating, outputting, keeping up to date*, and *backing up and moving projects*.

Interrogating

Interrogate means to *ask questions about something*. At the strategy levels of deciding how best to answer a research question, the entire analysis can be thought of as an interrogation of the data, with no limit to the range, uniqueness, and subtlety of interrogation activities. ATLAS.ti offers three broad kinds of software operations that support interrogation activities: *retrieving* groups of QUOTA-TIONS based on what they are linked to, *counting* things, and *displaying* COMPONENTS graphically in a NETWORK. These have been discussed individually in the context of the various COMPONENTS that they operate on.

Outputting

ATLAS.ti is well designed for working primarily on screen and navigating around its interconnected COMPONENTS. However, there are times when outputting information is very useful. For example, it is common when engaged in a challenging ANALYTIC TASK to need to think deeply about all the QUOTATIONS linked to a code or all the QUOTATIONS linked to a CODE that co-occur with another CODE. Sometimes there is no substitute for printing them out and doing the deep thinking with paper and pencil at a pleasant coffee shop before returning to navigate around the ATLAS.ti screen.

Outputs can be *displayed on screen* in a separate window, sent directly to a *printer*, saved as a *file*, or saved as a file and immediately *opened* in the appropriate program.

*   ***Lists of*** COMPONENTS. Simple listings of every COMPONENT can also be outputted by choosing various options for what should or should not be included. One exception is COMMENTS, which are not independent COMPONENTS and so cannot be outputted in a separate listing. COMMENTS are outputted along with the COMPONENT that they annotate.
*   *QUOTATIONS*. ATLAS.ti is a QUOTATION-oriented program, with all software operations ultimately resulting in a simple set of QUOTATIONS no matter the complexity of an ANALYTIC TASK or its resulting software operations. It is therefore not surprising that the workhorse output for many researchers is a listing of QUOTATIONS that are linked to one or more CODES or SMART-CODES. The output can include or exclude QUOTATION COMMENTS and any HYPERLINKED-QUOTATIONS, depending on the purpose.
*   *NETWORKS*. A graphical output of any NETWORK can be outputted to a printer or as a graphical file, with many options for adjusting the appearance of the displayed COMPONENTS. Outputs of NETWORKS are useful for communicating a graphical view of the analysis with other team members or project stakeholders, or for use in a presentation, publication, or report.
*   *DOCUMENTS*. A graphical output reproduces the text or graphics of any DOCUMENT or set of DOCUMENTS with the margin area displaying any CODES or MEMOS linked to QUOTATIONS, just as they appear in the workspace in the center of the screen.
*   ***Code-Document Table.*** This table can be outputted as a Microsoft Excel spreadsheet of CODED-QUOTATIONS for each chosen CODE, CODE-GROUP, or CODE-SMART-GROUP (as the rows or columns) in each chosen DOCUMENT, DOCUMENT-GROUP, or DOCUMENT-SMART-GROUP (as the columns or rows). Only the counts of CODED-QUOTATIONS are available for further analysis, not the underlying CODED-QUOTATIONS.

- **Code Co-occurrence Table.** This table displays the co-occurring QUOTATIONS for any pair of CODES, which means that there is a QUOTATION coded to the first CODE that overlaps to whatever degree with a QUOTATION coded to the second CODE. This is analogous to a correlation and is discussed more fully on p. 130. The table can be outputted as a Microsoft Excel spreadsheet for further analysis of just the numbers of co-occurring QUOTATIONS in each cell, without access to the underlying CODED-QUOTATIONS that are available when the table is viewed within the ATLAS.ti-PROJECT.
- **SPSS runnable job.** For researchers conducting numeric or statistical analysis on what has been done in ATLAS.ti, often as part of a mixed-methods project, the entire ATLAS.ti-PROJECT can be outputted as an SPSS runnable job with separate data and syntax files. In SPSS language, each QUOTATION becomes a case, and each CODE, SMART-CODE, and CODE-FAMILY becomes a variable.

Keeping Up to Date

ATLAS.ti releases major new versions every few years. These new versions have always maintained the same underlying philosophy and functionality of ATLAS.ti, so fortunately it has not been necessary to relearn how to use ATLAS.ti powerfully with each new version. Version 8 is a major rewriting of the entire program with an updated look-and-feel and the potential for the addition of many new features for some time to come.

Some users always buy the latest version to take advantage of new or more efficient features. Others continue with the current version they are happy with. One reason researchers delay upgrading is to ensure that all team members are using the same version. If one team member upgrades to Version 8 and others do not, it is not possible to merge everybody's work. This book is based on ATLAS.ti Version 8 for Windows.

Minor updates to correct bugs or add minor improvements come out every few weeks or months. Whenever you open the program ATLAS.ti checks to see if updates are available and invites you to update if this is the case. You can also update manually by going to the Windows Start menu, then to Scientific Software, and then choosing Check for ATLAS.ti 8.0 Updates.

Backing Up and Moving Projects

ATLAS.ti has features for *saving* your current work, for *backing up* an ATLAS.ti-PROJECT as a safeguard of your work or as an archive, and for *moving* an ATLAS.ti-PROJECT to another computer.

Saving Your Current Work

All work done in an ATLAS.ti-PROJECT is saved by ATLAS.ti in its standard hidden location. Saving your work therefore only requires pressing the Save button. There are no separate project files to save or to be concerned with. As there is no automatic backup, we press the Save button very regularly, sometimes every few minutes if in the midst of valuable work.

Another reason for saving is to freeze the ATLAS.ti-PROJECT at a moment in time, saving it with a different project name. You can then continue work in the current version and always be able to open and look back at a previous version of the project. Some researchers save these archive versions of their project regularly, which also creates an audit trail to help with the write-up of the methods of the project. Adding the date as part of the ATLAS.ti-PROJECT name in these archive versions allows easy selection of an earlier version of the project you may be interested in reviewing. All these versions of the project are saved by ATLAS.ti in its same hidden location, and all appear along with all your other projects whenever you open the program.

Backing Up a Project

Backing up a project means asking ATLAS.ti to create a compressed file called a Project Bundle that contains the ATLAS.ti-PROJECT and all its associated DOCUMENT files. You can save the Project Bundle file anywhere you wish: on your computer's hard drive, a computer network, a removable thumb drive, or a cloud service like Dropbox. The Project Bundle cannot be opened or used directly. Its purpose is to serve as an archive of the complete project—ATLAS.ti-PROJECT and DOCUMENTS—which can later be reinstated by importing it back into ATLAS.ti.

It makes sense to have a Project Bundle stored somewhere other than on your working computer so that it can be reinstated on a different computer should your working computer die.

Moving Projects

Moving a project to another computer simply means saving a Project Bundle file, copying this file to another computer, and then importing the Project Bundle in ATLAS.ti on the new computer. The ATLAS.ti-PROJECT will be saved by ATLAS.ti on the new computer in its usual hidden location, and the project will be available to open every time you open the program.

Importing Pre–Version 8 Projects

ATLAS.ti-PROJECTS originally conducted in Version 5, 6, or 7 of ATLAS.ti can be imported as a Legacy Project. The ATLAS.ti-PROJECT is converted to and saved as a Version 8 project. Once converted the project cannot be imported back and used in Version 5, 6, or 7.

In some cases older projects originally conducted in Version 5 have to be opened in and converted to Version 7, then exported as a Project Bundle (called a Copy Bundle in Version 7), and the Project Bundle imported as a Legacy Project to Version 8.

We now invite you to go to the companion website to view the *Component Orientation* video for *The* ATLAS.ti-PROJECT *as a whole*.

Working in Teams

Using ATLAS.ti in a team situation involves considering both the human aspect of *who does what* from a research perspective and the technical aspect of *merging each team member's contributions*. We discussed the human aspects of team working in Chapter 4. Here we describe the technicalities of the merging process.

ATLAS.ti is not a multiuser program, so each team member works independently on their own copy of the ATLAS.ti-PROJECT. As discussed in Chapter 4 there are different ways of assigning the analytic work among team members. However work is assigned, periodically each team member submits their ATLAS.ti-PROJECT for merging and stops work while all the ATLAS.ti-PROJECTS are merged. A copy of the newly merged ATLAS.ti-PROJECT containing everyone's work is then distributed back to each team member for their next round of work. Management of a team project therefore involves some kind of "merge cycle"—either ad hoc or on a routine schedule—for collecting all the ATLAS.ti-PROJECTS, merging them, and redistributing the merged ATLAS.ti-PROJECT.

Merging one ATLAS.ti-PROJECT with another is smooth and effortless from a technical point of view, involving little more than clicking a button. But if the merge cycle procedures are not thought through, the resulting merged ATLAS.ti-PROJECT can unintentionally include or exclude or duplicate some items and waste a great deal of time in sorting it out. Long experience with team projects has led us to adopt a "foolproof method." It requires no thinking—the same procedures are followed every time, leaving the thinking for the more important research activities. Arguments can be made that this foolproof approach is unnecessarily rigid, and some teams prefer to cut corners. We prefer not to.

Every team project is different in the details of implementing the foolproof method, but all follow the same general principles. We begin with the principles and then outline the procedures.

Everyone on the Same Cycle

Even if one team member has done no work between the last merge cycle and the current one, the foolproof method has them submit their ATLAS.ti-PROJECT for merging and not continue working until they receive the merged ATLAS.ti-PROJECT. In theory, missing a merge cycle if you have done no work since the last one should not be a problem, but the possibility for human error is great—in real life people just forget things that they have done.

What Happens When You Merge

When two ATLAS.ti-PROJECTS are merged, each COMPONENT is *added*, *unified*, or *ignored*. The key to making the right selections is knowing what these three actions mean:

- *Add* means that if a COMPONENT in one of the ATLAS.ti-PROJECTS to be merged has the same name as a COMPONENT in the other, a duplicate is created in the merged ATLAS.ti-PROJECT. This is generally not what you want to do or expect to happen, although it can be used for specialized purposes. For example, if there is a fixed set of CODES used by all team members, merging their separate ATLAS.ti-PROJECTS with the *add codes* option would produce multiple sets of identical CODES in the merged ATLAS.ti-PROJECT, one complete set for each team member.
- *Unify* means that if a COMPONENT in one of the ATLAS.ti-PROJECTS to be merged has the same name as a COMPONENT in the other, then the attributes of one are simply combined with the other. This is the intuitive meaning of merging—what you expect and hope will happen.
- *Ignore* leads to that COMPONENT not being merged. This is usually valuable for some ad hoc special-purpose merges rather than the team production kinds of merges we have been discussing.

Principles of the Foolproof Method

The foolproof method is intended to avoid errors by accomplishing the merge with the least amount of thinking, variation, or choices. The following general principles are always followed.

- *User system.* Each team member creates a new user name for themselves and logs in to the ATLAS.ti-PROJECT using that name. All COMPONENTS added or modified are then tagged with their user name, and in the merged ATLAS.ti-PROJECT it is possible to see who created or modified any COMPONENTS. However, it is not possible to know who took an action, such as linking a CODE to a QUOTATION.
- *The merge manager.* The foolproof method requires centralized management by a "merge manager," who becomes the team expert in the process. The right personality helps—detail oriented, control oriented, and proficient with keeping track of incoming Project Bundle files. The right person will automatically think to develop a naming convention for each team member's Project Bundle files and will create a log of when they arrive and when they are sent back out.

- *All ATLAS.ti-PROJECTS contain all DOCUMENTS.* If some team members add their own DOCU-MENTS to their ATLAS.ti-PROJECT (perhaps just the ones they work on) and others have a different selection of DOCUMENTS, the potential for ending up with duplicate DOCUMENTS and coding in the merged ATLAS.ti-PROJECT is great. The safest procedure is that only the merge manager is permitted to add new DOCUMENTS to a project immediately after each merge. This can be inconvenient, and it sometimes requires everyone stopping work for a merge only in order that the merge manager can merge and then add the new DOCUMENTS, but this is essential to eliminating human error. When this corner is cut, the potential for human error is great.
- *No editing DOCUMENTS.* If DOCUMENTS are edited from within ATLAS.ti by one team member, those DOCUMENTS will become different from other team members' copies of those DOCUMENTS, and that DOCUMENT will be added and thus duplicated, with part of the coding in one DOCU-MENT and part in the new duplicate. All this can be avoided by disallowing team members from editing their DOCUMENTS from within the ATLAS.ti-PROJECT. (*This was the case at the time of writing. Updates to ATLAS.ti Version 8 may make* DOCUMENT *editing possible for teams.*)

Procedures of the Foolproof Method

The following three steps are an ideal that is always followed overall, but each step is necessarily adapted to each situation. Although these steps may be accomplished somewhat differently, the adaptations should never violate any of the principles described earlier.

- Step 1: The next merge is announced. Each team member saves their work, creates a Project Bundle, sends it to the merge manager, and then stops work until they receive the next Project Bundle.
- Step 2: The merge manager opens each submitted ATLAS.ti-PROJECT to confirm that each one contains all DOCUMENTS and no additional DOCUMENTS Then she merges the ATLAS.ti-PROJECTS one by one, selecting *unify* for all COMPONENTS.
- Step 3: The merge manager adds any new DOCUMENTS to the merged ATLAS.ti-PROJECT and then makes a Project Bundle to send to each team member for the next round of work.

Inter-Rater Reliability

There is no general agreement about what it means to calculate the inter-rater reliability of quali-tative coding. ATLAS.ti does not have a formal means for assessing coding reliability, but future updates will include such a feature. In the *Component Orientation* video for *Working in Teams* we demonstrate some informal procedures for assessing, but not quantifying, coding reliability.

We now invite you to go to the companion website to view this *Component Orientation* video.

References

Charmaz, K. (2014). *Constructing grounded theory* (2nd ed.). Thousand Oaks, CA: Sage Publications.

Corbin, J., & Strauss, A. (2014). *Basics of qualitative research: Techniques and procedures for developing grounded theory* (4th ed.). Thousand Oaks, CA: Sage Publications.

Saldaña, J. (2015). *Thinking qualitatively: Methods of mind.* Thousand Oaks, CA: Sage Publications.

Saldaña, J. (2016). *The Coding Manual for Qualitative Researchers* (3rd ed.). London. Sage Publications

Woolf, N. H. (2015, July 6). *Different ways to write about larger themes or concepts in ATLAS.ti* [Blog post]. Retrieved from http://atlasti.com/2015/07/06/different-ways-to-write-about-larger-themes-or-concepts-in-atlas-ti/

6

MASTERING THE PROCESS OF TRANSLATION

This chapter provides practical instruction in the five steps of TRANSLATION. In Chapter 2 we described TRANSLATION very generally as the *transformation* of strategies into tactics, similar to translating from one language to another. This is true but not sufficiently detailed to actually know what to do. In Chapter 3 we described the process in more detail as *matching* the units of an ANALYTIC TASK to a COMPONENT of the software. This is also true but still not sufficiently detailed. TRANSLATION in practical terms means *representing* the UNITS of an ANALYTIC TASK by the most appropriate of all the possible COMPONENTS to which they could be matched, and this requires taking account of the purpose of the task and knowing the actions that can be taken on COMPONENTS.

This is a good moment to remind you that we are not inventing something new and complicated, but only describing what expert users of ATLAS.ti have come to do automatically and unconsciously so that you can begin to do it too. Initially we need to spell out the steps in detail, but once this detailed process is understood and used just a few times, it will become simple and automatic, and you will be able to draw productive analogies from our case illustrations to your own project and begin harnessing ATLAS.ti powerfully. You may choose to continue using the ANALYTIC PLANNING WORKSHEETS in your own projects, as many of our students do, or you may not feel it is necessary to do so. But for learning purposes it is an important TOOL.

We begin by explaining why TRANSLATION is a heuristic process. We then describe how to write ANALYTIC TASKS at an appropriate level of detail, and we introduce the ANALYTIC PLANNING WORKSHEET for planning, managing, and documenting *Five-Level QDA* projects. We then provide instruction in each of the five steps of TRANSLATION: *identifying units, describing purposes, identifying possible components, choosing appropriate components,* and *finalizing* SELECTED- *or* CONSTRUCTED-TOOLS. By necessity we present the steps of TRANSLATION in sequence. In practice, after some experience with the process, the steps become less separate and discrete than our presentation suggests. Each step includes examples and is illustrated with a running sample ANALYTIC TASK, with its ANALYTIC PLANNING WORKSHEET gradually being filled until it is complete at the end of Step 5. This instruction in each step of TRANSLATION will be sufficient if you already use ATLAS.ti and have some experience with qualitative research. If you are new to either ATLAS.ti or qualitative research, additional and more elaborated illustrations are provided in the appendices. These appendices will be especially useful when you are ready to conduct each step in your own project. The instruction and the various tables provided in each step are also a preparation for the video demonstrations of TRANSLATION on the companion website. These videos are described in more detail in Chapter 7.

Translation as a Heuristic Process

In Part I we highlighted the difference between the emergent nature of qualitative analysis and the cut-and-dried nature of computer software. TRANSLATION falls somewhere in the middle and involves a different kind of thinking or mind-set. When working at the strategy levels we are thinking with an emergent mind-set—once a task is completed the outcome suggests or leads to the next task without it being anticipated in detail in advance. At the tactics levels of operating the software, we are thinking with a step-by-step or algorithmic mind-set in which each operation, such as pressing a button or accessing a menu, has a predetermined and reliable outcome. Between the two, at the level of TRANSLATION, we are thinking in a third way with a heuristic mind-set, because TRANSLATION is more of an art than a science. One way of describing expertise in the *Five-Level QDA* method is the ability to naturally move among these three mind-sets without thinking too much about it. Figure 6.1 illustrates this.

A heuristic is like a rule of thumb, a practical or commonsense approach to solving a problem based on experience with similar problems. A heuristic has guidelines rather than a precise set of rules. That describes the TRANSLATION process quite well. A heuristic mind-set is a different way of thinking from the emergent mind-set at the strategy levels. At the strategy levels we allow the data in our projects to determine the emergence of each new step of strategy, rather than take examples of other projects as a heuristic for making analytic choices of our own. A heuristic mind-set is also a different way of thinking from the algorithmic mind-set we adopt when learning about and operating the software, which is a rules-based domain, with each action having a predetermined

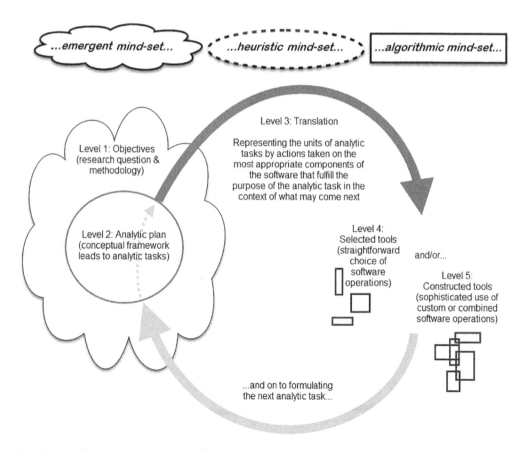

FIGURE 6.1   Emergent, heuristic, and algorithmic mind-sets

outcome. We will return to this issue of heuristic thinking as we point out how and why our examples of TRANSLATION are only examples and guidelines, not hard-and-fast rules. We call these *learning heuristics*—rules of thumb appropriate when starting out with the *Five-Level QDA* method. As your experience and expertise in TRANSLATION develop, your own rules of thumb for your own kind of data analysis will evolve accordingly.

Writing Analytic Tasks

Without an appropriately written ANALYTIC TASK, there is nothing to TRANSLATE. ANALYTIC TASKS are the smallest items of analytic activity. This is not a precise definition, and there is no neat and tidy procedure for deciding the best level of detail for writing an ANALYTIC TASK. In Chapter 2 when discussing the gourmet meal, we suggested that the best approach for deciding the appropriate level of detail for a task was to consider *what you plan to do next*, so that the outcome of the task most easily led to the next task. For example, *chop salad ingredients evenly* was most helpful in leading to the next task: *cut up fish*. Identifying a much broader task, such as *prep all the ingredients*, was too large a scale for suggesting a specific next step. Conversely, a task such as *open refrigerator door* was too detailed, requiring the next task to be something equally detailed, such as *get salad ingredients out of the fridge*, an absurdly unhelpful sequence of small-scale steps.

In the *Five-Level QDA* method the goal is to write ANALYTIC TASKS that readily reveal their UNITS and purpose in order to identify the appropriate software COMPONENTS to harness. Many researchers intimately know their strategies and what they want to do next in their project. But they initially find it difficult to write these intentions as ANALYTIC TASKS that are precise and specific, but not too specific, for the purposes of TRANSLATION.

As an example, consider the common task of familiarizing yourself with your data before beginning detailed analysis. In our workshops it is common for participants to express this as *find out what's going on in the data* or *explore the data with regard to content and meaning*. These are worthy tasks, but for the purposes of TRANSLATION they are too general—equivalent to the cooking task *prep all the ingredients*. In workshops we help participants rewrite these at a more detailed level by asking questions about the project—for example, what kind of data are being used, why is this something that needs to be achieved, and what has already been done and is intended to be done next? These are good questions to ask yourself. Depending on the answers we would rewrite their ANALYTIC TASKS to be more specific, but not too specific. In the context of an interview project, the task *find out what's going on in the data* might be rewritten more specifically as *read interview transcripts to identify potential concepts for coding*. This naturally leads to the next ANALYTIC TASK, which might be *organize and set up initial coding scheme*. But it is not so detailed as, for example, *read the first interview*, which is on a similar level of fine detail as *open refrigerator door*. At this fine level of detail way too many individual tasks would have to be written for no benefit.

Appendix 1 illustrates 14 examples of ANALYTIC TASKS from very different research contexts written at the appropriate level of detail for TRANSLATION. One of these tasks—*compare teachers' reactions to different kinds of bullying*—will serve as the running sample ANALYTIC TASK throughout this chapter. For each illustrative ANALYTIC TASK in Appendix 1, three columns display a version of the task that is too general (e.g., *find out what's going on in the data*), a version that is unnecessarily detailed (e.g., *read the first interview*), and a version at an appropriate level of detail for TRANSLATION (e.g., *read interview transcripts to identify potential concepts for coding*). When you are ready to write your own ANALYTIC TASKS, this appendix will be a helpful resource. The examples are grouped by five major kinds of analytic activity that occur in a qualitative analysis, as described by Silver and Lewins (2014):

- **Integrating.** Combining parts into a whole by bringing together the elements that make up a research project and thinking about how they relate to one another.

- *Organizing.* Creating structures related to objectives in order to reflect on meaningful aspects of the data in relation to project objectives.
- *Exploring.* Examining the content and structure of the data in order to consider the inherent nature of the data.
- *Reflecting.* Considering carefully and deeply about what is going on in the project in order to record analytic insights and the process.
- *Interrogating.* Asking questions about data in order to follow up on the work we have done so far.

Thinking in terms of these five analytic activities is helpful when developing an analytic plan and writing ANALYTIC TASKS at Level 2 of the *Five-Level QDA* method. As the strategy levels of qualitative research are not the subject of this book, we do not discuss analytic activities further, but we use them as a logical way of grouping our examples of ANALYTIC TASKS in the appendices. Appendix 2 provides a deeper look at the Silver and Lewins (2014) framework of five analytic activities.

The Analytic Planning Worksheet

The ANALYTIC PLANNING WORKSHEET is a display of the *Five-Level QDA* process in a standard format. It is primarily a learning TOOL for mastering the five steps of TRANSLATION as quickly and smoothly as possible. But it is also a working TOOL for managing and documenting a qualitative analysis. Having a standard format is useful for demonstrating the integrity and quality of a project (Tracy, 2010); for providing an audit trail through the different phases of a project (Lincoln & Guba, 1985); and for offering an opportunity to review the details of earlier steps of analysis, which are easily forgotten in the iterative and emergent unfolding of data analysis. Many researchers find it a helpful way to document progress on a project, and students use the worksheets to communicate the progress of a thesis or dissertation to their academic advisors. All the video demonstrations of ANALYTIC TASKS on the companion website are accompanied by completed ANALYTIC PLANNING WORKSHEETS, which can be printed or downloaded and are referred to in the videos. A template of the worksheet can also be printed or downloaded.

The Format of the Analytic Planning Worksheet

Each ANALYTIC PLANNING WORKSHEET displays a small number of ANALYTIC TASKS that, taken together, are a coherent set of related tasks that we call a *phase* of the analysis. A whole project will therefore have a succession of ANALYTIC PLANNING WORKSHEETS, one for each phase.

The format of the ANALYTIC PLANNING WORKSHEET follows the five levels of the *Five-Level QDA* method. The top two sections for Levels 1 and 2 serve as a reminder of the objectives, methodology, and current iteration of the analytic plan, which are best kept in mind as the details of the current ANALYTIC TASKS are thought out and entered into the worksheet. This is of particular value to researchers who are obliged to be away from their projects from time to time and need to efficiently reorient themselves on returning to the research. Also included in the top sections are the context of the current phase, consisting of a summary of what has been accomplished so far; the name of the current phase; and what is anticipated to happen next. Filling out these top sections is not a formality or bureaucratic exercise, but helps ensure the current analytic activity is congruent with the current iteration of the objectives, methodology, and analytic plan, which are updated as necessary in each successive ANALYTIC PLANNING WORKSHEET. These iterations of the project strategies in the top sections of the worksheet therefore also provide a record of their emergence through the life of the project. The lower sections of the worksheet document the process of TRANSLATION, recording the name of each ANALYTIC TASK, the steps of TRANSLATION, and the resulting SELECTED- and CONSTRUCTED-TOOLS that are used to fulfill each ANALYTIC TASK. Figure 6.2 displays an illustrated template of the ANALYTIC PLANNING WORKSHEET.

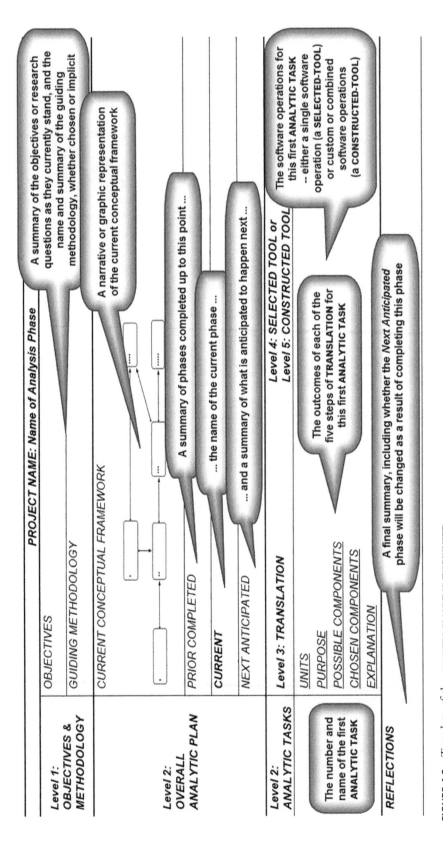

PROJECT NAME: *Name of Analysis Phase*

Level 1: OBJECTIVES & METHODOLOGY

OBJECTIVES

GUIDING METHODOLOGY

> A summary of the objectives or research questions as they currently stand, and the name and summary of the guiding methodology, whether chosen or implicit

CURRENT CONCEPTUAL FRAMEWORK

> A narrative or graphic representation of the current conceptual framework

Level 2: OVERALL ANALYTIC PLAN

PRIOR COMPLETED

> A summary of phases completed up to this point …

CURRENT

> … the name of the current phase …

NEXT ANTICIPATED

> … and a summary of what is anticipated to happen next …

Level 2: ANALYTIC TASKS

> The number and name of the first ANALYTIC TASK

Level 3: TRANSLATION

UNITS
PURPOSE
POSSIBLE COMPONENTS
CHOSEN COMPONENTS
EXPLANATION

> The outcomes of each of the five steps of TRANSLATION for this first ANALYTIC TASK

Level 4: SELECTED TOOL or
Level 5: CONSTRUCTED TOOL

> The software operations for this first ANALYTIC TASK -- either a single software operation (a SELECTED-TOOL) or custom or combined software operations (a CONSTRUCTED-TOOL)

REFLECTIONS

> A final summary, including whether the *Next Anticipated* phase will be changed as a result of completing this phase

FIGURE 6.2 Template of the ANALYTIC PLANNING WORKSHEET

Analytic Planning Worksheet for the Sample Analytic Task

Our sample ANALYTIC TASK is part of an imagined research project on bullying in schools, a topic of continuing research interest. Researchers have found that teachers' and pupils' definitions of bullying are different (Naylor, Cowie, Cossin, Bettencourt, & Lemme, 2006) and that teachers adopt a range of strategies to react to cases of reported bullying (Rigby, 2014). This imagined interview-based thematic-analysis study aims to understand teachers' reactions to different kinds of bullying in two contrasting schools in order to inform the design of a new evidence-based bullying intervention program.

Figure 6.3 displays the top section of the ANALYTIC PLANNING WORKSHEET for this project. The analytic plan is illustrated with a graphical conceptual framework, broken into planned phases. Our preference is for graphical conceptual frameworks—other researchers prefer lists, tables, or a short narrative in this section of the worksheet. This particular ANALYTIC PLANNING WORKSHEET is for the phase of analysis named *Explore teacher reactions to bullying*. The prior completed phase is indicated in the diagram, but the subsequent phase is tentative and will surely evolve. In a real-world project this diagram would therefore be updated in each iteration of the worksheet.

The Five Steps of Translation

Figure 6.4 displays the sequence of five steps of TRANSLATION. The first step is to *identify the units* in the ANALYTIC TASK. Units are the building blocks of any analysis. Identifying the units means listing the major entities that are *contained* within the ANALYTIC TASK. *Entities* refers broadly to *the kinds of things being analyzed* or *what is being looked for* in accomplishing the task. The second step is to *describe the purpose* of the ANALYTIC TASK—why the task is being done. The third step is to *identify possible* COMPONENTS that could represent the units. The fourth step is to *choose appropriate* COMPONENTS to accomplish the ANALYTIC TASK by considering its context, which includes what has been achieved previously and what is anticipated to come next. The final step is to finalize the software operations by SELECTING or CONSTRUCTING TOOLS. A TOOL is a combination of a COMPONENT and an action appropriate for a specific ANALYTIC TASK in its context. Whether there are more SELECTED-TOOLS or more CONSTRUCTED-TOOLS in a project does not indicate a more or less sophisticated analysis or more or less skill in harnessing ATLAS.ti. The choice depends solely on the specifics of each ANALYTIC TASK and its context. The remainder of this chapter consists of discussions and illustrations of each of these five steps.

Step 1—Identifying Units

In Chapter 3 we introduced the central idea of units in research for describing the things that are being analyzed (see p. 45). We discussed how the primary objective of a project would be reflected in a major unit, and there would generally be additional or secondary units either at the outset or that emerge as the analysis proceeds. We also indicated that it is not always standard practice in qualitative research to explicitly identify and name the units of analysis. One reason is because many styles of qualitative analysis are *grounded*, meaning that units emerge as the data are analyzed.

For purposes of the *Five-Level QDA* method, it is important to specify units, as these are what are TRANSLATED into SELECTED- and CONSTRUCTED-TOOLS. ANALYTIC TASKS must be written at a level of detail that is not too general but not too specific. This ensures that their units "jump out." If they do not jump out, the ANALYTIC TASK is rewritten until they do. To avoid ambiguity we use regular type when referring to the concept of units generally, but we use SMALL CAPS when discussing the UNITS we identify in individual ANALYTIC TASKS for the specific purpose of TRANSLATION.

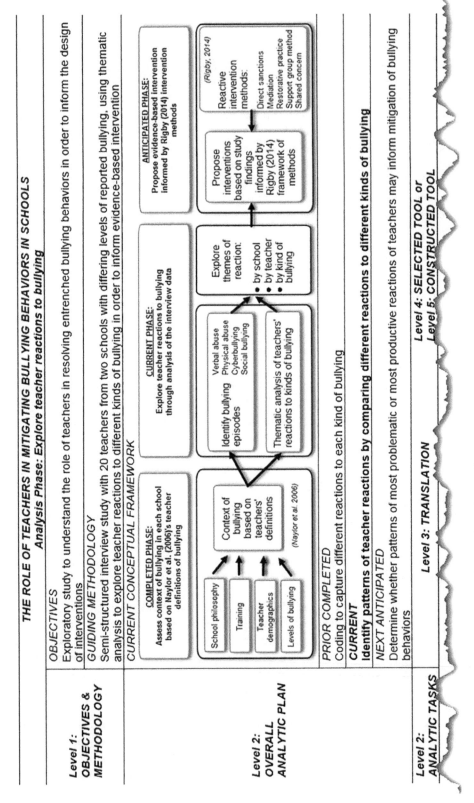

FIGURE 6.3 ANALYTIC PLANNING WORKSHEET for sample analytic task

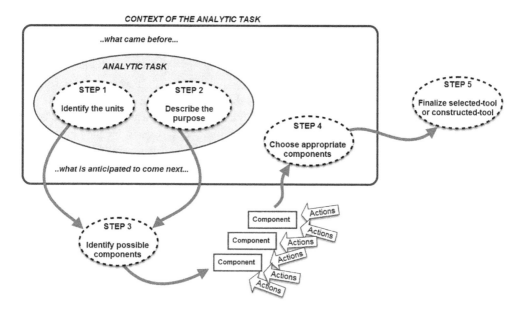

FIGURE 6.4   The steps of TRANSLATION

One stumbling block to internalizing the meaning of a unit is its ambiguity. *Unit* means something different at two different levels, so it helps to think of two separate terms: a *unit* and an *instance of a unit*. *School* is a unit—the name of a collection of things. "Santa Barbara High School" and "Gillingham Comprehensive School" are both schools, but they are instances of the unit, rather than the unit itself. Unit may have the connotation for us as a single thing, rather than a group of things. But in research "unit" refers to a collection of things of one kind, and "instance" refers to a particular example of the collection.

Think about each ANALYTIC TASK in terms of three types of units: *units of analysis*, which are the major entities that are the subject of the analysis; *units of data*, which indicate the form of the data that you have collected; and *units of meaning*, which are the parts of your data or the analytic entities you create that have meaning in your analysis. Other writers identify other types of units for different purposes (e.g., di Gregorio & Davidson, 2008, discuss their use of units of observation), but for our purposes units of analysis, data, and meaning have proved most helpful. These three types of units are distinct when ANALYTIC TASKS are straightforward, but they overlap in more sophisticated ANALYTIC TASKS.

Looking for these three types of units in your ANALYTIC TASKS helps you ask the right questions, which brings the idea of a unit alive so that so that the UNITS of your precisely written ANALYTIC TASKS jump out at you. Once a UNIT has been identified, it is entered into the ANALYTIC PLANNING WORKSHEET. The type of unit does not directly affect the following steps of TRANSLATION, but we enter the types into the ANALYTIC PLANNING WORKSHEET just as an aid in thinking through the following steps.

Units of Analysis

Units of analysis indicate the entities in a project that are the subject of the analysis. These could be anything—individuals, groups of individuals, organizations, parts of organizations, events, settings, programs, documents, artifacts, countries, places, etc. There is often one major unit of analysis and several additional units, but there is no ideal number of units of analysis to aspire to: it depends on the kind and complexity of the research questions.

In the bullying project we may be comparing episodes of bullying within two different schools, so there would be two units of analysis: *schools* and *episodes of bullying*. If we were also investigating teachers' responses to episodes of bullying, then we would additionally have *teachers* as a unit of analysis. These units let us know what the subject of the analysis is. But if instead we were investigating students' lived experiences of being bullied within one particular school, there would be one unit of analysis: *students*. If we were evaluating the effectiveness of programs designed to minimize bullying within schools located in a particular district of a large city, there would be four units of analysis: *programs*, *schools*, and two sets of individuals—*students* and *teachers*. If the focus of analysis changes as the project advances, additional units may be identified.

Units of Data

The data for this project also come in units. One factor in identifying units of data is the complexity of the data collection procedures. If data collection is straightforward, then the source of material may be the only unit of data. For example, if the bullying project involved in-depth interviews with individual teachers and also focus group discussions with many teachers, it would be typical to transcribe each interview and each focus group into its own Microsoft Word file. If the intention is to consider the data from the individual interviews and the focus groups as equivalent and to analyze all the data in the same way, then for TRANSLATION purposes *transcript* would be the single unit of data, and each interview and each focus group would be an instance of this one unit. But if the intention is to first analyze the focus group data and later use the conclusions to inform the analysis of the individual interviews, then there would be two different units of data: *interview* and *focus group*. Identifying units therefore involves both the form in which the data have been collected or prepared and the purpose to which they will be put. These principles apply in the same way to all kinds of data—for example, survey data containing qualitative responses, collections of images, video data, social media content, and so on.

Some projects are more sophisticated and involve more units of data. In the bullying project an additional objective may be to compare the responses of each person in the focus groups, perhaps because each respondent has been selected to represent a stakeholder group, such as an academic department. If the focus groups have been transcribed with a marker of some kind in the text to indicate who said what, then there are three units of data: *interview* and *focus group* for the first objective and *focus group respondent* for the second. In this case *focus group respondent* is also a unit of analysis—it is an "entity" in the project that is being analyzed. But this does not mean *focus group respondent* is two different units. Thinking separately about units of data and units of analysis is only helpful in identifying *focus group respondent* as a unit in the context of two different purposes. Once a unit is identified, it is not important whether it is a unit of data or a unit of analysis or both.

Units of Meaning

It is helpful to think of two kinds of units of meaning. The first are the meaningful concepts created for the analysis. As we discussed in Chapter 2 (p. 37), we use "concept" as the general term for all the different kinds of meaningful entities created in the analytic process. These are variously referred to in different methodologies and research traditions as codes, labels, topics, content areas, categories, themes, properties, dimensions, etc.

The second kind of unit of meaning are the segments of data that are meaningful because they are instances of concepts and are therefore conceptualized in some manner. For example, data segments could be tagged with a code name or interpreted in analytical writing. A unit of meaning of textual data could be a single word, a phrase, a sentence, a paragraph, many paragraphs, or a whole document. Some methodologies prescribe "line-by-line coding," although this is somewhat ambiguous with electronic data, as the number of words on a "line" depends on how wide the margin is set. In still images a unit of meaning may be based on the entire image, a selected portion of an image, or a series of images. In video recordings a unit of meaning may be the entire video, a scene, a clip, or a series of clips. In Twitter data a unit of meaning may be each individual tweet, all the tweets posted using a particular hashtag, all the tweets posted in response to another tweet, or all tweets posted on a topic in a particular time frame.

These units of meaning may appear to be similar to units of data. The difference is in their purpose. Units of data are identified based on how the data are organized. Segments of data are identified as units of meaning because they are instances of meaningful concepts. Yet both units may be based on the same data, with one embedded in the other. For example, a *transcript* of a document may be identified as a UNIT in an ANALYTIC TASK, and a *survey response* that appears in that document may be identified as a UNIT in a different ANALYTIC TASK. The *transcript* UNIT was identified when thinking about the ANALYTIC TASK in terms of units of data, and the *survey response* UNIT was identified when thinking about a different ANALYTIC TASK in terms of units of meaning. Types of units are helpful as an aid in identifying UNITS.

Appendix 3 provides numerous examples of the three types of units.

The Rule of Thumb of Two Units

At the levels of strategy—objectives, methodology, and analytic plan—a research project with fewer units suggests a more straightforward study, and a project with many units suggests greater complexity or a more sophisticated analysis. This does not follow for UNITS of ANALYTIC TASKS. The strategy levels deal with the analysis as a whole, the big picture; in contrast, the ANALYTIC TASK is the smallest item of analytic activity. For an individual ANALYTIC TASK, more than two UNITS is not a sign of sophistication, but only complicate the process of TRANSLATION. That is why when learning and initially practicing TRANSLATION, the rule of thumb is that no more than two UNITS should be identified for each ANALYTIC TASK.

If more than two UNITS are identified, there are two possibilities to consider. First, the ANALYTIC TASK may be too large. By rewriting the ANALYTIC TASK it is usually possible to divide it more conveniently into two smaller tasks. Second, there may be good reason for the ANALYTIC TASK to have more than two UNITS—that is why the rule of thumb is only a heuristic, not a firm rule that must not be broken. Our sample ANALYTIC TASK—*compare teachers' reactions to different kinds of bullying*—is a good example. As discussed in Appendix 1, this ANALYTIC TASK has three UNITS—*teacher, reactions,* and *kinds of bullying*—but is not amenable to being split into two separate tasks. Reducing the task to two units requires thinking about whether any pair of these three UNITS is really a single UNIT for the purposes of TRANSLATION. For example, is *teacher* a unit of analysis in the study that is independent of the teachers' *reactions* to different kinds of bullying, or are they a single unit? Similarly, are *reactions* to bullying and concepts about *kinds of bullying* best represented as a single unit of meaning—*reactions to different kinds of bullying*—or will subsequent ANALYTIC TASKS have different purposes and require two separate UNITS of meaning: *reactions* and *different kinds of bullying*? How do we know all this from the ANALYTIC TASK as written? We don't. We know it from the analytic plan, which is conveniently displayed in the ANALYTIC PLANNING WORKSHEET for reference as the analysis proceeds. Figure 6.5 displays the first iteration of the worksheet, which indicates that in this example three UNITS are called for—*teachers, reactions,* and *kinds of bullying*—based on the purpose of the task, which is the subject of the next section. We added the type of each unit to the worksheet in Figure 6.5 as a reminder of how we were thinking about the task, but this is optional as the type of unit is not used for TRANSLATION.

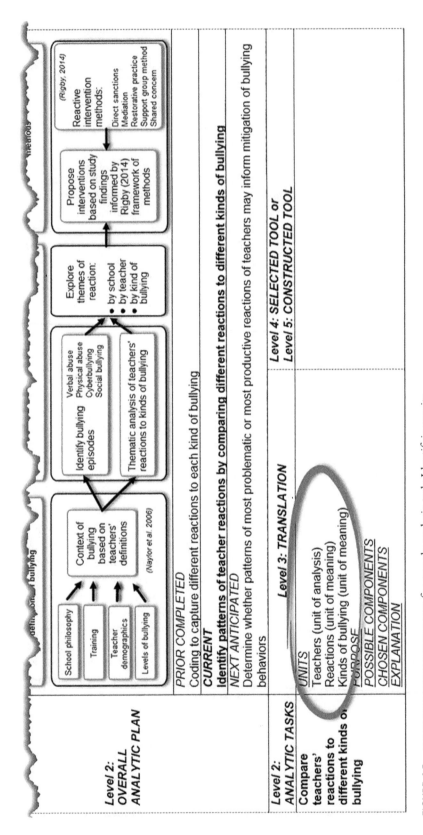

FIGURE 6.5 ANALYTIC PLANNING WORKSHEET for sample analytic task: Identifying units

For further illustration of identifying UNITS, Appendix 4 identifies and discusses the UNITS of our 14 example ANALYTIC TASKS. Appendix 4 will be a helpful resource when you are ready to identify the UNITS of your own ANALYTIC TASKS. Some of the examples follow the rule of thumb that an ANALYTIC TASK contains only one or two UNITS, and some do not. Some of these examples also demonstrate why the purpose of an ANALYTIC TASK must be known to properly identify its UNITS for TRANSLATION.

Step 2—Describing Purposes

Qualitative analysis is emergent to varying degrees, and it is common to feel unsure what to do next. Asking yourself *why* you need to accomplish an ANALYTIC TASK prevents you from acting without a focus or a reason. This question of *why* at the most detailed level of an ANALYTIC TASK mirrors the broadest question at the highest level of strategy: *Why* am I undertaking this research project? When that essential question is answered, the result is a clear, coherent research question that guides the entire project. When the *why* question is answered at the detailed level of an ANALYTIC TASK, the result is a clear purpose that is intimately involved in choosing the appropriate COMPONENTS from the identified list of possibilities for fulfilling the task. This will be discussed further in "Step 4, Choosing Appropriate COMPONENTS."

As in every step of TRANSLATION, there is a rule of thumb for describing purposes: an ANALYTIC TASK written at the most helpful level of detail tends to have a single purpose so that its outcome leads easily to identifying the next task. But as with all heuristics, this is not always the case.

The Difference Between a Purpose and an Action

One stumbling block to identifying the purposes of ANALYTIC TASKS is that it is easy to confuse a *purpose* with an *action*. Whereas a purpose is the reason *why* an ANALYTIC TASK is planned, an action is *how* it will be accomplished. We always include the purpose—the *why*—when writing ANALYTIC TASKS, but we only include the action—the *how*—when it is a help in the TRANSLATION process. Whether or not you include the action is influenced by the guiding methodology for the project, as well as the context of the task—what has come before and what is anticipated to come next. Deciding whether to include the action when writing an ANALYTIC TASK quickly becomes second nature after going through the TRANSLATION process a few times, but this initially requires some thought.

Consider again the ANALYTIC TASK from Appendix 1—*read interview transcripts to identify potential concepts for coding*. At first glance this has two purposes—to read the transcripts and to identify the potential concepts. But thinking of a purpose as *why* and an action as *how* makes clear that there is actually only one purpose: *to identify the concepts*. This is the *why* of the task—its purpose—and it is accomplished by the *how* of the task—the action of reading. This task therefore has a single purpose, which is the rule of thumb.

It may have been appropriate to include the action in the task—*read interview transcripts*—perhaps because the guiding methodology emphasizes that the researcher read the transcripts in their entirety before identifying any concepts. A different methodology with completely different objectives and methods for analyzing texts might emphasize identifying concepts in a different way, perhaps in a granular manner at the detailed level of each small segment of data or at a high-level based on the frequency of occurrence of key words. In these situations the ANALYTIC TASK might be better written as *identify potential concepts for coding*, which expresses the purpose but leaves open the action to fulfill the purpose. In the TRANSLATION process various possibilities for acting on COMPONENTS would then be identified in the software, some that involve close reading, but perhaps others that would not involve close reading, such as auto-coding or word-cloud operations.

Other examples of ANALYTIC TASKS in which it is helpful to include an action as well as a purpose are included in Appendix 5, which discusses the purposes of all 14 ANALYTIC TASKS introduced in Appendix 1.

The Rule of Thumb of One Purpose

A single purpose for an ANALYTIC TASK simplifies the process of TRANSLATION. This is because the TRANSLATION process takes account of what is anticipated to come next, and this is more complicated for a task with more than one purpose. A single purpose is therefore a helpful learning heuristic.

But often it is more productive to have two purposes than to split an ANALYTIC TASK in two. Consider this ANALYTIC TASK that has been written in sufficient detail to ensure there is a single purpose: *review codes and the coding scheme. Review* is a shorthand way of describing the purpose—*assess the codes that have been created in order to check they are of value within the coding scheme.* This single-purpose task easily leads to what we intend to do next—if we decide a CODE is not useful for some reason, we would do something about it. For example, we may rename it to more precisely reflect its characteristics, or we may merge it with another CODE that we realized represents the same concept, and so on. This following ANALYTIC TASK would be *refine codes and the coding scheme.* Although each ANALYTIC TASK indeed conforms to the learning heuristic of one purpose, in practice it would be difficult to *review codes and the coding scheme* and not at the same time *refine codes and the coding scheme* as needed, because this is an iterative process—refining one CODE influences the review of the next CODE. Reviewing all the codes (the first task) and then going back and refining them all (the second task) does not make sense. In this case it would be more appropriate to write an ANALYTIC TASK with two purposes, as they go hand in hand—for example, *review and refine codes and the coding scheme.* This is the way we have presented this ANALYTIC TASK in Appendices 1, 4, and 5.

Regarding our sample ANALYTIC TASK, *compare teachers' reactions to different kinds of bullying,* we noted in Step 1 when identifying UNITS that we don't know from the wording of the task alone whether to identify two UNITS—*teachers* and *reactions to kinds of bullying*—or three—*teachers, reactions,* and *kinds of bullying.* The purpose of the task lets us know. If the purpose is *to investigate how individual teachers react to different kinds of bullying,* the focus is on the kinds of bullying and two UNITS are most helpful. If the purpose is *to investigate whether individual teachers display similar or different reactions to different kinds of bullying,* then the reactions and kinds of bullying must be differentiated and three UNITS are called for—*teachers, reactions,* and *kinds of bullying.* The second purpose is the one assumed in our sample ANALYTIC TASK, as displayed in Figure 6.6, the second iteration of the ANALYTIC PLANNING WORKSHEET.

For further illustration, Appendix 5 discusses the purposes of each of the 14 example ANALYTIC TASKS. Appendix 5 will be a helpful resource when you are ready to identify the purposes of your own ANALYTIC TASKS. Some of the examples follow the one-purpose rule of thumb, and some do not.

Step 3—Identifying Possible Components

In Chapter 3 we introduced the idea of TRANSLATION as a simple *matching* of a unit of an ANALYTIC TASK to a COMPONENT of the software, but in practice TRANSLATION means something richer: *representing* the UNITS of an ANALYTIC TASK by the most appropriate of all the possible COMPONENTS to which they could be matched. This requires taking account of the context of the task and knowing the actions that can be taken on the COMPONENTS. For purposes of exposition and to provide a learning heuristic, we divide the process into two parts: first, *identifying* all the possible COMPONENTS that could be used to fulfil an ANALYTIC TASK (Step 3); and second, *choosing* the most appropriate COMPONENTS from among these possibilities (Step 4). When learning the process it is helpful to think about these two steps as distinct. After a small amount of experience our students come to think of these steps in the manner of experienced users of ATLAS.ti—as a single thought process—and it is likely you will too. But for learning purposes we begin by identifying the possible COMPONENTS that could be used to fulfil an ANALYTIC TASK.

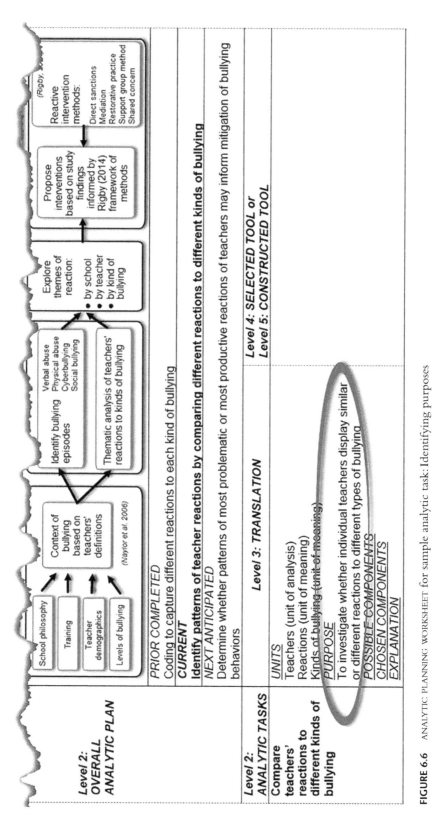

FIGURE 6.6   ANALYTIC PLANNING WORKSHEET for sample analytic task: Identifying purposes

In Chapter 3 (p. 49) we compared the TRANSLATION of ANALYTIC TASKS to the translation of languages. In language translation a simple word-by-word rendition of one language into another is called the *formal equivalence* of the words in each language. This may be adequate for asking directions or translating technical terms that don't involve shades of meaning. But a formal word-by-word translation is not sufficient for translating idioms or subtleties from one language to another. This requires *dynamic equivalence* between the original and the translated text. This means finding appropriate words in the second language that ensure that the original and the translated versions have roughly the same effect on their respective readers, something not accomplished by a mechanical word-by-word translation.

The distinction between *formal equivalence* and *dynamic equivalence* in language translation is the basis for our rule of thumb for identifying possible COMPONENTS. We first look for *formal equivalence*. This means a clear and obvious match between a UNIT and a COMPONENT that is suggested by the affordances of the software, meaning the way the software is designed and presented on the screen with this equivalence in mind. We then consider any *dynamically equivalent* COMPONENTS, meaning those that are not as obvious a match to a UNIT. This ensures that we take advantage of the full flexibility of ATLAS.ti and not limit ourselves to *formally equivalent* COMPONENTS that might not be the best candidate in a particular context.

The distinction between *formally equivalent* and *dynamically equivalent* COMPONENTS is a helpful learning heuristic, but it is not necessary to think too deeply about whether an equivalence between a UNIT and a COMPONENT is formal or dynamic. Knowing about this distinction is enough to prompt us to first identify the obvious matches suggested by the program's affordances and then identify out-of-the-box matches that may prove more productive. As experience grows and you become more familiar with using the various COMPONENTS, the distinction will fade. In the meantime, we use the terms *formal equivalence* and *dynamic equivalence* when necessary in the remainder of this section to draw attention to the different thinking processes.

We now return to the sample ANALYTIC TASK—*compare teachers' reactions to different kinds of bullying.* Table 6.1 summarizes all the possible COMPONENTS that could represent the UNITS of the task: *teachers,* which is a unit of analysis, and *reactions* and *kinds of bullying,* which are both units of

TABLE 6.1 Summary of possible components for "teachers," "reactions," and "kinds of bullying"

Component	*"Teachers"*	*"Reactions"*	*"Kinds of bullying"*
DOCUMENT	possible component		
DOCUMENT-GROUPS AND SMART-GROUPS	possible component		
QUOTATION		possible component	possible component
HYPER-LINKED-QUOTATION			
CODE	possible component	possible component	possible component
CODED-QUOTATION		possible component	possible component
CODE-GROUPS AND SMART-GROUPS		possible component	possible component
SMART-CODE		possible component	possible component
SMART-CODE-SNAPSHOT		possible component	possible component
COMMENT		possible component	possible component
MEMO	possible component	possible component	possible component
MEMO-GROUPS AND SMART-GROUPS			
NETWORK	possible component	possible component	possible component
NETWORK-GROUPS AND SMART-GROUPS			

meaning. Following Table 6.1 we discuss the rationale for identifying each possible COMPONENT, and we then display the updated ANALYTIC PLANNING WORKSHEET with the possible COMPONENTS entered.

Possible Components for First Unit

In this sample ANALYTIC TASK we are thinking of *teachers* as a UNIT of analysis independent of their reactions to different kinds of bullying (see Appendix 4). We therefore need to identify COMPONENTS that could be used to represent *teachers* independent of any other UNIT in the study.

Document

A DOCUMENT can be used to represent a teacher when the entirety of each teacher's contributions to the study is contained within one DOCUMENT. This would likely be the situation in an interview-based study in which each teacher had been interviewed once. The whole of each interview would have been transcribed into a separate Microsoft Word file and added to the ATLAS.ti-PROJECT as a separate DOCUMENT. There would thus be a *formal equivalence* between the UNIT of a teacher and the COMPONENT of a DOCUMENT.

Document-Groups and Document-Smart-Groups

A DOCUMENT-GROUP can be used to represent a teacher when there is more than one DOCUMENT per teacher. This may be the situation in a longitudinal project if each teacher had been interviewed on three separate occasions. In the ATLAS.ti-PROJECT we would therefore have three DOCUMENTS per teacher, so each DOCUMENT is not *formally equivalent* to the UNIT of teacher. We therefore need to seek a *dynamic equivalence* between the UNIT and a COMPONENT. We could use DOCUMENT-GROUPS for this purpose, one per teacher, into which we would add each teacher's three DOCUMENTS. We would then have created one COMPONENT, a DOCUMENT-GROUP to represent each UNIT, the teacher.

Code

A CODE can be used to represent a teacher when several teachers' contributions to the study are contained within a single DOCUMENT. This may be the situation in a focus group study when several teachers come together to discuss bullying in a moderated discussion. The focus group discussion would be added to the ATLAS.ti-PROJECT as one DOCUMENT. There would not be a *formal equivalence* between the UNIT of a teacher and each DOCUMENT, because the DOCUMENT includes the voices of multiple teachers. In this situation CODES can be used to create a *dynamic equivalence* between the UNIT and the COMPONENT because we could create one CODE to represent each teacher, linking all their contributions throughout the DOCUMENT to their own CODE.

Memo

A MEMO can be used to represent the UNIT *teachers* when it is appropriate for all the researcher's insights about an individual teacher to be written up in one space. This is a natural use for a MEMO, and this *formal equivalence* may be appropriate in many types of study—for example, an analytic plan may call for summarizing teachers' reactions by writing analytic interpretations about each teacher separately.

This use of MEMOS is independent of data collection strategies. *Teachers* may also be represented by other COMPONENTS for other purposes. There is no reason that a UNIT cannot be represented in multiple ways for different purposes.

Network

A NETWORK is the most flexible of COMPONENTS. Any other COMPONENTS can be displayed and worked on in a visual manner in a NETWORK. A NETWORK can therefore be used as a *dynamic equivalent* for any UNIT. In the example of *teachers* with three interviews each, a NETWORK can be created to display all three DOCUMENTS, and a variety of tasks can be undertaken in this visual display if it is determined in Step 4 that this is more appropriate than other ways of working.

Possible Components for the Second Unit

Reviewing the ANALYTIC PLANNING WORKSHEET for our sample ANALYTIC TASK, we know that teachers' *reactions* and *kinds of bullying* are considered separate UNITS of meaning, rather than a single UNIT of *reactions to kinds of bullying*, based on the purpose of the task (p. 113). Because both UNITS are of the same type, the thought processes involved in identifying possible COMPONENTS are the same. In this section we only discuss the UNIT *reactions* to avoid unnecessary duplication.

Quotation

A QUOTATION unlinked to any other COMPONENT is called a free QUOTATION. If several *reactions* are expressed within one DOCUMENT, a free QUOTATION can be used to represent each reaction, and each QUOTATION can be named to reflect the type of reaction expressed. For example, we may rename one QUOTATION *disapproval* and another *censure*. This somewhat unusual *dynamic equivalence* between a renamed free QUOTATION and a unit of meaning can be a useful substitute for the early coding stages in some methodologies, allowing you to avoid large numbers of unnecessary initial codes. An added advantage is that several QUOTATIONS can have the same name without problems—each QUOTATION already has a unique identifying number to distinguish it from others. This approach can be used whether the DOCUMENT contains text, graphical, audio, or video data.

Code

A CODE representing a concept or a unit of meaning is the most obvious *formal equivalence*. A CODE can be used to represent a teacher's *reaction* when it is anticipated that several instances of each kind of reaction will be identified across different DOCUMENTS and there is a need to gather them all together or retrieve them. This would likely be the situation if several different teachers had been interviewed, observed, or taken part in focus group discussions. A CODE would be created and named for each reaction and linked to QUOTATIONS where those concepts were explicitly stated or implied by teachers, for example, *disapproval* and *censure*.

Coded-Quotation

If CODES were used to represent teachers' *reactions*, then linking the CODES to QUOTATIONS produces CODED-QUOTATIONS that are instances of each *reaction*. For some purposes these CODED-QUOTATIONS that represent the instances of reactions in the data may be acted upon independently.

Code-Groups and Code-Smart-Groups

A CODE-GROUP could be used to represent different types of *reactions*, if CODES had first been used to represent teachers' *reactions*. For example a CODE-GROUP named *passive reactions* could contain the CODES *disapproval, censure,* or *regret,* and another CODE-GROUP called *active reactions* could contain the CODES *physical restraint* and *exclusion.* CODE-GROUPS may therefore represent higher-level concepts in order to work separately with all passive reactions and all active reactions.

A CODE-SMART-GROUP could be used to represent teachers' *reactions* if the concept being represented is at the next higher level of abstraction. For example, various CODES may represent different teacher *reactions* to three kinds of bullying: *physical, verbal,* and *cyber* bullying. These three sets of *reaction* codes can be grouped into three CODE-GROUPS of the same names. This is one level of abstraction higher than the individual *reaction* CODES. If the purpose of an ANALYTIC TASK is to retrieve data only related to face-to-face bullying (i.e., physical or verbal but not cyber bullying), then a CODE-SMART-GROUP could be created to be *formally equivalent* to the concept of *face-to-face bullying.* The two relevant CODE-GROUPS—*physical bullying* and *verbal bullying*—can be combined to create a CODE-SMART-GROUP that can be used to retrieve all CODED-QUOTATIONS from the CODES in the two face-to-face bullying CODE-GROUPS.

Smart-Code

When the Query Tool retrieves CODED-QUOTATIONS from two or more CODES, a SMART-CODE can be created to represent the resulting concept. For example, if it was necessary to think about just some of the *active reactions* together, but not all of them, we could use the Query Tool to combine the CODES *short-term exclusion* and *permanent exclusion* and save it as a SMART-CODE.

Smart-Code-Snapshot

A SMART-CODE-SNAPSHOT can be used to represent a particular set of teachers' *reactions* by freezing a SMART-CODE that combines any of the sets and groupings of CODES described earlier that have been created to serve the purpose of an ANALYTIC TASK. This is particularly useful in longitudinal projects, for example, if there is a need to compare teachers' *reactions* at the end of each wave of data collection.

Comment

If a renamed free QUOTATION is used to represent a teacher's *reaction*, a possible *dynamic equivalence* described earlier, then the COMMENT area of the QUOTATION is the natural space to write the researcher's insights about this specific reaction. The COMMENT will always be available wherever the QUOTATION is viewed, whether onscreen or in printed or exported form. Similarly, if a CODE is used to represent a teacher's *reaction* in a formal equivalence, the COMMENT area of the CODE is the natural space to record analytic insights and commentary about the evolution of the concept as more QUOTATIONS are linked to the CODE.

Memo

A MEMO can be used to represent a teacher's *reaction* when all the researcher's insights about each reaction need to be written up in a separate space. This is a natural use for a MEMO, and this *formal equivalence* may be appropriate in many types of study—for example, an analytic plan may call for summarizing teachers' *reactions* by writing analytic interpretations about each reaction separately and then analyzing these summaries rather than the original data.

Network

As described earlier, a NETWORK is the most flexible of COMPONENTS and can be used as a *dynamic equivalent* for any UNIT. Any of the COMPONENTS discussed earlier to represent teachers' *reactions* can be displayed in a NETWORK, and tasks can be undertaken in this visual display if it is determined in Step 4 that this is more appropriate than other ways of working.

In summary, ATLAS.ti is flexible when harnessed powerfully. There is no fixed one-to-one relationship between a particular UNIT and a particular COMPONENT. The same UNIT of an ANALYTIC TASK can often be represented by several different COMPONENTS, and conversely, the same COMPONENT can represent different UNITS in the same ATLAS.ti-PROJECT. Additionally, the use of COMPONENTS can change as an analysis proceeds. For example, one UNIT may be represented by more than one COMPONENT if it is required for different ANALYTIC TASKS at different stages of a project. Identifying COMPONENTS is therefore not done once and set in stone, but is an emergent process that parallels the emergent process at the strategy levels.

Additional Possible Components When Purposes Require Writing or Visualizing

In addition to UNITS, purposes can play a role in identifying COMPONENTS. This is the case when the UNITS of an ANALYTIC TASK do not call for COMPONENTS that involve writing or visualizing, yet the purpose of the task does require writing or visualizing. For example, five of the 14 ANALYTIC TASKS in Appendix 5 have writing or visualizing purposes that stand alone from the UNITS of the task identified in Appendix 4. For these five ANALYTIC TASKS the purpose suggests additional needed COMPONENTS for *explaining, summarizing,* or *interpreting*:

- Compare theoretical and emerging concepts and *explain* their similarities and differences
- Review field notes to *summarize* athletes' body language with same- and opposite-gender coaches
- Create and *explain* relationships between concepts
- *Summarize* differences in verbal and nonverbal interactions between doctors and patients
- *Interpret* media representations of local politicians in relation to attitudes expressed by focus group respondents

When identifying possible COMPONENTS we therefore ask ourselves a final question: *Does the purpose of the* ANALYTIC TASK *call for additional possible* COMPONENTS *to support writing or visualizing?* For example, these actions of *explaining, summarizing,* or *interpreting* indicate a need to either write about or graphically represent what is seen while undertaking the task. Therefore COMMENTS, MEMOS, and NETWORKS are common additional possible COMPONENTS for these tasks as *formal equivalents* to their purposes. Other COMPONENTS may also come into play—for example, HYPERLINKED-QUOTATIONS may facilitate interpretation and writing purposes by linking conceptually related QUOTATIONS and allowing you easily to move between them.

In the case of our sample ANALYTIC TASK, these COMPONENTS have already been identified. However, for some ANALYTIC TASKS these COMPONENTS may not have been identified from the UNITS and therefore it is always important to consider whether the purpose of the task calls for additional COMPONENTS to support writing or visualizing.

Figure 6.7 displays all the possible COMPONENTS that we have identified in the third iteration of the ANALYTIC PLANNING WORKSHEET.

ANALYTIC PLAN

Levels of bullying (Naylor et al. 2006) → ...reactions to kinds of bullying → ...bullying → ...framework of methods → Restorative practice / Support group method / Shared concern

	PRIOR COMPLETED Coding to capture different reactions to each kind of bullying **CURRENT** **Identify patterns of teacher reactions by comparing different reactions to different kinds of bullying** *NEXT ANTICIPATED* Determine whether patterns of most problematic or most productive reactions of teachers may inform mitigation of bullying behaviors
Level 2: **ANALYTIC TASKS**	*Level 3: TRANSLATION* *Level 4: SELECTED TOOL or* *Level 5: CONSTRUCTED TOOL*
Compare teachers' reactions to different kinds of bullying	<u>UNITS</u> Teachers (unit of analysis) Reactions (unit of meaning) Kinds of bullying (unit of meaning) <u>PURPOSE</u> To investigate whether individual teachers display similar or different reactions to different types of bullying <u>POSSIBLE COMPONENTS</u> **Teachers** – DOCUMENT, DOCUMENT-GROUP, CODE, MEMO, NETWORK **Reactions** – QUOTATION, CODE, CODED-QUOTATION, CODE-GROUP & CODE-SMART-GROUP, SMART-CODE, SMART-CODE-SNAPSHOT, COMMENT, MEMO, NETWORK **Kinds of bullying** - QUOTATION, CODE, CODED-QUOTATION, CODE-GROUP & CODE-SMART-GROUP, SMART-CODE, SMART-CODE-SNAPSHOT, COMMENT, MEMO, NETWORK <u>CHOSEN COMPONENTS</u> <u>EXPLANATION</u>

FIGURE 6.7 ANALYTIC PLANNING WORKSHEET for sample analytic task: Identifying possible components

Step 4—Choosing Appropriate Components

Step 4 involves choosing the appropriate COMPONENTS to fulfill an ANALYTIC TASK. This means evaluating the possible COMPONENTS identified in Step 3 in terms of the *actions* that can be taken on those COMPONENTS and the *context* of the task. The context of an ANALYTIC TASK consists of three elements: its purpose, what has been accomplished previously, and what is anticipated to happen next.

We illustrate Steps 4 and 5 differently from Steps 1, 2, and 3, so we begin by discussing the differences. We then describe all the actions that can be taken on COMPONENTS in ATLAS.ti and illustrate the process of choosing appropriate COMPONENTS.

Illustrations for Steps 4 and 5

In the first three steps of TRANSLATION we provided a variety of illustrations in the chapter text as well as further examples for each of the 14 ANALYTIC TASKS in the appendices. Our purpose was to facilitate this way of thinking through multiple examples that offer models to be adapted and transferred to your own project. Steps 4 and 5, however, are different. These last two steps describe in detail a way of thinking about the completion of the TRANSLATION process using our straightforward sample ANALYTIC TASK. How this thinking is applied in different contexts is extremely varied because every project is so different and there are many possible contexts for each ANALYTIC TASK. For this reason we cannot provide a range of written illustrations wide enough to serve as models to be adapted for Steps 4 and 5, and therefore there is no appendix of additional examples for these steps of TRANSLATION. Instead, Steps 4 and 5 are preparation for the video demonstrations in Part III that illustrate TRANSLATION of a selection of ANALYTIC TASKS in real-world projects. Chapter 7 provides more detail about the videos and how to learn from the case illustrations.

Steps 4 and 5 are the heart of the practical instruction in TRANSLATION. Table 6.2 reviews the sequence of this practical instruction.

TABLE 6.2 The sequence of practical instruction in ATLAS.ti's components

Chapter 5 and accompanying *Component Orientation* videos	Chapter 5 and accompanying videos are organized by COMPONENT and focus on the mechanics of each COMPONENT—how they are designed and how they work. These resources can be used at any time to remind yourself how a particular COMPONENT functions.
Chapter 6 Steps 3, 4, and 5	Steps 1 and 2 prepare the groundwork for TRANSLATION, identifying UNITS and purposes in ANALYTIC TASKS. Steps 3, 4, and 5 focus on the COMPONENTS. Step 3—*identifying possible components*—is presented in a similar manner to Steps 1 and 2, with a comprehensive review of all of the commonly used COMPONENTS.
	Steps 4 and 5 do not attempt to provide a comprehensive range of examples, but instead focus on the detailed thinking process in one straightforward example of TRANSLATION. The learning objective is to understand the process. The video demonstrations in Part III provide a range of examples of this thinking process in real-world projects that you can adapt to your own work.
Chapters 8 and 9 and accompanying *Case Illustration* videos	Chapters 8 and 9 provide two fully documented real-world case illustrations. The accompanying video demonstrations include examples of real-world TRANSLATION of ANALYTIC TASKS as they occurred in each project.
Harnessing Components videos	The final set of *Harnessing Components* videos is the culmination of the instruction. These videos are organized by COMPONENT and demonstrate contrasting ways to harness COMPONENTS in different contexts.

Actions That Can Be Taken on Components

You already have an understanding of ATLAS.ti's 14 COMPONENTS from Chapter 5 and the accompanying *Component Orientation* videos. The definitions of each COMPONENT are found in Table 5.2 (p. 67). But you also need to know what actions can be taken on COMPONENTS. Some actions can be taken on all COMPONENTS, which we call *common actions*. These are listed in Table 6.3. Other actions are specific to particular COMPONENTS. These *component-specific actions* are listed in Table 6.4. We only list actions that are relevant for analytic purposes. We do not list every possible routine or housekeeping action, such as *open* a window, *close* a window, *save*, *print*, *output*, *delete*, etc. These two tables of analytic actions are referred to in the coming sections and in all the video demonstrations on the companion website.

Note that *any* analytic action can be taken at *any* time in ATLAS.ti. For example, the action *Add or import* DOCUMENTS is not restricted to the beginning of a project; additional DOCUMENTS can be added or imported at any time as the project proceeds.

The Context of Analytic Tasks

Qualitative analysis is iterative—we continually reconsider what we are currently doing in light of what has already been done so that the individual parts of an analysis develop together as a whole. The rule of thumb for Step 4 is that the choice of appropriate COMPONENTS for an ANALYTIC TASK is informed by the three elements of its context: what has been accomplished previously, the purpose of the task, and what is anticipated to happen next. This is a guide, not a step-by-step procedure, and in each situation the role of these context elements will vary. A learning heuristic is to consider each of the following points in turn when choosing appropriate COMPONENTS:

- Review objectives and analytic plan
- Consider previous ANALYTIC TASK
- Evaluate previous ANALYTIC TASK in terms of current purpose
- Choose COMPONENTS in terms of anticipated next task

TABLE 6.3 Analytic actions that can be taken on all components

Common Actions	
Create new	Create a new COMPONENT at any time. There is never a need to think in advance of all the COMPONENTS that need to be created before beginning work.
Rename	Rename COMPONENTS at any time. COMPONENTS are given names when they are created. In some cases we provide the names, such as for new CODES or MEMOS, and in other cases ATLAS.ti supplies a name, such as for QUOTATIONS. Regardless, we can change the name of any COMPONENT at any time.
Search	Search for any string of characters in the name, the content, the COMMENT of any individual COMPONENT or COMPONENT-GROUP, or any set of individual COMPONENTS or COMPONENT-GROUPS. A listing is produced of all the items that meet the search criteria.
Write	Write a COMMENT on any COMPONENT, write in a MEMO, or use the program's *edit mode* to write in a DOCUMENT.
Sort	Sort lists of COMPONENTS in various ways, including by any column header.
Visualize in networks	Display and work with COMPONENTS visually. The NETWORK view of COMPONENTS is not independent of the rest of the ATLAS.ti-PROJECT. Any action carried out in a NETWORK, such as renaming a CODE or linking a CODE to a MEMO, is immediately put into effect throughout the ATLAS.ti-PROJECT.

TABLE 6.4 Component-specific analytic actions

Component	Component-specific analytic actions
DOCUMENT	***Add or import*** into the ATLAS.ti-PROJECT. ***Edit*** to change the content (text DOCUMENTS only). ***Group*** into DOCUMENT-GROUPS OR SMART-GROUPS. ***Filter*** to focus attention or limit an operation to only some DOCUMENTS. ***Interrogate*** DOCUMENTS.
DOCUMENT-GROUPS and SMART-GROUPS	***Add or remove*** members. ***Filter*** to focus attention or limit an operation to only some DOCUMENT-GROUPS OR SMART-GROUPS. ***Combine*** DOCUMENT-GROUPS or SMART-GROUPS into a new SMART-GROUP. ***Interrogate*** a DOCUMENT-GROUP or SMART-GROUP.
QUOTATION	***Link*** to CODES, other QUOTATIONS, or MEMOS. ***Resize*** to include more or less data. ***Rename*** from the default name given when created to a more analytically meaningful name.
HYPERLINKED-QUOTATION	***Jump*** between HYPERLINKED-QUOTATIONS. ***Change*** relation.
CODE	***Group*** into CODE-GROUPS and CODE-SMART-GROUPS. ***Link*** to QUOTATIONS, other CODES, SMART-CODES, or MEMOS. ***Filter*** to focus attention or limit an operation to only some CODES. ***Interrogate*** CODES.
CODED-QUOTATION	***Retrieve*** sets of QUOTATIONS based on how they are coded. ***Link*** to other QUOTATIONS, other CODES, or MEMOS. ***Interrogate*** a DOCUMENT.
CODE-GROUPS AND SMART-GROUPS	***Add or remove*** members. ***Filter*** to focus attention or limit an operation to only some CODE-GROUPS or SMART-GROUPS. ***Combine*** CODE-GROUPS or SMART-GROUPS into a new SMART-GROUP. ***Interrogate*** CODE-GROUPS and CODE-SMART-GROUPS.
SMART-CODE	***Link*** to other CODES or SMART-CODES or MEMOS. ***Interrogate*** SMART-CODES.
SMART-CODE-SNAPSHOT	***Link*** to quotations, other CODES, SMART-CODES, or MEMOS. ***Interrogate*** SMART-CODE-SNAPSHOTS.
COMMENT	*A COMMENT is a space in which to write about any COMPONENT. Other than the action of writing in them, COMMENTS cannot be acted on independently.*
MEMO	***Link*** to other MEMOS, QUOTATIONS, CODES, or SMART-CODES. ***Convert*** into a DOCUMENT.
MEMO-GROUPS AND SMART-GROUPS	***Add or remove*** members. ***Filter*** to focus attention or limit an operation to only some MEMO-GROUPS or SMART-GROUPS. ***Combine*** MEMO-GROUPS or SMART-GROUPS into a new SMART-GROUP.
NETWORK	*A NETWORK is a display of other COMPONENTS. Actions are taken on the COMPONENTS displayed within a NETWORK, not on the NETWORK itself.*
NETWORK-GROUPS AND SMART-GROUPS	***Add or remove*** members. ***Filter*** to focus attention on only some NETWORK-GROUPS or SMART-GROUPS. ***Combine*** NETWORK-GROUPS or SMART-GROUPS into a new SMART-GROUP.

Review Objectives and Analytic Plan

In qualitative research the analytic plan evolves as the project progresses. In some methodologies even the objectives may change based on the progress of the analysis. It is therefore important to first review the current iteration of the analytic plan, especially if there has been a gap in time since last working on the project.

The objectives and current analytic plan for our sample ANALYTIC TASK are found in the upper part of its ANALYTIC PLANNING WORKSHEET in Figure 6.3 (p. 106). In summary, this project is an interview-based study of teachers in two schools with differing levels of bullying, using thematic analysis to understand the role of teachers in resolving entrenched bullying. Figure 6.3 also indicates that the current analysis phase will *explore teacher reactions to bullying*, and the graphical conceptual framework presents the current plan for accomplishing this. The prior completed task and next anticipated task are noted. This review of the worksheet has brought us up to date on the overall context for the ANALYTIC TASK we are now working on: *compare teachers' reactions to different kinds of bullying*.

Consider Previous Analytic Task

The ANALYTIC PLANNING WORKSHEET for this phase, displayed in Figure 6.3, shows us that the prior completed task involved coding to capture different reactions to each kind of bullying. A review of that prior worksheet would show us that in addition to one unit of analysis—*teachers*—we had identified two separate units of meaning—*teachers' reactions* and *kinds of bullying*. This led to creating two sets of CODES. One set represented the different kinds of bullying we had identified in the literature—*verbal abuse, physical abuse, cyber bullying*, etc., and another set represented each type of reaction we found in the interview data—*disapproval, censure, sympathy*, etc.

Each teacher's interview transcript had been added to the ATLAS.ti-PROJECT as a separate DOCUMENT. Each teacher was interviewed only once, and the interviewer had asked short questions and used simple prompts to encourage them to elaborate. So the vast majority of text within each DOCUMENT consisted of the teacher speaking, and therefore each teacher could be represented by a single DOCUMENT. The focus of the thematic analysis was to identify themes by interpreting what was implied as well as what was explicit in the teachers' responses. Therefore the coding had been accomplished by reading through each DOCUMENT and applying CODES to QUOTATIONS one by one, without the use of any auto-coding procedure. There is therefore no reason to consider an alternative COMPONENT for representing *teachers* from the possible COMPONENTS we had considered in Step 3.

Reviewing the prior ANALYTIC TASK in this way reminds us of the available building blocks of analysis that have already been created. These building blocks serve as the context for designing the activities in the current task.

Evaluate Previous Task in Terms of Current Purpose

The building blocks made available by the previous ANALYTIC TASK must now be evaluated in terms of the purpose of the current ANALYTIC TASK. The purpose had been entered into the ANALYTIC PLANNING WORKSHEET in Step 2, displayed in Figure 6.6 (p. 113). The purpose is *to investigate whether individual teachers display similar or different reactions to different types of bullying*. This requires a fine-grained set of comparisons that distinguish and compare each type of reaction to each kind of bullying. The issue is whether the building blocks from the prior ANALYTIC TASK will serve this purpose.

We already have each *teacher* represented as a DOCUMENT from the previous task, so we can continue to use DOCUMENTS to represent this UNIT for the current ANALYTIC TASK.

Regarding the COMPONENTS to represent the *similar or different reactions to different kinds of bullying*, we must now consider if the choices made in the prior ANALYTIC TASK are consistent with the purposes of the current task. In the prior task we had settled on two separate units of meaning—*reactions* and *kinds of bullying*—and coded accordingly. These separate sets of CODES from the prior task provide enough differentiation to support the fine-grained comparisons we intend to perform in the current task because the two elements we want to compare—*reactions* and *kinds of bullying*—have been captured independently from one another. In this straightforward example, there is therefore no reason to consider alternative COMPONENTS from the numerous possible COMPONENTS we had identified in Step 3 for representing *reactions* and *kinds of bullying*. We can proceed with the comparisons by using the building blocks created in the prior task.

Looking ahead: This straightforward progress of the analysis is not always the case. It is common to discover that the prior ANALYTIC TASK has been fulfilled in a way that does not make the current task so straightforward. In the final part of Step 5 we will consider the complications that would arise if we had made different choices in the prior task.

Choose Components in Terms of Anticipated Next Task

In order to make the most appropriate decisions about SELECTING or CONSTRUCTING a TOOL, we must also consider what we anticipate doing next. This is the third element of the context of an ANALYTIC TASK.

Thinking ahead reduces the likelihood that we will need to backtrack later. We already know that we made a good choice in the prior task by coding at a sufficient level of detail, creating sets of CODES for two UNITS of meaning—*reactions* and *kinds of bullying*—rather than a single set of CODES for the single UNIT *reactions to different kinds of bullying*. This choice permitted us to move ahead easily with the current task of comparing teacher's reactions to different kinds of bullying, as we have separate sets of CODES for each UNIT. From the ANALYTIC PLANNING WORKSHEET we also know the purpose of the current task and the actions available to take on the COMPONENTS representing our UNITS. We have almost everything we need to choose how to finalize SELECTED- or CONSTRUCTED-TOOLS in order to fulfill this ANALYTIC TASK in the software.

One more thing to consider: what is anticipated to come next. Because qualitative analysis is emergent, anticipating what may come next is not always possible. Therefore it is tempting to think: *What happens next depends on the outcome of the current investigations of similar and different reactions. That is the point at which I will decide what happens next.* But when TRANSLATING ANALYTIC TASKS, we should always attempt to anticipate the next task more specifically because this focuses our current actions and helps ensure that we make the most appropriate choices. This is not the same as predetermining the next task, but rather choosing the best current action in the context of our best current anticipation of what may come next. This is part of the iterative process of qualitative analysis.

We have an overall analytic plan at strategy Level 2 in the ANALYTIC PLANNING WORKSHEET. This area of the worksheet is designed to facilitate thinking in an emergent manner about what happens next. Figure 6.8 displays schematically these areas of the worksheet. In the central area of the worksheet, at Level 2, we see the general purpose of the current phase that emerged from prior analytic activity: *identify patterns of teacher reactions by comparing different reactions to different kinds of bullying*. The first ANALYTIC TASK in this current phase begins to fulfill this general purpose: *compare teachers' reactions to different kinds of bullying*. Figure 6.8 also indicates the next anticipated phase. This suggests a possible way forward by next considering the extremes of teacher reactions and their impact—the most problematic and the most productive reactions of teachers—perhaps based on prior research. The next anticipated phase indicated in Figure 6.8 is therefore to *determine whether patterns of most problematic or most productive reactions of teachers may inform mitigation of bullying behaviors*. This possible way forward for the next phase is entered into the ANALYTIC PLANNING WORKSHEET because it needs to be considered in the current phase. We do this by thinking through how to integrate this possible way forward while fulfilling the current task, and we come up with a question to ask ourselves as we conduct the analysis: *Do the patterns of teacher reactions that we discover in the current phase help determine whether the most problematic and the most helpful teacher reactions emerge as a helpful way of informing ways to mitigate bullying?* This will be an assessment of the patterns we discover in the current task, and is therefore consistent with our TRANSLATION plans so far. But a new thought also comes to mind. Because we selected two schools with contrasting

THE ROLE OF TEACHERS IN MITIGATING BULLYING BEHAVIORS IN SCHOOLS

Analysis Phase: Explore teacher reactions to bullying

The highest or most general level of the analytic plan expresses graphically in overall terms how the project objectives will be achieved, but with plenty of scope for the details to emerge

...to understand the role of teachers in resolving entrenched bullying behaviors in order to inform the ...ions

The next level of detail describes the *PRIOR*, *CURRENT* and *ANTICIPATED* analysis phases, but still in general terms, allowing the specific **ANALYTIC TASKS** to emerge within each phase.

...of reported bullying, using thematic ...ence-based intervention

...emergent mind-set...

...algorithmic mind-set...

**Level 2:
OVERALL
ANALYTIC PLAN**

PRIOR COMPLETED
Coding to capture different reactions to each kind of bullying

CURRENT
Identify patterns of teacher reactions by comparing different reactions to different kinds of bullying

NEXT ANTICIPATED
Determine whether patterns of most problematic or most productive reactions of teachers may inform mitigation of bullying behaviors

Level 3: TRANSLATION

Level 4: SELECTED TOOL or
Level 5: CONSTRUCTED TOOL

The next level of detail specifies individual **ANALYTIC TASKS** to fulfill the *CURRENT* analysis phase above, using the various rules of thumb of the five steps of *TRANSLATION*

UNITS

PURPOSE

...SSIBLE COMPON...
...MPONENTS

**Level 2:
ANALYTIC TASKS**

Compare teachers' reactions to different kinds of bull...

...heuristic mind-set...

REFLECTIONS

FIGURE 6.8 Schematic Level 2 of the ANALYTIC PLANNING WORKSHEET reports of entrenched bullying, we may find that distinguishing schools, not just teachers, may be helpful in identifying patterns of problematic and helpful teacher reactions. We now realize that we have neglected to consider *school* as a UNIT—it just slipped through the net until this point. However, we know that every teacher teaches at one school or the other. A school is therefore a group of teachers, and so the *school* as a UNIT is simply a higher-level organization of *teachers* as a UNIT. We therefore have confidence that if we decide to go ahead with this new ANALYTIC TASK, we can take account of the new UNIT in Step 5 when we finalize the SELECTED- or CONSTRUCTED-TOOLS for that task.

Considering what is anticipated next is part of the iterative process of making choices about the present task in light of anticipated future tasks. This ensures that our current actions do not preclude anticipated tasks and informs our thinking about the current task. Considering what is anticipated next is therefore not the same as predetermining the next task. In our example, we have been alerted to the possibility that patterns of bullying at the school level may be considered in the next task, and so we will be sensitive to this possibility when analyzing reactions at the teacher level in the current task. This may seem obvious in retrospect, but the best insights are often simple rather than complex and often do feel obvious. In this case the insight came from linking the idea of considering the most problematic and most helpful reactions—which may not have been part of the original research design—to the selection of schools with widely varying bullying reports.

In conclusion, if we do not think through what is anticipated next—the third element of the context of an ANALYTIC TASK—we may miss analytic opportunities. Having had this insight we want to make sure it is not lost, which can easily happen with so many things to think about as the analysis progresses. We therefore note the insight in the *Reflections* box of the ANALYTIC PLANNING WORKSHEET. Figure 6.9 displays these reflections, as well as our final choice of appropriate COMPONENTS, in the fourth iteration of the ANALYTIC PLANNING WORKSHEET.

Step 5—Finalizing Selected- or Constructed-Tools

The final step of TRANSLATION is finalizing SELECTED- or CONSTRUCTED-TOOLS that act on the chosen COMPONENTS, thereby fulfilling an ANALYTIC TASK. We use the term TOOL to mean an action taken on a COMPONENT. Figure 2.1 (p. 27) displays the two kinds of TOOLS as Levels 4 and 5 of the *Five-Level QDA* method. This section therefore marks the end of our elaboration of the method.

We begin by distinguishing SELECTED- and CONSTRUCTED-TOOLS, and then we provide an example for each of the circumstances that calls for either one. We end each section with a more thoroughly worked example of the sample ANALYTIC TASK in the bullying study.

The Distinction Between Selected- and Constructed-Tools

The distinction between SELECTED- and CONSTRUCTED-TOOLS is only a learning heuristic. It is easy to provide a formal distinction—a SELECTED-TOOL is a *straightforward choice of individual software operations*, and a CONSTRUCTED-TOOL is a *sophisticated use of software by combining operations or using them in a custom way*. But with growing experience the distinction between the two fades. The evolving way in which humans experience the passage of time is a helpful analogy. Babies and children experience time passing very slowly because each perception is a new experience; there are so many new perceptions that each day feels like an eternity. As we get older perceptions and experiences accumulate and are repeated. They start to clump together so that they are experienced as larger events. We therefore perceive fewer of them each day, and the day feels like it passes more quickly. By the time we are elderly we have seen almost everything already, and experiences are connected and clumped into much larger events. The days and weeks and years fly by with far fewer (but larger) individual events perceived each day.

Level 2: ANALYTIC TASKS	Level 3: TRANSLATION	Level 4: SELECTED TOOL or Level 5: CONSTRUCTED TOOL
	bullying behaviors	
Compare teachers' reactions to different kinds of bullying	<u>UNITS</u> Teachers (unit of analysis) Reactions (unit of meaning) Kinds of bullying (unit of meaning) <u>PURPOSE</u> To investigate whether individual teachers display similar or different reactions to different types of bullying <u>POSSIBLE COMPONENTS</u> **Teachers** – DOCUMENT, DOCUMENT-GROUP, CODE, MEMO, NETWORK **Reactions** – QUOTATION, CODE, CODED-QUOTATION, CODE-GROUP & CODE-SMART-GROUP, SMART-CODE, SMART-CODE-SNAPSHOT, COMMENT, MEMO, NETWORK **Kinds of bullying** – QUOTATION, CODE, CODED-QUOTATION, CODE-GROUP & CODE-SMART-GROUP, SMART-CODE, SMART-CODE and SMART, COMMENT, MEMO, NETWORK <u>CHOSEN COMPONENTS</u> Teachers = DOCUMENT Reactions = CODE (resulting in CODED-QUOTATIONS) Kinds of bullying = CODE (resulting in CODED-QUOTATIONS) <u>EXPLANATION</u>	

REFLECTIONS Remember to bear in mind which school the teachers come from when looking at patterns of reactions – this may help in the next step for deciding whether the most problematic or most productive sets of teacher reactions are related to their schools

FIGURE 6.9 ANALYTIC PLANNING WORKSHEET for sample analytic task: Choosing appropriate components

In a similar way, when starting out with the *Five-Level QDA* method we stick to the rules of thumb whenever possible—a couple of UNITS and a single purpose per ANALYTIC TASK—because this simplifies the process. We use many SELECTED-TOOLS and just a few CONSTRUCTED-TOOLS where SELECTED-TOOLS are not available. As experience grows we gradually leave the rules of thumb behind and find ourselves not thinking too much about whether we are using a SELECTED- or CONSTRUCTED-TOOL. More and more of the SELECTED-TOOLS we are using will start to clump into larger CONSTRUCTED-TOOLS. For the expert ATLAS.ti user, the entire project becomes an amorphous, giant CONSTRUCTED-TOOL.

We do not write this to encourage you to hurry past the stage of identifying many SELECTED-TOOLS—that would be counterproductive. We mention this because you may wonder why a particular example of an action taken on a COMPONENT in the following sections or in the videos is considered a SELECTED-TOOL rather than part of a larger CONSTRUCTED-TOOL. The answer is that it helps you learn the process. As you gain experience it is of no concern whether you are thinking in terms of SELECTED-TOOLS or CONSTRUCTED-TOOLS to fulfill your ANALYTIC TASKS. A project with mainly SELECTED-TOOLS most certainly does not imply less sophistication or complexity than a project with mainly CONSTRUCTED-TOOLS, and vice versa.

Next we describe the circumstances for finalizing either a SELECTED- or a CONSTRUCTED-TOOL. We provide an example of each circumstance and how it is documented and explained in its ANALYTIC PLANNING WORKSHEET, and then we describe the thinking process in greater detail for the sample ANALYTIC TASK in the bullying study. Your ANALYTIC TASKS will certainly be very different from all these examples, but once the process is learned, it can be applied to your own tasks, in conjunction with the following:

- The list of COMPONENTS (Table 5.2, p. 68)
- The actions that can be taken on COMPONENTS (Tables 6.3 and 6.4, pp. 121–122)
- The video demonstrations of the TRANSLATION of real-world ANALYTIC TASKS from a wide variety of research projects (described in Chapter 7)

When to Use a Selected-Tool

The rule of thumb for using a SELECTED-TOOL—a *straightforward choice of individual software operations*—is to do so in one of two circumstances. The first circumstance is a chain of one-to-one relationships between UNITS, COMPONENTS, actions, and purposes. The second circumstance is when an affordance of the program can fulfill the purpose of the ANALYTIC TASK.

Using a Selected-Tool When There Is a Chain of One-to-One Relationships

Recognizing a chain of one-to-one relationships means looking for three straightforward conditions:

- An ANALYTIC TASK has only one or two UNITS
- There is a *formal equivalence* between each UNIT and a COMPONENT
- A single action on each COMPONENT accomplishes the purpose of the task

A straightforward ANALYTIC TASK from the 14 example tasks is *read interview transcripts to identify potential concepts for coding*. We determined in Appendix 4 that this task has two UNITS and in Appendix 5 that it has one purpose. After identifying possible COMPONENTS for this task and reviewing the analytic actions that can be taken on them (displayed in Tables 6.3 and 6.4, pp. 121–122), we choose two COMPONENTS for this task: DOCUMENTS and COMMENTS (Figure 6.10). We determine that the task can be fulfilled with a single action: *writing* in each DOCUMENT COMMENT. The ANALYTIC TASK therefore can be fulfilled using a SELECTED-TOOL. The details are described succinctly in the ANALYTIC PLANNING WORKSHEET in Figure 6.10. This completed worksheet includes not only the UNITS, purpose,

Level 2: ANALYTIC TASKS	Level 3: TRANSLATION	Level 4: SELECTED TOOL or Level 5: CONSTRUCTED TOOL
Read interview transcripts to identify potential concepts for coding	_UNITS_ Interview transcripts (unit of data) Potential concepts (unit of meaning) _PURPOSE_ To identify concepts that may be potential candidates for coding interview transcripts _POSSIBLE COMPONENTS_ _(Not included for this illustration)_ _CHOSEN COMPONENTS_ Interview transcripts = DOCUMENT Potential concepts = COMMENT _EXPLANATION_ This task is exploratory and the next anticipated task is to test the identified concepts in a first round of coding. For testing it will help to know which transcripts produced the potential concepts. We will therefore record them in the COMMENT of the DOCUMENT that inspired them. We can output all the COMMENTS for all DOCUMENTS	(Selected tool) Open and read a DOCUMENT, write and output COMMENTS: • Open a DOCUMENT and its associated COMMENT floating window • Read the transcript and write potential concepts in the COMMENT window • Output the COMMENTS for all DOCUMENTS

FIGURE 6.10 First example of a SELECTED-TOOL

and COMPONENTS chosen, but also an explanation of how the COMPONENTS will be harnessed and the actions we plan to take in ATLAS.ti. This is how ANALYTIC PLANNING WORKSHEETS will appear on the companion website to accompany the video demonstrations of TRANSLATION.

Using a Selected-Tool With an Affordance of the Program

The second circumstance that calls for a SELECTED-TOOL is when an affordance of the program has been specifically designed for the purpose of the ANALYTIC TASK. An affordance is an existing combination of actions and COMPONENTS presented on the screen as a single feature. For example, another straightforward ANALYTIC TASK from the 14 example tasks is *search newspaper articles for the use of evocative terms*. We determine that this task also has two UNITS and one purpose (displayed in Appendices 4 and 5), and as shown in the ANALYTIC PLANNING WORKSHEETS in Figure 6.11, we choose two COMPONENTS for this task: DOCUMENTS and MEMOS. The next step is to review the analytic actions that can be taken on these COMPONENTS (displayed in Tables 6.3 and 6.4, pp. 121–122). We determine that the task can be fulfilled with a single action on each component: *interrogating* DOCUMENTS and *writing* in MEMOS. We then determine that ATLAS.ti's Word Cloud feature (p. 74) will serve to interrogate the DOCUMENTS in a manner that permits us to identify the evocative terms while we *write* in a MEMO either a simple list of the terms we identify or perhaps our first reflections on them. Figure 6.11 displays the details of this SELECTED-TOOL in the ANALYTIC PLANNING WORKSHEET in a similar manner to the previous example, including the explanation and the actions to be taken in ATLAS.ti.

Selected-Tool for the Sample Analytic Task

We now return to the sample ANALYTIC TASK to describe in more detail the thinking process for finalizing a SELECTED-TOOL. The purpose of the task is *to investigate whether individual teachers display similar or different reactions to different kinds of bullying*, which was the reason that *reactions* and *kinds of bullying* were differentiated as separate UNITS in Step 1. Including *teachers* as a unit of analysis, the ANALYTIC TASK therefore has three UNITS and one purpose. This is more than the rule of thumb, but in the earlier discussion in Step 1 we decided this was the best way to go, and we anticipate fulfilling the task with a SELECTED-TOOL. (Having three units and one purpose also allows us to explore other implications of this choice later in the chapter).

We next review the analytic actions displayed in Tables 6.3 and 6.4 (pp. 121–122) and decide to consider how to use ATLAS.ti for *interrogating* DOCUMENTS and *interrogating* CODES. This requires thinking through the purpose of the task in more detail and then evaluating options for interrogating.

To investigate similar or different *reactions* to different *kinds of bullying*—which is the strategy—we need to find quotations coded to each *reaction* code for each *kind of bullying* code—which comprise the tactics. The outcome will be a set of CODED-QUOTATIONS for each combination of *reaction* code, such as *disapproval*, and *kind of bullying* code, such as *verbal abuse*. The next strategy is to read the CODED-QUOTATIONS for each pair of combined CODES to investigate the similarities and differences both within and between the sets of CODED-QUOTATIONS. This sequence of activities puts into effect a journey around the circular path of *Five-Level QDA* strategies and tactics, as illustrated in Figure 3.9 (p. 56). We can't say more about how we will go about investigating the similarities and differences, because this is an emergent activity at the strategy levels, and we don't know in advance where the similarities or differences may lie. But we can say more about the cut-and-dried tactics because this will be a definite procedure determined by the design of the software.

We have decided to fulfill the purpose of this analytic task by seeking out *co-occurring* QUOTATIONS. In ATLAS.ti, co-occurring QUOTATIONS are pairs of QUOTATIONS in which one QUOTATION is coded to one CODE and an overlapping QUOTATION is coded to another CODE. The two CODES are therefore

Level 2: ANALYTIC TASKS	Level 3: TRANSLATION	Level 4: SELECTED TOOL or Level 5: CONSTRUCTED TOOL
Search newspaper articles for the use of evocative terms	<u>UNITS</u> Newspaper articles (unit of data) Evocative terms (unit of meaning) <u>PURPOSE</u> To find terms within newspaper articles that can be considered evocative <u>POSSIBLE COMPONENTS</u> (Not included for this illustration) <u>CHOSEN COMPONENTS</u> Newspaper articles = DOCUMENT Evocative terms = MEMO <u>EXPLANATION</u> The initial search for evocative words can be fulfilled by the Word Cloud which can sort all words used in selected DOCUMENTS by length and indicate relative frequency and thus their salience. Evocative words tend to be longer, so the list can be scanned from the longest words and the relatively frequently used evocative terms can easily be typed into an open MEMO.	Selected tool: Scan a Word Cloud on newspaper article DOCUMENTS and record relatively frequently used evocative terms in a MEMO • Create a MEMO in a floating window • Open the DOCUMENT Manager and select all newspaper articles • Produce typewriter-style Word Cloud, sorted longest first • Scan word list for relatively frequently used evocative terms and type into MEMO

FIGURE 6.11   Second example of a SELECTED-TOOL

found in the same area of the coded data, so they may have some relationship to one another, somewhat similar to a correlation. The overlap of the QUOTATIONS can be of any degree. Just one word or even one character that is common to both QUOTATIONS constitutes an overlap, all the way up to a complete overlap, meaning we have a single QUOTATION coded to two CODES. If we can retrieve all co-occurring QUOTATIONS for each combination of the *reaction* CODES and the *types of bullying* CODES, this will provide the material for conducting our similarities and differences investigation.

We now consider the three capabilities of ATLAS.ti that allow working with co-occurring QUOTATIONS: the Query Tool, the NETWORKS, and the Code Co-occurrence Table. If you are new to ATLAS.ti, the following discussions are only intended to illustrate a thinking process, not to provide comprehensive instruction in operating ATLAS.ti. Each of the capabilities discussed next is demonstrated in the *Harnessing Components* videos on the companion website, but in this section it is the thinking process that is most important.

If we used the Query Tool (p. 84), we could retrieve co-occurring QUOTATIONS between one pair of CODES at a time, such as *disapproval* and *verbal abuse*, then *disapproval* and *physical abuse*, then *disapproval and cyber bullying*, and so on, until one by one we had retrieved each possible combination of a *reaction* CODE and *kind of bullying* CODE. The Query Tool is very useful for many tasks because of additional capabilities that are not relevant to the task at hand. But as our current task has so many combinations of *reactions* and *kinds of bullying*, the process of working with each pair of CODES one at a time would be both cumbersome and problematic for visualizing patterns of co-occurrence.

A NETWORK would allow visualizing patterns of co-occurrence by importing co-occurring *types of bullying* CODES for each *reaction* CODE and then importing the co-occurring QUOTATIONS. But there are three disadvantages of a NETWORK for the purpose of our task. First, we would not easily be able to identify CODES that had no co-occurrences, which might be important for assessing similarities and differences. Second, we would import irrelevant co-occurring CODES and QUOTATIONS (i.e., from other areas of the coding scheme). Third, we would not have frequency information to assess the prevalence of each pair of CODES because frequencies are not displayed in NETWORKS.

We are left with the Code Co-occurrence Table (p. 130), which allows the retrieval of CODED-QUOTATIONS for each pair of CODES in two chosen sets. One set of CODES can be chosen for the rows of the table—for example, the *reaction* CODES—and another set of CODES for the columns—for example, the *types of bullying* CODES. Each cell of the table shows the number of co-occurring QUOTATIONS for the CODE in the row and the CODE in the column. The co-occurring QUOTATIONS can be directly accessed and viewed from the cells of the table. This will serve the purposes of our ANALYTIC TASK. And this is all the material we need to travel around the circular path of *Five-Level QDA* strategies and tactics and begin to investigate the similarities and differences, both within and between these sets of CODED-QUOTATIONS. Following this analytic activity at the strategy levels of the project, the next ANALYTIC TASK will emerge to be translated in turn into SELECTED- or CONSTRUCTED-tools.

Figure 6.12 displays this fifth iteration of the ANALYTIC PLANNING WORKSHEET—using a SELECTED-TOOL. As we have described the thinking process in detail, the worksheet does not include a summary explanation in the TRANSLATION column.

When to Use Constructed-Tools

The rule of thumb for using a CONSTRUCTED-TOOL—a *sophisticated use of the software by combining software operations or using them in a custom way*—is to do so in one of two circumstances. The first circumstance is when a "larger" ANALYTIC TASK has more UNITS or purposes than the rules of thumb suggest, but the task is better fulfilled by combining multiple TOOLS into a single larger CONSTRUCTED-TOOL rather than artificially splitting the ANALYTIC TASK into two separate tasks. The second circumstance is when a custom way of combining actions and COMPONENTS is needed to fulfill a task.

Level 2: ANALYTIC TASKS	Level 3: TRANSLATION	Level 4: SELECTED TOOL or Level 5: CONSTRUCTED TOOL

Identify patterns of teacher reactions by comparing different reactions to different kinds of bullying

NEXT ANTICIPATED
Determine whether patterns of most problematic or most productive reactions of teachers may inform mitigation of bullying behaviors

Compare teachers' reactions to different kinds of bullying

UNITS
Teachers (unit of analysis)
Reactions (unit of meaning)
Kinds of bullying (unit of meaning)

PURPOSE
To investigate whether individual teachers display similar or different reactions to different types of bullying

POSSIBLE COMPONENTS
(Not included for this illustration)

CHOSEN COMPONENTS
Teachers = DOCUMENT
Reactions = CODE (resulting in CODED-QUOTATIONS)
Kinds of bullying = CODE (resulting in CODED-QUOTATIONS)

EXPLANATION
(Full explanation in the chapter text)

Selected tool:

Use the Code Co-occurrence Table to investigate co-occurrences between the *reactions* CODES and the *kinds of bullying* CODES.

- Select all the *reaction* CODES for the rows of the table

- Select all the *kinds of bullying* CODES for the columns of the table

FIGURE 6.12 ANALYTIC PLANNING WORKSHEET for sample analytic task: SELECTED-TOOL

Using Constructed-Tools for "Larger" Analytic Tasks

One reason to use a CONSTRUCTED-TOOL is to avoid artificially breaking an ANALYTIC TASK into multiple tasks, where each follows the rules of thumb, just to make the TRANSLATION process simpler. Soon, with more experience, translating "larger" ANALYTIC TASKS will become as straightforward as TRANSLATING "smaller" tasks, so splitting tasks that are better fulfilled as a whole is not the habit we want to develop.

One ANALYTIC TASK from the 14 example tasks is *watch videos of math lessons to identify types of interaction between students and teachers*. We identify one purpose for the task in Appendix 5—*to identify how students and teachers interact during math lessons*. In Appendix 4 we identify four UNITS to fulfill this purpose: *videos of math lessons, types of interaction, students*, and *teachers*. We discuss these multiple UNITS at length in Appendix 4. In summary, one approach would be to consider students and teachers as instances of a single UNIT, *participants*, leading to two separate tasks, each conforming to the rule of thumb. The first task would be to identify *types of interaction* without regard to *students* and *teachers*, and the second would require going back to identify each type of interaction in relation to *students* and *teachers*. Splitting the task in this way would simplify TRANSLATION into two SELECTED-TOOLS, but at a cost. The two-step process would be cumbersome and also implies this easy separation of *types of interaction* from the people who are interacting. We conclude that the best way forward is not to split the task but to consider both dimensions—*types of interaction* and *who is interacting*—in the same task.

We assume that in a prior ANALYTIC TASK we created CODED-QUOTATIONS by segmenting every student–teacher interaction in the video DOCUMENTS of math classes. We assume that each QUOTATION has been coded with two CODES: one for the name of the teacher (there is therefore a set of teacher CODES) and one for the name of the student (there is therefore a set of student CODES).

We decide to fulfill the current ANALYTIC TASK in an iterative manner. We first watch and interpret each QUOTATION in the video DOCUMENTS, coding each student–teacher interaction to a CODE that represents the style of interaction. As we proceed, each CODED-QUOTATION is hyperlinked (i.e., directly linked) to all other QUOTATIONS coded to this style of interaction for this teacher, if there are any. This set of HYPERLINKED-QUOTATIONS is then displayed in a NETWORK, which will allow reviewing the video QUOTATIONS from within the NETWORK without going back and forth among the DOCUMENTS. There will be many NETWORKS—one for each teacher interacting with a variety of students in a particular style. Similarities and differences in the manner in which this teacher interacts are interpreted and written in the NETWORK COMMENT, with a summary added to the accumulating writing in the comment of this teacher's CODE. We then return to the video QUOTATION at the beginning of this sequence of activities and reinterpret the interaction in this video QUOTATION in light of the other student interactions of this teacher we had studied in the NETWORK. We then write our reinterpretations in the QUOTATION COMMENT. The process would be repeated for each NETWORK, with varying amounts of iterative recoding and writing as required.

We refer to this set of software operations as a CONSTRUCTED-TOOL because they are a combination of separate uses of the software conducted together. We have described the process we chose to fulfill this ANALYTIC TASK at a high level to indicate what a CONSTRUCTED-TOOL is like—we do not expect you to be able to reproduce the process from this description. That is the purpose of the *Harnessing Components* videos on the companion website, which lend themselves to demonstration of the detailed steps to fulfill ANALYTIC TASKS similar to this one.

Figure 6.13 displays the ANALYTIC PLANNING WORKSHEET for this task. This shows that there are additional chosen COMPONENTS for the writing and visualizing purposes of the task, as well as the COMPONENTS representing the UNITS of the task. These include NETWORKS and COMMENTS for writing and HYPERLINKED-QUOTATIONS to support the interpretation and writing purpose. Figure 6.13 displays a description of the sequence of planned actions that comprise the CONSTRUCTED-TOOL in the *Level 4/5* column.

Level 2: ANALYTIC TASKS	Level 3: TRANSLATION	Level 4: SELECTED TOOL or Level 5: CONSTRUCTED TOOL
Watch videos of math lessons to identify types of interaction between students and teachers	<u>UNITS</u> Videos of math lessons (unit of data) Types of interaction (unit of meaning) Students (unit of analysis) Teachers (unit of analysis) <u>PURPOSE</u> To identify how students and teachers interact during math lessons <u>POSSIBLE COMPONENTS</u> *(Not included for this illustration)* <u>CHOSEN COMPONENTS</u> Videos of math lessons = DOCUMENT Types of interaction = CODE (resulting in CODED-QUOTATIONS) Students = CODE Teachers = CODE *Additional components from writing/visualizing purpose of task* Interpretation of interactions = HYPER-LINKED-QUOTATIONS, NETWORK, NETWORK-COMMENTS, CODE-COMMENTS, QUOTATION-COMMENTS <u>EXPLANATION</u> *(Full explanation in the chapter text).*	Constructed tool: • View video QUOTATIONS and code to new or existing *style of interaction* CODE • Hyperlink to QUOTATIONS also coded to this *style of interaction* in other DOCUMENTS for this teacher • Display all HYPER-LINKED-QUOTATIONS for this teacher in a NETWORK, view QUOTATIONS from within NETWORK, and write interpretations of similarities and differences in NETWORK COMMENT • Navigate to each QUOTATION and update QUOTATION COMMENTS in light of new interpretations of all quotations for this teacher

FIGURE 6.13 First example of a CONSTRUCTED-TOOL

Using Constructed-Tools as a Customized Way to Harness the Program

Some ANALYTIC TASKS call for a customized way to harness the program, regardless of the number of UNITS and purposes. This means that the straightforward way to use the COMPONENTS does not seem to offer a solution to the requirements of a task. By *straightforward* we mean simple and obvious; by *customized* we mean creative or unusual. Once a customized way of using a COMPONENT has served you well, it will join the category of simple and obvious.

To illustrate a custom use of COMPONENTS, we continue with the last ANALYTIC TASK: *watch videos of math lessons to identify types of interaction between students and teachers*. The CONSTRUCTED-TOOL we designed for this task, described earlier in Figure 6.13, led to a great deal of iterative analytic activity. One finding of this ANALYTIC TASK is that there is a great deal of difference in styles of interaction between teachers who interact with all students in a consistent style (teacher group 1) and those who interact very differently with students with apparently higher and lower math abilities (teacher group 2). To follow up this observation we obtain math ability information from the school, and we rename each student CODE with a prefix that indicates either higher or lower math ability.

As a result of all this analytic activity, a new ANALYTIC TASK emerged: *synthesize a general style of interaction typical of group 1 and group 2 teachers*. The purpose is *to characterize typical styles of student–teacher interaction among teachers with a consistent style toward all students and teachers whose style varies with students of different math ability*. We decide that typical styles in each teacher group are indicated by the most prevalent styles adopted by those teachers. Fulfilling this task involves three steps. First we would determine the prevalence of each style of interaction adopted by *group 1* and *group 2* teachers. Next we would view the video CODED-QUOTATIONS and read the QUOTATION COMMENTS for the most prevalent of these styles for each teacher group. Finally, we would synthesize this information into a general style of interaction for each teacher group.

It is beyond the scope of this chapter to illustrate the full range of possible ways to TRANSLATE this ANALYTIC TASK into CONSTRUCTED-TOOLS—that is the purpose of the *Harnessing Components* videos on the companion website. The purpose of this example is only to illustrate what a customized CONSTRUCTED-TOOL is like. Here we describe one way to fulfill the current task using the Code Co-occurrence Table in a customized manner.

We could put all our teacher CODES as rows and all the styles of interaction CODES as columns in the Co-occurrence Table. But we don't want rows for all the teachers—there may be dozens. We want just two rows in the table: one for the *group 1* teachers and one for the *group 2* teachers. We can do this with a customized use of DOCUMENTS. We can create a QUOTATION that spans the entire length of each video DOCUMENT, effectively turning the DOCUMENT into a CODED-QUOTATION. We can then code each of these quotations to either *group 1* or *group 2*, depending on whether the teacher is a *group 1* or *group 2* teacher. We can then select these two CODES as the rows of the Co-occurrence Table, leaving the columns as before for each *style of interaction* CODE. We now have the number of co-occurring QUOTATIONS in each cell that we want in order to determine their prevalence for each group of teachers, and we can easily navigate to and watch each individual video QUOTATION and read its COMMENT to begin our synthesis of a general style of interaction for each teacher group. As we watch more videos and accumulate insights about each group of teachers, we add notes to a MEMO for that teacher group. We have already created these MEMOS, one for each teacher group, because the purpose of this task—*to characterize the typical styles of student–teacher interaction*—called for MEMOS as an additional COMPONENT in which to write the synthesis.

Figure 6.14 displays the ANALYTIC PLANNING WORKSHEET for this task, indicating the new purpose, the new chosen COMPONENTS, and a description of the actions planned for this CONSTRUCTED-TOOL in the Level 4/5 column.

Level 2: ANALYTIC TASKS	Level 3: TRANSLATION	Level 4: SELECTED TOOL or Level 5: CONSTRUCTED TOOL
Synthesize a general style of interaction typical of group 1 and group 2 teachers	*UNITS* Videos of math lessons (unit of data) Types of interaction (unit of meaning) Teacher (unit of analysis) Teacher groups (unit of analysis) *PURPOSE* To characterize typical styles of student-teacher interaction among teachers with a consistent style (group 1) and teachers with a variable style (group 2) POSSIBLE COMPONENTS (Not included for this illustration) CHOSEN COMPONENTS Videos of math lessons = DOCUMENT, CODED-QUOTATIONS (of whole DOCUMENTS) Kinds of bullying = CODE (resulting in CODED-QUOTATIONS) Teacher-groups = CODE *Additional components from writing/visualizing purpose of task* Synthesis of typical styles = MEMO *EXPLANATION (Full explanation in the chapter text)*	Constructed tool: • Select the entirety of a video DOCUMENT and create a QUOTATION for the entire selection. • Code this QUOTATION to one of the two teacher-group CODES (*group 1* or *group 2*). Repeat for all video DOCUMENTS • In the Co-occurrence Table select the two teacher-group CODES as rows, and all the *kinds of bullying* CODES as columns. • Record notes and write final synthesis in a MEMO for each teacher group

FIGURE 6.14 Second example of a CONSTRUCTED-TOOL

Constructed-Tools for the Sample Analytic Task

Our discussions about the sample ANALYTIC TASK—*compare teachers' reactions to different kinds of bullying*—have all assumed that in the prior task we thought of *reactions* and *kinds of bullying* as two separate units of meaning. What if the TRANSLATION of the previous task had not been sufficiently guided by what was anticipated to come next, and we had decided to stick to the rule of thumb of two UNITS? The purpose of that previous task might have been well served by a single unit of meaning—*teachers' reactions to different kinds of bullying*—along with *teachers* as UNIT of analysis. We would have created CODES that specified in the code name both the nature of the reaction and the kind of bullying, such as *disapproval of verbal abuse, censure of physical abuse, sympathy to cyber bullying,* and so on. This may have been efficient for the prior task, but not for the current task of investigating teacher reactions stimulated by different kinds of bullying, because the CODES do not distinguish *reactions* from *kinds of bullying.*

This sort of situation is common. No matter how much thought you give to the context of an ANALYTIC TASK and the actions that can be taken on its COMPONENTS in Step 4, unexpected new purposes emerge, and in hindsight the prior decisions are not always the most appropriate. We could go back and recode every QUOTATION to separate CODES for each reaction and kind of bullying, but this would be time consuming and perhaps demoralizing. In our experience an inability to work out a better solution leads researchers to stop using the software. Yet ATLAS.ti is flexible enough to easily fulfill our ANALYTIC TASK by CONSTRUCTING a TOOL. In this example we would do this by combining software operations, rather than by using the software in a customized way.

If our coding scheme has combined *reactions* and *kinds of bullying* into single CODES, we somehow need to separate them for our new purpose of investigating all the possible combinations of *reactions* and *types of bullying.* In this case the Query Tool—which did not suit our purpose in the earlier example (p. 132)—will be just right, because it allows us to create SMART-CODES—combinations of other CODES connected by *operators.* For example, we can create a SMART-CODE called *disapproval* that combines all the CODES for the disapproval reaction—*disapproval of verbal abuse, disapproval of physical abuse,* etc.—by using the operator *OR.* We can repeat the process to create SMART-CODES for each *reaction* and each *type of bullying.* Then we can use the Co-occurrence Table as before, but this time choosing the *reaction* SMART-CODES for the rows and the *types of bullying* SMART-CODES for the columns.

We refer to this as a CONSTRUCTED-TOOL, rather than a pair of SELECTED-TOOLS performed one after the other, only because the two operations had to be thought out together in order to solve the problem. Once you are performing operations in the software, the distinction between SELECTED- and CONSTRUCTED-TOOLS is irrelevant. The distinction is only an aid to making better choices for harnessing ATLAS.ti powerfully. Figure 6.15 displays the sixth and final iteration of the ANALYTIC PLANNING WORKSHEET for the sample ANALYTIC TASK using a CONSTRUCTED-TOOL. As we have described the thinking process in detail, the worksheet in Figure 6.15 does not include a summary explanation in the TRANSLATION column.

This completes our instruction in the five steps of TRANSLATION. It also completes Part II, the application of the principles of the *Five-Level QDA* method that were introduced and described in Part I. In Part III and the accompanying video demonstrations on the companion website, we illustrate these principles in a variety of real-world research projects. Chapter 7 begins by suggesting how you can best take advantage of these illustrations.

	Identify patterns of teacher reactions by comparing different reactions to different kinds of bullying

	Level 3: TRANSLATION	Level 4: SELECTED TOOL or Level 5: CONSTRUCTED TOOL
	NEXT ANTICIPATED Determine whether patterns of most problematic or most productive reactions of teachers may inform mitigation of bullying behaviors	

Level 2: ***ANALYTIC TASKS***	**Level 3: *TRANSLATION***	*Constructed tool:*
Compare teachers' reactions to different kinds of bullying	*UNITS* Teachers (unit of analysis) Reactions to kinds of bullying (unit of meaning) *PURPOSE* To investigate whether individual teachers display similar or different reactions to different types of bullying *POSSIBLE COMPONENTS* *(Not included for this illustration)* *CHOSEN COMPONENTS* Teachers = DOCUMENT Reactions = SMART-CODE (resulting in CODED-QUOTATIONS) Kinds of bullying = SMART-CODE (resulting in CODED-QUOTATIONS) *EXPLANATION* *(Full explanation in the chapter text)*	• Create SMART-CODES for each set of CODES with the same *reaction*, and for each set of CODES with the same *kind of bullying* • Co-occurrence table: Select the *reaction* SMART-codes as rows, and the *kinds of bullying* SMART-CODES, as columns.

FIGURE 6.15 ANALYTIC PLANNING WORKSHEET for sample analytic task: CONSTRUCTED-TOOL

References

di Gregorio, S., & Davidson, J. (2008). *Qualitative research design for software users.* Maidenhead, UK: McGraw Hill/Open University Press.

Lincoln, Y. S., & Guba, E. G. (1985). *Naturalistic inquiry.* Thousand Oaks, CA: Sage.

Naylor, P., Cowie, H., Cossin, F., Bettencourt, R., & Lemme, F. (2006). Teachers' and pupils' definitions of bullying. *British Journal of Educational Psychology*, 76(3), 553–576.

Rigby, K. (2014). How teachers address cases of bullying in schools: A comparison of five reactive approaches. *Educational Psychology in Practice*, 30(4), 409–419.

Silver, C., & Lewins, A. (2014). *Using software in qualitative research: A step-by-step guide* (2nd ed.). Thousand Oaks, CA: Sage.

Tracy, S. J. (2010). Qualitative quality: Eight 'big-tent' criteria for excellent qualitative research. *Qualitative Inquiry*, 16(10), 837–851.

PART III
Case Illustrations

Part III illustrates the *Five-Level QDA* method in a variety of real-world qualitative research projects. These projects are unlikely to be exactly the same as your own projects in terms of methodology or content. Chapter 7 explains how to learn by analogy from these case illustrations in order to transfer the underlying process to your own work. Chapter 7 also describes the content of the three sets of video demonstrations on the companion website (www.routledgetextbooks. com/textbooks/5LQDA) that accompany the case illustrations. Chapters 8 and 9 contain the complete documentation of two full-case illustrations that are referred to in the video demonstrations. The documentation of many additional mini-cases is available with their videos on the companion website.

7

ORIENTATION TO CASE ILLUSTRATIONS

Case illustrations bring the *Five-Level QDA* method to life by illustrating the process in real-world research projects with accompanying video demonstrations that can be used as a guide in your own work. In this chapter we describe how these resources are organized and how they can be accessed. We first describe the characteristics of the case illustrations and how best to learn from them. Second, we describe the three series of video demonstrations available on the companion website and our format for presenting the full-case illustrations in Chapters 8 and 9.

Learning From Case Illustrations

A case illustration is not the same as a case study. A case study describes a real-world problem in order to reflect on the content of the case and learn to think like an expert in that field (Ertmer, Quinn, & Glazewski, 2014). The case study method is an established method of learning—the Harvard MBA program famously organizes its entire curriculum around a series of case studies. But in this book we are not studying the content of research methods or the strategy levels of research projects. We are instead studying the process of TRANSLATING from strategy to tactics. Successful TRANSLATION of an ANALYTIC TASK requires knowing its context—what has come before and what you plan to do next. We therefore need to know the full subject matter of these real-world research projects to provide the context for TRANSLATION. But we are not primarily focused on studying the projects themselves; we are only using them to teach the TRANSLATION of individual ANALYTIC TASKS, and in doing so, to demonstrate how ATLAS.ti can be harnessed powerfully throughout an entire project. We therefore call the projects *case illustrations*, and we draw on the content of the case as context for the instruction. In other words, we are interested here in process rather than content, but we need to be aware of the content to understand the process.

There is no comprehensive generic list of ANALYTIC TASKS that can be picked from and copied. ANALYTIC TASKS are the most specific level of detail in an analytic plan, specific to the context of a particular research project. This creates a quandary for illustrating the process of TRANSLATION. We cannot provide sufficient illustrations so that there will always be an ANALYTIC TASK within a project from the same discipline, guided by the same methodology, seeking to answer the same kind of research question with the same style of analysis that can then be directly copied to your project. Instead we provide a range of illustrations, which will likely be different from your project in many ways but can be used as analogies. But they must be "productive analogies"—those that shed new light on what they are being compared with (Vosniadou & Ortony, 1989, p. 14). We must therefore consider how best to learn by analogy.

Learning by Analogy

Reasoning by analogy is a much-studied psychological process (Gentner, Holyoak, & Kokinov, 2001). Analogies are based on the similarity between two things, which allows inferences to be drawn from one to the other. If a friend tells you that she felt like a fish out of water at a formal opera gala, you infer she was not comfortable in the alien surroundings. Thinking in this way is not a special skill but is at the core of our mental processes, as the "spotting of analogies pervades every moment of our thought" (Hofstadter & Sander, 2013, p. 18). This does not mean that all analogies are appropriate, correct, or helpful (Sunstein, 1993). If a student is told that the solar system is like an atom, which has electrons circling around its nucleus, he may wrongly infer that planets jump out of their orbits when he is taught in another class that electrons jump from orbit to orbit around the nucleus.

We cannot know the context of the ANALYTIC TASKS in your own project and how you are drawing analogies from the ANALYTIC TASKS in our case illustrations. But we can draw attention to some aspects of learning by analogy. The most important issue is whether the similarity you see between a case illustration and your own project is based on *structural characteristics* of the case illustration or on its *surface features* (Gentner, 1989). Surface features refer to the individual details of a situation. The surface features of the fish out of water example are the fish and the wet and dry environments. The structural characteristic refers to the *relationships* among the surface features—the fish is not comfortable because it is out of water, or more generally, an alien environment produces discomfort. Drawing a productive analogy is based on noticing the similarity of the structural characteristics—that your friend felt discomfort because she was in unfamiliar surroundings. But drawing an analogy based on the surface features would lead you astray. If you concluded that your friend felt like a fish out of water because she is usually wet, perhaps spending most of her time swimming or walking in the rain, but is now feeling uncomfortable because she is dry, that would not have been the intention of her analogy and clearly makes no sense.

We have belabored the issue of needing to seek structural similarities rather than surface similarities, because psychologists report that in real situations people do not always spontaneously draw relevant, productive analogies from situations that are very different from their own (Holyoak & Koh, 1987, p. 334). The surface features of our case illustrations are the specifics of the projects—the discipline, methodology, type of research question, style of analysis, etc.—and are likely to be very different from your own. If you focus on these surface features, you may not find many ANALYTIC TASKS with the exact same combination of these surface features as in your own project. Conversely, shared surface features between projects do not imply that there are ANALYTIC TASKS with the same structural characteristics as your own. We know from Chapter 6 that the structural features of an ANALYTIC TASK are its units and purposes. If these features of an ANALYTIC TASK in a case illustration seem similar to a task in your own project, we suggest that you not be concerned whether the surface features—the discipline, methodology, type of project, or research question—are similar to or different from your own project.

The conclusion we can draw from the psychological research on analogies is that intentionally seeking analogies in case illustrations that are structurally similar to your own, regardless of whether there are any surface features in common, will make the analogy productive. It is beyond the scope of this chapter to go further into learning by analogy. For a fuller description of how to identify the structural characteristics of situations analogous to your own, see Mayer (1992).

Authentic Learning

The *Five-Level QDA* method is concerned with managing the contradiction between the emergent nature of qualitative analysis and the cut-and-dried nature of software. A similar contrast holds between learning the skill of TRANSLATION and learning to operate the software effectively.

Donald Schön (1990) identified the problems of applying cut-and-dried technical knowledge to practice areas that are emergent in nature. Schön (1990) proposed that educational methods in these areas required the kind of practical knowledge only gained by engagement with real-world problems. In our field, learning to operate ATLAS.ti effectively requires technical knowledge of how the program works. But learning the process of TRANSLATION between strategies and tactics is based on the practical knowledge that only comes from engaging with real-world research projects. We therefore do not invent projects or fragments of projects to illustrate an idealized example of qualitative analysis or TRANSLATION. Instead we present projects that have been undertaken by experienced qualitative researchers who use ATLAS.ti. These contributing researchers have kindly described the entire progress of their qualitative analysis in the sequence that it occurred. Their project descriptions have two characteristics: they are *messy* and they are *unsanitized.*

In this context *messy* means *does not proceed in a straight line.* A qualitative project is a journey from a research question to a finding or a conclusion. This journey is not a predetermined series of steps, but to some degree iterative and emergent: the outcome of one analytic activity leading to reconsideration of what has gone before as part of the determination of what to do next. This sometimes proceeds smoothly, sometimes in fits and starts, and sometimes requires retracing of steps and adopting course corrections—all are part of a systematic yet emergent qualitative analysis process. We include this full messiness in our case illustrations so that the authentic structural characteristics of the ANALYTIC TASKS that we demonstrate are available for you to draw analogies to your own, inevitably messy, projects. The case illustrations are not intended as model or exemplar research projects, but simply real-world examples of a process.

We also present the case illustrations unsanitized. Our students consistently report that they do not learn much transferable knowledge from reading concise, highly ordered descriptions of a qualitative analysis in the methods sections of journal articles. In the interests of space these methods sections are boiled down to the main steps of analysis, bypassing the detours that did not contribute to the findings in a direct way. They serve a different purpose from our case illustrations. For learning purposes we describe how a qualitative analysis actually progressed, including the detours that are not mistakes but an intimate part of the process, in the order in which they occurred. This is particularly important regarding ATLAS.ti, as the inevitable detours involve harnessing the software in ways that may have an impact on what comes next and how the exit from the detour is accomplished.

Most of the case illustrations are completed projects with published articles. Some are still in progress at the time of writing, and others reached a certain point and will never be completed, either because the funding ran out or for some other reason. Whatever the current status of the project, the progress that was made and reported was authentically done.

Learning From Multiple Illustrations

In the video demonstrations of TRANSLATION we always include a pair of contrasting examples. There are two reasons for this. One purpose of the *Five-Level QDA* method is to counteract the wrong impression that there is a "correct" way to use ATLAS.ti. This may be due to what we call the default software mind-set: that there is always a correct way to use software that must be discovered. Our demonstrations of TRANSLATING an ANALYTIC TASK inevitably lead to harnessing particular COMPONENTS, which contributes to an inappropriate assumption that this is how those COMPONENTS should always be used, or this is the only way this ANALYTIC TASK could be accomplished. We therefore always include a contrasting demonstration of a different way to use the COMPONENTS or a different way to fulfill the ANALYTIC TASK to show that this is not the case.

A second reason for including multiple ANALYTIC TASKS in each video demonstration is based on the recommendations of educational psychologists. Qualitative analysis is an example of an "ill-structured activity." "Ill" does not mean that there is anything wrong with it, but that there is uncertainty or incomplete information about how a conclusion can be reached, and no single correct outcome can be considered "correct"—almost a definition of qualitative analysis (see Box 1.1, p. 15). Gaining skill in such ill-structured activities requires learning multiple perspectives using multiple contrasting examples, which Spiro, Coulson, Feltovich, and Anderson (1988) refer to as "criss-crossing the conceptual landscape" (p. 6). For both reasons we therefore ensure that each demonstration of the TRANSLATION of an ANALYTIC TASK is accompanied by a contrasting example.

Video Demonstrations of Case Illustrations

This book has three sets of video demonstrations. The first set—the *Component Orientation* videos—provides a short orientation to how each COMPONENT works. These videos are described in Chapter 5. The second set—*Case Illustration* videos—demonstrates the two full cases documented in Chapters 8 and 9. The third set—the *Harnessing Components* videos—demonstrates both the two full cases and a series of mini-cases documented on the companion website. Here we describe the second and third sets of videos and the full-cases and mini-cases. Figure 7.1 provides an overview of the different sets of videos.

Case Illustration Videos

The *Case Illustration* videos demonstrate the two full cases described in Chapters 8 and 9. Both are real-world projects conducted using ATLAS.ti. The first, described in Chapter 8, is a more straightforward project contributed by Elizabeth Pope, a PhD candidate at the University of Georgia. The second, described in Chapter 9, is a more sophisticated project contributed by Professor Trena Paulus, University of Georgia, and Assistant Professor Mary Alice Varga, University of West Georgia. The purpose of the chapters and the *Case Illustration* videos is to demonstrate the progress of these real-world projects in the sequence in which the analytic activities occurred. Your current project may not be like either of these studies, but as we discussed earlier, the surface features do not have to be similar in order for productive analogies to be drawn.

Accompanying the *Case Illustration* videos are *Translating an Analytic Task* videos that demonstrate in detail the TRANSLATION process for a selection of the ANALYTIC TASKS in the project. The associated ANALYTIC PLANNING WORKSHEETS that are demonstrated in the videos are also downloadable as PDF documents.

There Is Often More Than One Way to Fulfill an Analytic Task

It is likely that harnessing one COMPONENT to fulfill an ANALYTIC TASK will be more effective than harnessing another, based on the context—what has been accomplished previously, the purpose of the ANALYTIC TASK, and what is anticipated to come next. But there will also be alternative ways. In the *Translating an Analytic Task* videos for the more sophisticated project in Chapter 9 we therefore demonstrate contrasting ways to TRANSLATE the same ANALYTIC TASK, and we discuss the pros and cons of each with the case contributor, Dr. Paulus. This ensures that there is no misunderstanding that there is a single "correct" way to accomplish an ANALYTIC TASK.

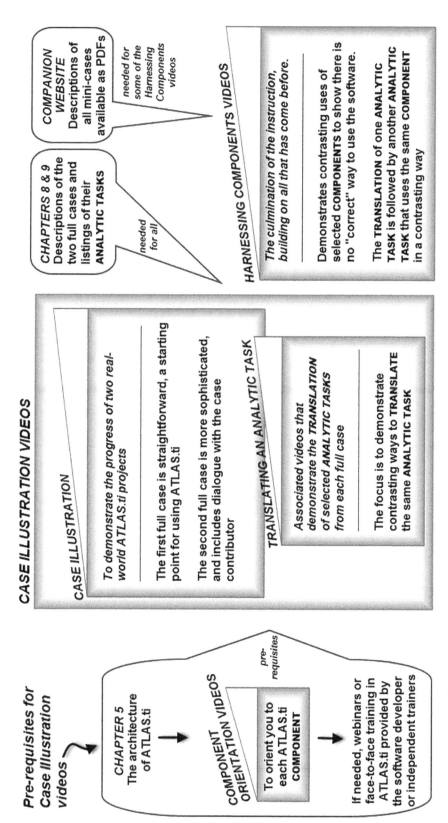

FIGURE 7.1 Overview of video demonstrations

Harnessing Components Videos

The *Harnessing Components* videos are the culmination of the book—they build on everything that has come before to demonstrate different ways to harness ATLAS.ti powerfully. These videos are organized by COMPONENT. Each video demonstrates how a COMPONENT can be harnessed by TRANSLATING an ANALYTIC TASK into SELECTED- or CONSTRUCTED-TOOLS that use that COMPONENT.

There Is No One Correct Way to Harness a Component

Each COMPONENT can be harnessed in different ways based on the units and the purpose of an ANALYTIC TASK. In the *Harnessing Components* videos we therefore demonstrate contrasting examples of the use of a selection of the COMPONENTS to illustrate that there is no single "correct" way to harness that COMPONENT. This emphasizes that the use of the software is driven by the needs of the analysis, not by the "correct" use of the software. To accomplish this in the *Harnessing Components* videos we begin by choosing one ANALYTIC TASK of interest from a case illustration. We then select a second ANALYTIC TASK that harnesses the same COMPONENT in a different way or for a different purpose. We then demonstrate the TRANSLATION of both ANALYTIC TASKS, going through the ANALYTIC PLANNING WORKSHEETS, which are also downloadable as PDF documents.

The two full-case illustrations in Chapters 8 and 9 do not provide sufficient variety for all the necessary contrasting examples for all COMPONENTS. We therefore illustrate ANALYTIC TASKS from additional mini-cases that are not described in the book. We provide descriptions of these mini-cases in PDFs on the companion website in the same format as Chapters 8 and 9, but in abbreviated form, with a short summary of the project's purpose, methodology, and ANALYTIC STRATEGIES. These mini-case descriptions are two-page overviews that provide the necessary context for the *Harnessing Components* videos.

Accessing Video Demonstrations

All video demonstrations and associated PDF documents are available at the companion website. To register and log in go to www.routledgetextbooks.com/textbooks/5LQDA. You will be directed to choose *Component Orientation, Case Illustration,* or *Harnessing Components* videos. Within each category you will then be directed to choose among the available videos.

The Two Full-Case Illustrations

Chapters 8 and 9 describe the full cases in a standard format. Each chapter begins with a narrative overview of the entire project in straightforward language without any terms or jargon words that would not be understood outside that field. The purpose is to facilitate productive analogies without any required knowledge of the surface features of the research topic, discipline, or methodology. The narrative overview includes the background of the project, the objectives and methodology, and any unexpected and unplanned detours that occurred. This is the same format that is used in abbreviated form for the mini-cases, which are available on the companion website.

Following the narrative overview we list all the project's ANALYTIC TASKS in a standard format. In collaboration with the contributors we have grouped all the ANALYTIC TASKS for a project into a number of analytic phases, or simply *phases*, in which each phase reflects a coherent set of tasks. For more convenient demonstration in the videos, all the phases of the project have been further grouped into a small number of *stages* of the project, so that each stage can be demonstrated in a separate video. The videos refer to the written descriptions of the stages, phases, and ANALYTIC TASKS in Chapters 8 and 9. Figure 7.2 displays a schematic of these stages, phases, and ANALYTIC TASKS, and Figure 7.3 explains their presentation in Chapters 8 and 9.

Chapters 8 and 9 are a collaboration between the case contributors and the authors of this book. The text of each chapter is a synthesis of the contributors' initial descriptions of their projects, the authors' questions and comments, and the contributors' responses. The contributors have approved the final text as an accurate representation of what occurred. The video demonstrations rely on the text of these chapters, as they provide the context for the videos, as well as the detailed listing of ANALYTIC TASKS in each stage of the project. Neither the chapters nor the accompanying videos are intended to be independent standalone instruction; they are intended to be read and viewed together in order to be meaningful.

Case Illustration 1: A Literature Review

The first full case in Chapter 8 is a more straightforward project, a literature review conducted as part of a PhD dissertation. This project provides a starting point for those with little or no experience in qualitative research or for those with no prior experience in using ATLAS.ti. The *Case Illustration* and *Translating an Analytic Task* videos demonstrate on screen the progress of the project described in the chapter, and we assume that you have read the chapter prior to watching the

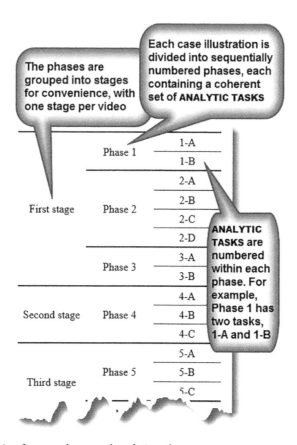

FIGURE 7.2 Schematic of stages, phases, and analytic tasks

Phase 4: Construct a re[...]	This figure displays Phases 4 and 5 from Chapter 9. These phases each have two ANALYTIC TASKS: 4-A & 4-B, and 5-A & 5-B
4-A	*Identify data for* [...] • We accessed the [...] identified posts in the forum on *"loss of a spouse, partner or significant other"*. *This forum was chosen because it was the most active forum on the site.* • *We downloaded the 107 most recent threads from this forum*
4-B	Create an analytic worksp[...] • We created a new master AT[...] profiles and log-in details [...] • We created and nam[...] pasted the content into t[...] • We pasted the URL link [...] DOCUMENT to access the original content.

ANALYTIC TASKS in *italics* do not involve the use of ATLAS.ti

ANALYTIC TASKS in *regular type* are TRANSLATED into software operations using ATLAS.ti

Phase 5: Set up parameters of the analysis	
5-A	Create and define conversational features and discursive moves to be used to analyze threads • We created the eight discursive [...] es identified in the First Stage as CODES and defined them [...] COMMENTS. • We created a "Variable" MEMO [...] about posts that seemed to be [...] functioning differently from [...] • We create [...] QUOTATION out[...] thread so tha [...] ould each [...] exactly the sam[...] mean[...]
5-B	Duplica[...] • We c[...] • So [...] on.

The *names* of the ANALYTIC TASKS in Chapters 8 & 9 are the same as on the ANALYTIC PLANNING WORKSHEETS on the Companion Website...

... but the *summary descriptions* of the tasks in Chapters 8 & 9 are replaced by the details of the TRANSLATION process in the ANALYTIC PLANNING WORKSHEETS on the Companion Website

FIGURE 7.3   Presentation of stages, phases, and analytic tasks in Chapters 8 and 9

videos. Although this case illustration is intended for those with no prior experience of ATLAS.ti, we hope that those with more experience will also find the videos helpful in becoming encultur-ated into *Five-Level QDA* thinking.

Case Illustration 2: A Discourse Analysis Study

The second full case in Chapter 9 is a more sophisticated project, a discourse analysis study. This is intended for those with some experience in both qualitative research and ATLAS.ti. This also serves as a second step of learning for those who have watched the videos of Case Illustration 1.

In addition to demonstrating the progress of the project on screen, the *Translating an Analytic Task* videos include a dialogue with the case contributor, Dr. Paulus, an experienced qualitative researcher and professor of research methods. The dialogue focuses primarily on the extent and manner to which ATLAS.ti was harnessed powerfully, rather than on the project's strategy—the objectives, research questions, and development of the analytic plan. Discussions include the pros and cons of the choices made in this project's research context compared with other contexts, and the pros and cons of possible alternative choices for fulfilling the analytic plan. The purpose is to explore the implications and consequences of alternative ways to harness the program.

References

Ertmer, P. A., Quinn, J. A., & Glazewski, K. D. (Eds.). (2014). *The ID casebook: Case studies in instructional design* (4th ed.). Boston: Pearson.

Gentner, D. (1989). The mechanisms of analogical learning. In S. Vosniadou & A. Ortony (Eds.), *Similarity and analogical reasoning* (pp. 199–241). New York: Cambridge University Press.

Gentner, D., Holyoak, K. J., & Kokinov, B. N. (2001). *The analogical mind: Perspectives from cognitive science.* Cambridge, MA: MIT press.

Hofstadter, D., & Sander, E. (2013). *Surfaces and essences: Analogy as the fuel and fire of thinking.* New York: Basic Books.

Holyoak, K. J., & Koh, K. (1987). Surface and structural similarity in analogical transfer. *Memory & Cognition,* 15(4), 332–340.

Mayer, R. E. (1992). Chapter 14: Analogical reasoning. *Thinking, problem solving, cognition* (2nd. Ed., pp. 415–454). New York: W. H. Freeman and Company.

Schön, D. A. (1990). *Educating the reflective practitioner: Toward a new design and teaching and learning in the professions.* San Francisco: Jossey-Bass.

Spiro, R. J., Coulson, R. L., Feltovich, P. J., & Anderson, D. (1988). *Cognitive flexibility theory: Advanced knowledge acquisition in ill-structured domains.* Paper presented at the Proceedings of the 10th Annual Conference of the Cognitive Science Society. Montreal, Quebec, Canada.

Sunstein, C. R. (1993). On analogical reasoning. *Harvard Law Review,* 106(3), 741–791.

Vosniadou, S., & Ortony, A. (1989). Similarity and analogical reasoning: A synthesis. In S. Vosniadou & A. Ortony (Eds.), *Similarity and analogical reasoning* (pp. 1–17). New York: Cambridge University Press.

8

CASE ILLUSTRATION — AN EXPLORATORY LITERATURE REVIEW

Exploring the Literature on Interfaith Dialogue

Elizabeth M. Pope

This chapter and the accompanying videos illustrate what a straightforward, real-world qualitative analysis executed in ATLAS.ti is like. The contributor, Elizabeth Pope, is a PhD candidate in Adult Education at a major U.S. research university. We asked Elizabeth to contribute this case from her dissertation because PhD students take their dissertation projects very seriously—it is their first piece of original research and they want to make sure it is an example of good scholarship. Elizabeth's project is therefore documented in detail, and it is easy to follow how she moved the project forward. Her dissertation is a qualitative case study examining an interfaith dialogue group between Jewish, Christian, and Muslim adults. This chapter illustrates only the literature review part of her dissertation. However, a literature review is a qualitative research project in itself, as it takes a large body of unstructured materials—articles, books, etc.—in order to make sense of them and provide a framework for the research project.

The purpose of the chapter is to provide the context for the ANALYTIC TASKS that are referred to in the video demonstrations. The first section of the chapter—"Analytic Strategies"—contains the objectives and guiding methodology of the project, that is, Level 1 of the *Five-Level QDA* method. The second section—"Stages of the Analysis"—is Level 2, the analytic plan, which unfolds in six stages, including the generation of ANALYTIC TASKS at each stage. This is the point at which Level 3 begins, that is, TRANSLATING the ANALYTIC TASKS into software operations. Each stage is demonstrated in a separate video, including commentary on the choices made and on possible alternative choices for fulfilling the analytic plan using ATLAS.ti. To view a video after reading a stage, please go to www.routledgetextbooks.com/textbooks/5LQDA and follow the on-screen instructions.

Elizabeth originally conducted her project using ATLAS.ti 7. We have converted her project to ATLAS.ti 8, which led to no changes in process or procedure, except for changing the names of the COMPONENTS to their ATLAS.ti Version 8 names.

Now we turn over the chapter to Elizabeth.

Analytic Strategies

I have presented the context for the case illustration in three sections—"Background," describing my dissertation as a whole; "Focus of This Case Illustration," describing the conceptual framework for my dissertation, which determined the scope for the literature review; and "Guiding Methodology" for the literature review.

Background

This literature review is for my dissertation, a qualitative case study titled '*This Is a Head, Hearts, and Hands Enterprise:' Interfaith Dialogue and Perspective Transformation*. The study was conducted in the southeastern United States and explored a community-based interfaith dialogue program between Jewish, Christian, and Muslim adults.

The context for the study is the continuing problem of religious conflict. The history of violence, fear, prejudice and bigotry, misunderstandings, misinformation, and a general lack of knowledge about different faith traditions has led to negative perceptions of the "religious other." Many scholars of religion believe that interfaith dialogue could be an invaluable method for resolving religious discord. But although interfaith dialogue can be successful, it can just as often fail. One explanation is the many idealized and varied goals of interfaith dialogue. Unanticipated challenges in practice and implementation can also be a detriment. And Jewish–Christian–Muslim dialogue has its own particular difficulties, including the expectation that each group is speaking on behalf of an entire faith tradition, a lack of trust between participants, historical disagreements, etc.

Most academic literature on interfaith dialogue is conceptual, aiming to understand the impact of interfaith experiences. There is little empirical research that examines the effects and process of interfaith dialogue, the nature of learning in such an interfaith experience, or how perceptions of the "religious other" can be transformed through interfaith dialogue. The need for research into these issues is the rationale for my dissertation.

Focus of This Case Illustration

The purpose of my dissertation is twofold. First, it is to examine the nature of learning in interfaith dialogue. Second, to understand if, and how, "perspective transformation" in people of different faiths occurs through interfaith dialogue. The research questions guiding the study are:

1. What happens when Jewish, Christian, and Muslim adults engage in interfaith dialogue?
2. How do facilitators of interfaith dialogue prepare for and guide group meetings?
3. In what ways, if any, does interfaith dialogue foster perspective transformation with regard to the religious other?

Before beginning the research I needed to review the existing literature about interfaith dialogue across academic fields. In this chapter I use the term *literature* interchangeably with *resources* to mean all items I gathered, whether journal articles, books, or other electronic resources. This literature review gave me an extensive overview of interfaith studies and allowed me to understand how interfaith dialogue has and has not been researched in a wide variety of disciplines.

Prior to conducting the literature review I created a conceptual framework for the whole dissertation to serve as the "analytic lens" through which I would view and interpret my data and conduct my analysis. This determined what literature I would need to review, and so I begin by describing how I created this conceptual framework. I began with two main elements: the concept of "dialogue" and the concept of "transformational learning." I based my understanding of dialogue on Martin Buber's (1923) seminal work *I and Thou*. Buber (1923) distinguishes two types of dialogic relationships: the "I-It" and "I-Thou" relationships. In the "I-It" relationship, the "It" is a person seen as an object to be used to achieve a certain goal. In the "I-Thou" relationship, in contrast, there is a "mutual and holistic existence of two entities" (Morgan & Guilherme, 2012, p. 982) between people. I based my understanding of transformational learning on Mezirow's (2012) "transformative learning theory," which defines transformational learning as a process that

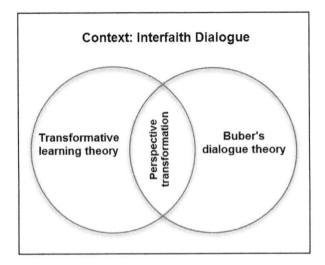

FIGURE 8.1 Theoretical framework for dissertation

"transforms our taken-for-granted frames of reference to make them more inclusive, discriminating, open, emotionally capable of change, and reflective" (p. 76). Within transformative learning theory one concept plays a crucial role, that of "transforming perspectives of the world." For my conceptual framework I proposed that the transformation of perspectives toward the "religious other" during interfaith dialogue can be understood through the intersection of Buber's (1923) and Mezirow's (2012) theoretical standpoints. Combined, these theories provide a way to conceptualize "perspective transformation" in interfaith dialogue groups in terms of both the individual experience of transformation and the relational experience of dialogue. Figure 8.1 illustrates a big-picture view of this framework.

Guiding Methodology

The guiding methodology described here concerns just the conduct of the literature review, not the entire dissertation. First I thought through the purpose of the review. The conceptual framework for the dissertation indicated that I needed to review the academic literature that used transformative learning and/or Buber's dialogue theory to examine intercultural or interfaith interactions. I also needed to identify any gaps in the literature regarding adult learning through interfaith dialogue in order to find areas in which further study was necessary. This search introduced me to resources in a wide variety of academic fields. I paid particular attention to the theoretical frameworks, data collection methods, analytical methodologies, and findings of these empirical articles in order to learn from and build on the existing research in this field.

I primarily searched for resources electronically, but I noticed that when I went to the library with a list of books to find, I often ended up finding other relevant resources through physical proximity to the books I was looking for. Visiting the library led to a serendipitous literature review that did not happen with electronic searching, and this became part of my personal guiding methodology.

My literature review was exploratory because my conceptual framework consisted of the intersection of two separate theories, and I was not aware of any existing framework that combined these theories which could be used to analyze the disparate items of literature. I therefore sought an inductive approach to the analysis, as inductive approaches do not start with a predetermined analytic frame, but rather start with specific observations or statements in the data and move logically to a more general explanation. I chose the inductive thematic analysis approach described by Braun and Clarke (2006), which is based on the work of Boyatzis (1998), as my guiding methodology because in the absence of an existing framework that combined transformative learning theory and dialogue theory I needed to generate data-driven themes. This approach is a "bottom–up" coding of the data to identify themes and patterns that are strongly linked to the data, which in this case are the various literature resources. This allowed me to note key themes and moments of importance as they became clear through my reading of the literature rather than relying on a predetermined coding frame to interpret them.

I implemented Braun and Clarke's (2006) methods in practice by first immersing myself in the literature with wide reading and marking segments of text that struck me as interesting. I then created descriptive codes to capture the concepts I was seeing in the literature and applied them to the segments I had identified as interesting. During this phase I generated 141 descriptive codes. I then grouped these codes into higher-level categories to indicate similarities and differences among the descriptive codes and to organize the relationships I was identifying between them. During this phase I reduced the number of descriptive codes to 139 by merging those that essentially represented the same concept and grouped them into 12 categories. Finally, I identified themes for representing a holistic picture of the broad literature on interfaith dialogue. The result was the creation of eight higher-level themes that grouped the categorized codes.

My process was informed by my general understanding of grounded theory methodology. In writing up my literature review methodology I felt I needed to name the stages of my process using established terms. I therefore borrowed two grounded theory terms to describe my process. I referred to the descriptive coding phase as "open coding," which I took to mean the creation of tentative labels for the concepts identified that summarize what is discussed. However, I only coded segments within the literature that related to the focus of my review, rather than coding all of each resource, which is typically how "open coding" is described in grounded theory texts. In the next step, I created the categories in an intuitive way, but referred to this as "axial coding" (Grbich, 2013), as this process of relating codes to one another is the second stage of grounded theory (Strauss & Corbin, 1998) and well describes what I did. My use of grounded theory terms ended there, because my intention in developing themes did not have the purpose of generating a core theory that reflects all the data in the analysis, as a grounded theory analysis does. Rather, I developed several themes that reflected how interfaith dialogue is discussed and has been researched across academic disciplines.

Stages of the Analysis

The analytic plan for reviewing the literature evolved as the work progressed. There were six stages of analysis, with each stage planned in light of the outcome of the previous stage and my current thinking about the literature. The six stages reflect turning points in the progress of the literature review, and I named the stages after the fact when reflecting on the process for this chapter. The six stages are listed in Table 8.1.

The first stage was like a mini-review in order to produce a first draft of my literature review during a course on how to conduct a literature review offered in my program. This initially involved lots of paper, and I soon realized I needed to use some kind of software to manage all the resources. After consulting Professor Paulus, one of my teachers at the University of Georgia (and the author of the next case illustration in Chapter 9), I chose ATLAS.ti and continued the project in that software package.

TABLE 8.1 The six stages of analysis

Stages of the project (one video on the companion website for each stage)	
Stage 1: Preliminary partial literature review	Analysis of initial resources gathered in order to complete first draft for literature review class.
Stage 2: Review and rationalize the first stage	Reconsideration of the analysis produced in the first stage and refinement and reorganization of the process for continued analysis to be included in dissertation prospectus.
Stage 3: Expand the scope of the literature review	Addition of more literature into the review and integration of it into the analysis.
Stage 4: Identify themes in the literature	Development of themes that came to frame the rewriting of the literature review.
Stage 5: Rewrite the literature review	Integration of the new analysis to the initial literature review to complete dissertation prospectus.
Stage 6: Ongoing expansion of the literature review	Continued adding of literature as identified.

When I came back to the project several months after the class had ended I discovered that I couldn't get back into my original thinking due to the lack of organization in my analytic process. This led to rationalizing the analysis, meaning that I reconsidered the first approach and reorganized the process; otherwise, I would be continuing to add to the disorganization. This was time consuming but turned out to be beneficial. The subsequent stages are similar to the first stage, but are more refined and systematic, and always included defining codes and making notes continuously about insights and the process. The result of these later stages was the development of themes which are now framing the dissertation data analysis. The literature review has been ongoing throughout my dissertation, and my refined and more precise process now allows me to easily add new resources into the framework whenever additional literature is published in the various academic fields.

First Stage: Preliminary Partial Literature Review

I submitted my dissertation prospectus for approval, including a first major draft of the literature review, during the spring semester of 2016. I began collecting literature in the spring semester of 2015 during a graduate course called "Critique of the Literature in Adult Education." The first stage of the project involved reviewing these resources for the purpose of this course. In retrospect this was the first iteration of the literature review.

The course taught doctoral students the steps of completing a literature review for their dissertations and how to examine and critique research questions and conceptual frameworks. During the class I collected 56 articles using the "multi-search" capability of the university library's website, which searched all available databases that the university subscribed to. I used the key terms *interfaith*, *interreligious*, *transform**, and *dialog** to identify resources. At this early stage I needed to get "the lay of the land" and sought a broad range of conceptual, experiential, and empirical literature. I understand conceptual literature to mean theoretical articles about the process or effects of interfaith and intercultural experiences. Experiential literature describes the author's experience within an interfaith or intercultural context. Empirical literature means research on human subjects to examine interfaith or intercultural interactions and contexts. As the purpose of my dissertation is to add to the scholarly understanding of interfaith dialogue through empirical research, I was particularly interested in finding empirical studies involving interfaith or intercultural interactions using transformative learning or dialogue theory in their conceptual frameworks. The search identified both electronic and print resources. All electronic resources identified by the university's multi-search capability are automatically available as full-text PDF downloads, and all the print resources identified were available for checking out in the library or were obtained by the library for me through interlibrary loan.

I read the downloaded PDF files of articles in Adobe Acrobat Reader, highlighting interesting sections of text and bibliographical information, and sometimes annotating sections using the comment tool. As I read and marked the resources I wrote an appraisal of each one in a separate Microsoft Word file. At this stage, this appraisal writing was not very systematic—sometimes it was a summary of the resource, and sometimes an abstract, a synopsis, or just notes about my initial reflections.

After reading, marking up, and appraising the resources, I imported all the PDF files into ATLAS.ti as individual DOCUMENTS and organized them using DOCUMENT-GROUPS in topical areas such as *Adult Learning Theory*, *Dialogue Theory*, and *Transformative Learning Theory*. The highlighting carried over into ATLAS.ti, but the annotations I had written using the comments tool in Adobe did not. I had highlighted sections to help familiarize myself with the literature, but this also served as a precoding process, because once inside ATLAS.ti, the highlighted portions served as triggers for sections that would probably require coding, and this acted as a roadmap of pertinent information later in the review process.

In the COMMENT for each DOCUMENT within ATLAS.ti I recorded the full citation and pasted in the article abstract and notes I had written about my initial impressions of the article. This was very time consuming, but I felt it was an important task because it would later help me to reference the resources and access my initial thoughts about each article.

I began coding this first set of articles in ATLAS.ti by creating 141 descriptive codes based on the text. By "descriptive code" I mean a single word or very brief phrase that identifies the topic of a particular portion of the resource. As a major purpose of my literature review was to understand and catalogue what literature existed on interfaith dialogue, using descriptive coding was my natural research instinct. Initially I did not organize or define the CODES in any way, as I thought they were self-explanatory and that I would remember their meaning from the short code name. I later realized the codes were of different types and needed to be organized to reflect this and that it was necessary to define new codes at the time of creating them to avoid reviewing this coding work in detail later in order to make sense of what I had done and be able to build on it in later stages, that occurred months later.

After all the articles were coded, I reviewed all the CODED-QUOTATIONS and organized the CODES into higher-level categories by adding prefixes to the CODE names to indicate category names. I organized most of the CODES into categories in this way, but a few remained uncategorized because I thought of them as categories in their own right. Examples of uncategorized CODES were "Empathy," "Effects of Globalization and Modernity," and "Pluralism."

When I had finished categorizing the CODES I exported all the CODED-QUOTATIONS associated with each CODE as a text file. I used this to write the first draft of my literature review, which was organized by the categories I had created using my prefix system. However, I also had the hard-copy resources I had gathered with accompanying Word files of appraisals, separate from ATLAS.ti. While writing my first draft based on the outputs of coded PDFs from ATLAS.ti I also flipped through the separate hard-copy resource, looking at the areas I had marked in order to fit the relevant topics into the draft of the literature review. This was extremely unsystematic and inefficient, which is why in later phases of the project I extended the color-coding system from ATLAS.ti to the hard-copy resources.

This stage of the project contained eight ANALYTIC TASKS. For ease of presentation in Table 8.2 and in the video demonstrations, I have grouped these ANALYTIC TASKS into three analysis phases. Figures 7.2 and 7.3, pp. 149–150, review the format and numbering system for stages, phases, and ANALYTIC TASKS. Note that bullet points in italics do not involve the use of ATLAS.ti.

TABLE 8.2 First Stage (Phases 1–3): Preliminary partial literature review

Phase 1: Identify and become familiar with resources

1-A	*Collect literature to review*
	• *I used the UGA Library's multi-search capability to identify literature that relates to the dimensions of the conceptual framework (see Figure 8.1) using the following key terms: interfaith, interreligious, transform*, and dialog*.*
	• *This process identified 56 relevant electronic resources which I saved as PDF files on my computer hard drive.*
	• *I renamed each file using a consistent naming protocol (Author, Date, Title) and saved them in folders representing three types of resource: Conceptual, Experiential, and Empirical.*
	• *In addition I identified relevant hard-copy resources (either books or book chapters). I purchased my own copies of most of these and took the others out of the UGA Library.*
1-B	*Become familiar with literature and mark interesting sections*
	• *I read each resource and marked interesting sections of text and bibliographic information that related to the dimensions of my conceptual framework.*
	• *For the electronic resources I did this in Adobe Acrobat Reader, using the text highlighting feature. Sometimes I made notes about the highlighted sections using the Adobe commenting feature.*
	• *For the hard-copy resources that I owned I used highlighter pens and made notes in the margins. For the hard-copy resources I took out of the library I made notes in a hard-copy notebook.*
	• *I created a Microsoft Word file for each resource in which I wrote an appraisal about each one. Sometimes this was a summary of the content, and sometimes I also wrote a synopsis and reflection.*

Phase 2: Organize and initially categorize resources

2-A	*Create an analytic workspace to store literature and notes*
	• I created and saved an ATLAS.ti-PROJECT and imported all the marked-up electronic resources into it as individual DOCUMENTS. Because of the way I had named the DOCUMENTS they listed alphabetically by author in the Documents Manager.
	• I recorded the full citation and abstract for each electronic resource and pasted the appraisal I had written about each one in 1-B into its DOCUMENT-COMMENT.
2-B	*Organize literature resources into subject areas*
	• I created nine DOCUMENT-GROUPS to represent the broad subject areas covered by the resources (e.g., "Adult Learning Theory," "Dialogue Theory," "Transformative Learning Theory," "Muslim and Christian Interfaith Dialogue," etc.) and assigned each DOCUMENT to the relevant DOCUMENT-GROUP. These DOCUMENT-GROUPS were mutually exclusive (i.e., each electronic resource belonged to only one DOCUMENT-GROUP).
2-C	*Apply descriptive codes to the relevant segments of literature and take notes*
	• I opened each DOCUMENT and coded the sections I had highlighted in 1-B to new descriptive CODES. This resulted in 141 descriptive CODES. Most reflected relevant concepts I identified (for example "Intercultural Communication," "Learning and Faith," and "Value of Interfaith Dialogue"). However, some were more practical (for example, "Design," "Hole in Literature," and "Future Research").
	• The vast majority of QUOTATIONS were coded to only one descriptive CODE.
	• I created MEMOS to record my thoughts as I was coding, for example, "Challenge of Method and Design," "Community Organization," and "Challenge of Language and Culture." One MEMO called "Problem of Sameness" summarized my thinking about the literature so far, as this was a common challenge I had noticed in the conceptual literature. An additional set of notes about "What Is Faith?" that I had written in a Microsoft Word file was pasted into a MEMO.
2-D	*Organize descriptive codes into initial categories*
	• I retrieved the QUOTATIONS coded to each CODE and reviewed them for equivalence, changing any coding where necessary.
	• I organized the descriptive CODES into categories by adding prefixes to their names, so that they were listed alphabetically in the Code Manager according to their category. Examples of categories are "Aims," "Definitions," "Categories," and "Outcomes."

TABLE 8.2 (Continued)

	Phase 3: Write first draft of literature review
3-A	*Extract coded literature by category* • Every CODE created in Analysis Phase 2 was outputted with all their CODED-QUOTATIONS into the ATLAS.ti Output Editor.
3-B	*Write a first-draft literature review* • *Using this output I wrote the first draft of my literature review. I displayed the ATLAS.ti output on one side of my computer screen and opened a Microsoft Word file on the other side. Referring to the coded-quotations in the output and the content of the memos I had written I wrote my review, which I organized according to the categories created in 2-C.*

Second Stage: Review and Rationalize the First Stage

I came back to the project several months after writing the first draft of the literature review to continue adding new resources and to use the project to help prepare for my comprehensive exams. However, I discovered that I couldn't get back into my original thinking by simply reviewing the ATLAS.ti-PROJECT as it was not well organized and I hadn't defined the CODES or made notes of my analytic process. It became clear that my previous assumption that the CODES were self-evident was not correct, and I had to review all my previous work in detail before planning how to continue and build on what I had previously done.

The review and rationalization process involved retrieving all the CODED-QUOTATIONS at each CODE, merging any CODES that represented the same concept, and then defining each CODE in its COMMENT. I dated the definitions so that if I later redefined them I would be able to track the development of my thinking. Reviewing each CODE involved reconsidering the categories I had created in the first stage to ensure they adequately grouped the descriptive CODES, but I only made one change to the categories.

I also reviewed the DOCUMENT-GROUPS I had created to store the literature and combined some of them so that they more meaningfully represented the way I was now thinking about collections of resources. While reviewing the work I had previously done and making changes to the ATLAS.ti-PROJECT I was fully re-engaging with the literature. I began making analytical notes to keep track of my insights and in particular the relationships I was seeing among the resources. For example, I wrote about individual articles, themes I was noticing across articles, and areas of disconnect or discord in the literature.

This second stage was time consuming yet immensely beneficial because it both reimmersed me in the literature and forced me to reflect upon the analytical decisions I had made at the outset of the project. I recognized that if during the first stage I had written about the analytical decisions I was making, I may not have struggled as I did when returning to the project months later. As a result of this stage, the next stages of my review were much more focused because the reconsideration of my earlier approach meant that I refined and reorganized the process. This ensured that I did not continue to add to the disorganization that I had created in the first stage.

Table 8.3 displays this stage of the project, which contains three ANALYTIC TASKS in a single analytic phase. These three ANALYTIC TASKS actually happened simultaneously, but they are presented as separate tasks to illustrate the process clearly.

Third Stage: Expand the Scope of the Literature Review

From the summer of 2015 to the early spring of 2016 I added more articles to the project in a piecemeal fashion. I used the same search criteria to identify additional resources as I had used in the first stage and followed the same process of downloading the article, reading it in Adobe,

TABLE 8.3 Second Stage (Phase 4): Review and rationalize the first stage

Phase 4: Review and reorganize the analytic workspace	
4-A	*Review and refine coding and the coding scheme* • I retrieved all the CODED-QUOTATIONS coded to each CODE in the first stage and, based on these, defined each CODE using CODE-COMMENTS, adding dates to the definitions. • Any CODES that I identified as repetitive or linked to CODED-QUOTATIONS that represented the same concept were merged. • Most of the CODE name prefixes that I had created in 2-B remained the same, other than renaming the "Aims" prefix as "Purpose." This resulted in a rationalized list of 139 CODES.
4-B	*Review and refine broad subject-areas covered by literature resources* • I reviewed the DOCUMENT-GROUPS created in 2-A and combined some of them to reduce the number from nine to five: "Adult Learning," "Buber and Dialogue Theory," "Empirical Studies on Interfaith Dialogue," "Interfaith Dialogue and Interactions," and "Transformative Learning."
4-C	*Reflect on the literature and coding achieved so far* • While undertaking 4-A, I appended the DOCUMENT-COMMENTS created in 2-A with additional insights about each electronic resource. • I also added commentary to the analytical MEMOS I had created in 2-C, concerning areas of disconnect or discord I was seeing. This led to two additional analytic MEMOS to capture insights relating to "Tolerance" and "Communicative Learning."

highlighting as necessary, adding the resource to the ATLAS.ti-PROJECT and coding the highlighted portions. I no longer made annotations using the comment feature in Adobe, as I now knew they would not transfer into ATLAS.ti, so I wrote all my notes about the articles as I read them in a Microsoft Word file. I also decided to add the new resources to the ATLAS.ti-PROJECT in smaller batches, around 10 at a time, and coded those articles before bringing in the next batch. This was a practical decision to avoid the tedium of adding the citation, abstracts, and notes to the DOCUMENT-COMMENTS for several dozen resources at a time, and because I found it overwhelming to code more than 10 documents at a time.

Each batch of resources was coded to the existing categorized CODES that had been rationalized in the second stage. Because I had just completed the review and rationalization of the project, I was very familiar with the categorized CODES and therefore this process was straightforward. Where I identified text in a resource for which I did not yet have a CODE, I immediately categorized the new CODE into one of the existing categories when I created it. The review and rationalization that I had undergone in the second stage meant I was now able to think at a higher level of abstraction when reading new literature. I no longer needed to first create a descriptive label for a new CODE and then think about which category this CODE belonged to, but could conceptualize segments of text into my scheme immediately. This meant the process of coding the new literature was both quicker and more analytically focused than had been the case in the first stage.

Table 8.4 displays this stage of the project, which contains four ANALYTIC TASKS grouped into two analytic phases. Because I was adding new resources to the ATLAS.ti-PROJECT in small batches, I repeated these tasks several times, so this stage comprises several iterative cycles of identifying resources, familiarizing with resources, integrating resources, and categorizing resources.

Fourth Stage: Identify Major Themes in the Literature

This stage focused on identifying the major themes in the literature and was based on the categorization process undertaken in the second stage. In order to generate themes I reflected on my

TABLE 8.4 Third Stage (Phases 5–6): Expand the scope of the literature review

---

Phase 5: Add resources to the analytic workspace

5-A	*Overview: The same process as outlined in 1-A was used to identify additional relevant resources, except that now I scanned hard-copy resources and added them to the hu along with electronic articles. Eight additional books were included in the review at this stage.* *Collect literature to review (ANALYTIC TASK 1-A repeated)* • *I used the UGA Library's multi-search capability to identify literature that relates to the dimensions of the conceptual framework (see Figure 8.1) using the following key terms: interfaith, interreligious, transform★, and dialog★.* • *This process identified additional relevant electronic resources which I saved as PDF files on my computer hard drive.* • *I renamed each file using a consistent naming protocol (Author, Date, Title) and saved them in folders representing three types of resource: Conceptual, Experiential and Empirical.* • *In addition I identified relevant hard-copy resources (either books or book chapters). I purchased my own copies of most of these and took the others out of the UGA Library.*
5-B	*Overview: The same process as outlined in 1-B was used to become familiar with identified new resources.* *Become familiar with resources (ANALYTIC TASK 1-B repeated)* • *I read each resource and marked interesting sections of text and bibliographic information that related to the dimensions of my conceptual framework.* • *For the electronic resources I did this in Adobe Acrobat Reader, using the text highlighting feature.* • *For the hard-copy resources that I owned I used highlighter pens and made notes in the margins. For the hard-copy resources I took out of the library I made notes in a hard-copy notebook.*
5-C	*Integrate additional resources into the analytic workspace* • I added newly identified electronic resources to the ATLAS.ti-PROJECT as DOCUMENTS. • I assigned each resource to the relevant DOCUMENT-GROUPS and recorded the full citation and abstract for each electronic resource in its DOCUMENT-COMMENT in the same way as I had done in 2-A.

Phase 6: Categorize new resources and adjust existing coding scheme

6-A	*Apply categorized codes to the relevant segments of literature and take notes* • After each new electronic resource had been added to the ATLAS.ti-PROJECT the sections highlighted in 5-B were CODED to the existing CODES rationalized in 4-A. • Where new concepts were identified in highlighted sections, CODES to represent them were created and defined using CODE-COMMENTS. These new CODES were immediately organized into categories by using the prefixes rationalized in 4-A.

previous work, and in doing so I began identifying relationships between the categorized codes. To capture these relationships I linked CODES to one another using named relations and created CODE-GROUPS.

Representing relationships within and between categories involved using relations such as "is associated with," "is part of," "is an outcome of," "is a cause of," and "contradicts" to link CODES. I chose to link CODES with the appropriate relation through the menus in the Code Manager rather than in a NETWORK view because I think hierarchically rather than visually. I created a total of 23 pairs of linked CODES in this way. Most of the relationships I created were between CODES within the same category, for example:

• "DEF: Dialogue *is part of* DEF: Discourse" (where DEF is the prefix for the category "Definitions")
• "CHAL: Culture and context *is associated with* CHAL: Language and translation" (where CHAL is the prefix for the category "Challenge of Dialogue")

- "ALT: Ambivalence *contradicts* ALT: Ambiguity" (where ALT is the prefix for the category "Adult Learning Theory")

Linking CODES in this way helped me to think about how the categorized CODES related to one another, and this informed the development of the themes. To represent the themes I created and named CODE-GROUPS and added categorized CODES into them. I created eight themes. Each theme was mutually exclusive rather than overlapping, meaning that no CODE belonged to more than one theme. This was because the themes served to represent the core aspects of interfaith dialogue in terms of how it has been discussed in the literature and previously researched. I developed the themes to identify the gaps and clusters in the focus of research on interfaith dialogue and to reach an understanding of the current status of scientific knowledge in this area. My thematic analysis was inductive in that the CODES, categories, and themes I developed were grounded in the data. However, it was not about generating a theory from the data, but to map out and analyze patterns in previous work on interfaith dialogue. For this reason mutually exclusive themes represented by CODE-GROUPS were most appropriate. Although no one CODE belonged to more than one theme, some of my themes did contain CODES from different prefixed categories. For example, the theme "The Practice of Interfaith Dialogue" included the CODES belonging to the following categories: "challenges of interfaith dialogue," "impact factors on dialogue," "outcomes of dialogue," "purposes of dialogue," and "types of interfaith dialogue."

As I organized my categorized CODES into themes, I also color-coded them. These colors served two purposes. First, they were a signal of the theme to which each CODE belonged, which appeared in the margin area where they were applied to quotations, and this was helpful when reviewing DOCUMENTS. Second, and more importantly, they corresponded to the colors of highlighting and tabs I used in the hard-copy books. Although my literature review is 95 percent paperless, I used several print books. Coloring the themes meant that I was able to directly relate work done within ATLAS.ti to my paper-based work.

Because I had organized my CODES categorically using prefixes, I continued to work with a long list of CODES throughout the project. I did not reduce the number of CODES as I moved from the descriptive "open coding" phase, through the categorization "axial coding" phase, into the phase of developing the themes. At this stage I was working with 168 CODES, because during the third stage when I expanded the literature review I generated almost 30 new CODES. Some of the CODES were repeated within the categories because the categorical system determined the situation within which the CODE was used. For example, the CODE "mutual learning" appears in both the category of "outcomes of interfaith dialogue" and the category of "purposes of interfaith dialogue." But the definition of "mutual learning" is different in each category and applied to different types of text segments.

- **OUTCOME: *Mutual Learning*—**An outcome of interfaith dialogue is that individuals learn about other traditions while the members of other traditions learn about them.
- **PURPOSE: *Mutual Learning*—**A purpose of interfaith dialogue is to promote mutual learning, which means that while you are learning about and from another religious tradition, you are also learning about your own, and the other participants of interfaith dialogue are doing the same.

These two "mutual learning" codes reflect different concepts in how interfaith dialogue is discussed in the literature. This way of working with codes provided me with a way to represent the nuances of the literature in my codebook. The way I organized CODES into categories and themes

TABLE 8.5 Fourth Stage (Phase 7): Identify major themes in the literature

Phase 7: Recategorization	
7-A	*Reflect on coding and analysis* • I revisited hard-copy resources, retrieved CODED-QUOTATIONS, and reviewed COMMENTS assigned to the categorized CODES. • I added to COMMENTS and MEMOS in relation to potential higher-level themes.
7-B	*Create and explain relationships between codes within categories* • I linked CODES to one another in the code list to express relationships between the CODES within the categories, using semantic links such as "is part of," "is associated with," and "is an outcome of." • I wrote about the relationships I was seeing and the links I was making in MEMOS.
7-C	*Generate and explain themes* • I created CODE-FAMILIES to represent potential themes; at this stage I had four themes: "Adult Learning and Theory in Interfaith Dialogue," "Empirical Research on Interfaith Dialogue," "The Practice of Interfaith Dialogue," and "Transformative Learning." • I assigned categorized CODES to the relevant CODE-FAMILIES and assigned colors to CODES based on the CODE-FAMILY they were assigned to. • All the CODES belonging to each code-family were assigned the same color so that the themes were reflected in the code list. • In MEMOS I wrote about the themes and reflected on the links between CODES and categories. The tasks undertaken in 7-A, 7-B, and 7-C were repeated until I had identified eight themes that accurately reflected the conceptual, experiential, and empirical emphasis of the literature. Themes were mutually exclusive, meaning each CODE only belongs to one CODE-FAMILY, but CODES with different category prefixes belong to different CODE-FAMILIES.
7-D	*Integrate hard-copy resources into themes* • *I reorganized the hard-copy resources so sections relevant to each of the themes identified in 7-C were easily retrievable, using tabs in the same colors.*

meant that the number of CODES never became overwhelming for me. I included a high level of detail within my coding scheme, which now that I was defining my concepts, I was able to easily keep track of my thinking, and the high level of detail contained within the coding scheme became very useful when writing up my findings in the next stage.

Table 8.5 displays this stage of the project, which contains four ANALYTIC TASKS in a single analytic phase.

Fifth Stage: Rewrite the Literature Review

To write up my findings from my literature review, I exported my themes by generating outputs of my CODE-GROUPS. I organized the outputs by CODES rather than QUOTATIONS or DOCUMENTS because the CODES represented the nuances of my themes. Because I was writing a thematic literature review, organizing the output in this way was most conducive to writing up my findings. I included MEMOS, COMMENTS, and CODED-QUOTATIONS in the outputs, so I had each step in my analysis process in the output and could therefore use the output file as the basis for my literature review. Because I had used the same colors for themes within ATLAS.ti and for tagging the print books, the organization and structure of my ATLAS.ti project actually organized the physical books I used in my literature review. This was invaluable when writing up my findings, as I could follow a system of colors to be sure each resource was considered in the write-up at the appropriate time. It also allowed me to keep the same organization system across my in-print books and my electronic articles, which led to a harmonious relationship between my two types of resources.

In rewriting the review, the CODE definitions informed my explanation of the nuances within each theme and category, and the exported quotations provided an easily accessible list of citations. As a result the writing-up process in this stage was streamlined, and I was able to complete a draft over the course of a few days.

Table 8.6 displays this stage of the project, which contains two ANALYTIC TASKS in a single analytic phase.

Sixth Stage: Ongoing Expansion of the Literature Review

At the time of writing this chapter, I am continuing to add to my literature review. I continue to add no more than 10 articles to the ATLAS.ti-PROJECT at a time. I aim to read several articles each week, add them to the ATLAS.ti-PROJECT, and integrate them into my analytic structure as described earlier. Because of the detailed setup of the coding system, it is a seamless process to bring newly identified literature into the analytical framework. The extensive work I did in the early stages of the literature, particularly the first and second stages, with regard to organizing and interrogating my coding system, has made the longitudinal nature of my literature review extremely manageable. My use of ATLAS.ti is integral to this process, as I do not believe that I would be able to complete as comprehensive a literature review if I was not using such a program.

I am currently analyzing the data I generated for my dissertation through observations, interviews, focus groups, and gathering documents, and I currently have a separate ATLAS.ti-PROJECT for the literature review and the data analysis portions of my dissertation. Upon completion of the data analysis I will be able to compare and contrast my analysis with what exists in current literature. I do not plan to combine my literature review and dissertation data ATLAS.ti-PROJECTS because the volume of materials in each may become unmanageable. Additionally, each ATLAS.ti-PROJECT has its own analysis plan, and I do not anticipate these merging successfully. I intend this examination to enhance the discussion chapter of my dissertation, providing a clearer understanding of how my findings compare to, contrast with, and contribute to the existing body of scholarship on interfaith dialogue. Table 8.7 displays this stage of the project, which contains a single ANALYTIC TASK, and Table 8.8 provides a closing summary of all nine phases.

TABLE 8.6 Fifth Stage (Phase 8): Rewrite the literature review

Phase 8: Rewrite the literature review	
8-A	*Extract coded data by categories and themes*
	• I outputted all CODED-QUOTATIONS, with linked MEMOS and COMMENTS, theme by theme into the ATLAS.ti Output Editor.
8-B	*Rewrite the literature review*
	• Using this output I wrote the second draft of my literature review. I displayed the ATLAS.ti output on one side of my computer screen and opened a Microsoft Word file on the other side. Referring to the CODED-QUOTATIONS in the output and the memos, I rewrote my review, which I now organized according to the themes created in 7–C.

TABLE 8.7 Sixth Stage (Phase 9): Ongoing expansion of the literature review

Phase 9: Integrate new resources cumulatively	
9-A	*Repeat analytic process as new relevant resources are identified*
	• Every few months I searched the UGA Library catalog, and when new relevant resources are identified I repeat phases 5 to 7 and integrate new knowledge into my literature review.

TABLE 8.8 Summary of the nine phases of analysis

Stages of the project (one video on the companion website for each stage)	Phases within each stage (one ANALYTIC PLANNING WORKSHEET on the companion website for each phase, describing the TRANSLATION of each of its ANALYTIC TASKS)
Stage 1: Preliminary partial literature review	Phase 1: Identify and become familiar with resources Phase 2: Organize and initially categorize resources Phase 3: Write first draft of literature review
Stage 2: Review and rationalize the first stage	Phase 4: Review and reorganize the analytic workspace
Stage 3: Expand the scope of the literature review	Phase 5: Add additional resources to the analytic workspace Phase 6: Categorize new resources and adjust existing coding scheme
Stage 4: Identify themes in the literature	Phase 7: Recategorization
Stage 5: Rewrite the literature review	Phase 8: Rewrite the literature review
Stage 6: Ongoing expansion of the literature review	Phase 9: Integrate new resources cumulatively

Acknowledgments

I would like to thank my committee members, Dr. Aliki Nicolaides, Dr. Kathryn Roulston, and Dr. Carolyn Jones-Medine, as well as Dr. Trena Paulus at the University of Georgia for their guidance and consideration throughout the course of my research.

References

Boyatzis, R. E. (1998). *Transforming qualitative information: Thematic analysis and code development.* Thousand Oaks, CA: Sage.

Braun, V., & Clarke, V. (2006). Using thematic analysis in psychology. *Qualitative Research in Psychology, 3*(2), 77–101.

Buber, M. (1958). *I and thou* (R. G. Smith, Trans.). New York: Scribner. (Original work published in 1923).

Grbich, C. (2013). *Qualitative data analysis: An introduction.* Thousand Oaks, CA: SAGE.

Mezirow, J. (2012). Learning to think like an adult: Core concepts of transformation theory. In E. Taylor & P. Cranton (Eds.), *The handbook of transformative learning: Theory, research, and practice* (pp. 73–95). San Francisco, CA: Jossey-Bass.

Morgan, W. J., & Guilherme, A. (2012). I and thou: The educational lessons of Martin Buber's dialogue with the conflicts of his times. *Educational Philosophy and Theory, 44*(9), 979–996.

Strauss, A., & Corbin, J. (1998). *Basics of qualitative research: Procedures and techniques for developing grounded theory* (2nd ed.). Newbury Park, CA: Sage.

9

CASE ILLUSTRATION — A DISCOURSE ANALYSIS STUDY

The Construction of Grief in an Online Support Group

Trena M. Paulus and Mary Alice Varga

This chapter and the accompanying videos illustrate a real-world discourse analysis executed in ATLAS.ti. The contributors are Trena M. Paulus, Professor of Qualitative Research Methods and Interdisciplinary Qualitative Studies at the University of Georgia, and Mary Alice Varga, an Assistant Professor at The University of West Georgia. We asked Drs. Paulus and Varga to contribute this case because of their long experience with discourse analysis, with teaching qualitative methods, and with using and teaching ATLAS.ti.

The purpose of the chapter is to provide the context for the ANALYTIC TASKS that are referred to in the video demonstrations. The first section of the chapter—"Analytic Strategies"—contains the objectives and guiding methodology of the project, that is, Level 1 of the Five-Level QDA method. The second section—"Stages of the Analysis"—is Level 2, the analytic plan, which unfolds in four stages, including the generation of ANALYTIC TASKS at each stage. This is the point at which Level 3 begins, that is, TRANSLATING the ANALYTIC TASKS into software operations. Each stage is demonstrated in a separate video and includes dialogue with Trena and Mary Alice about the pros and cons of possible alternative choices for fulfilling the analytic plan using ATLAS.ti. To view a video after reading a stage, please go to www.routledgetextbooks.com/textbooks/5LQDA and follow the on-screen instructions.

Trena and Mary Alice started their project using ATLAS.ti 6 and halfway through upgraded to 7 in which they completed the analysis. We have converted their project to ATLAS.ti 8, which led to no changes in process or procedure, except for changing the names of the COMPONENTS to their ATLAS.ti 8 names. To avoid confusion for readers who have not used ATLAS.ti 6 or ATLAS.ti 7, we have used the ATLAS.ti 8 names for COMPONENTS even when discussing ATLAS.ti 6 or ATLAS.ti 7 operations.

Now we turn over the chapter to Trena and Mary Alice.

Project in Brief

A growing number of grieving individuals seek out online support, and it is therefore important for those in the grief counseling field to understand what is happening in these virtual spaces and how they provide support to the bereaved. We were interested in how grief is socially constructed through talk in online environments, and we analyzed a selection of posts to an online support group to do so. Our analysis focused on the discourses evident in the posts and how newcomers and established members of the group negotiate membership. First we analyzed initial posts by newcomers to the group to identify how they displayed their eligibility for membership. Then we examined the first responses to the initial posts to understand how newcomers' bids for membership were taken up by current members of the group. The discursive focus of our analysis sheds light on how online communities respond to the newly bereaved and provides insight into how "normal" bereavement is negotiated in these environments. The project resulted in the publication of two articles: Varga and Paulus (2014) and Paulus and Varga (2015).

Analytic Strategies

We have presented the context for the case illustration in two sections—"Overall Objectives," a brief discussion of our overarching purpose in conducting the study, and "Guiding Methodology," in which we discuss the nature and purpose of discourse analysis, our overall approach to the data analysis, and the broad and more specific research questions that sensitized the analysis.

Overall Objectives

Our overarching objective was to understand how "grief" is constructed in online support groups, and to explore this topic we decided to analyze posts to one public support group with several different forums for different types of grief. The project objectives became more focused as the study evolved. Initially our objective was to better understand how group members support each other in these online groups. We became particularly interested in how first-time posters introduced themselves to the group because we found the way they described their grief to be quite interesting. We then refocused the study to concentrate on the initial posts newcomers made to just one forum, which concerns the loss of a spouse or significant other. This resulted in the publication of the first article: Varga and Paulus (2014). We then extended our analysis to focus on the first response to each initial post in the same forum, which resulted in the publication of the second article: Paulus and Varga (2015). This analysis provided further insight into the social construction of grief and highlights how online grief discourse deviates from grief discourse in the offline world.

Guiding Methodology

The study was a discourse analysis of posts to an online grief support group undertaken by two researchers. It was grounded in a social constructionist stance in which online support groups are considered spaces where grief is constructed through persistent conversations. We took a discursive psychology perspective, which assumes "talk is action" (Edwards & Potter, 1992), and this provided a theoretical framework and methodological procedures for investigating the phenomenon of grief in online environments. Discourse analysis is an interpretive methodology in which claims are warranted through criteria of trustworthiness and soundness, such as keeping a detailed audit trail and demonstrating the analysis for the reader through the reanalysis of the data in the findings section. We focused on how the posts were constructed, analyzing for patterns and themes related to our interest in the construction of grief.

The online support group was publicly visible, not requiring membership to view posts, and users are explicitly made aware of the public nature of their posts. Our Institutional Review Board (IRB) did not consider the study to constitute human subjects research, and so we were exempt from review, and because the site is in the public domain we did not need to seek informed consent. However, as the study progressed we faced ethical dilemmas about the appropriateness of analyzing this type of data, regardless of the stance of the IRB. Although we do not discuss these ethical dilemmas here, we have presented on this topic (Paulus & Varga, 2013), and the ethics of research in online grief and bereavement practices continues to be one of Dr. Vargas's areas of scholarship.

We took a collaborative and iterative approach to the analysis. We identified discursive features in the posts and generated interpretations of what the discursive features accomplished through the following steps:

- Repeated readings
- Selection, organization, and identification of patterns of discursive features
- Generation of explanations of what the features were accomplishing
- Reflexive and transparent documentation of claims through a reworking of the analysis

We undertook the analysis in separate ATLAS.ti-PROJECTS and met regularly to review posts and record and discuss our developing interpretations. The following questions sensitized our analytic process:

- What are the participants doing/accomplishing with their language? Specifically, when the study was focused on the posts from a single forum, how do newcomers make bids for membership, and how are these bids for membership being taken up by current members?
- How are they constructing their language in order to achieve this? Specifically, how are the initial posts and responses constructed in order to do this?
- What discursive resources are being used to perform these tasks?

Stages of the Analysis

We conducted the study from 2011 to 2013, and the analytic plan evolved as the work progressed. In terms of the *Five-Level QDA* method there were four stages of analysis, with each stage planned in light of the previous stage based on our developing understanding of the discursive features present and how they were being used. The four stages reflect turning points in the progress of the project, and we named the stages after the fact when reflecting on the process for this chapter.

We refocused the project in the second stage in response to feedback from reviewers to an article reporting our findings that we submitted to a journal at the end of the first stage. This resulted in narrowing our focus to consider in more detail the initial posts to only one forum: loss of a spouse or significant other. The four stages are listed in Table 9.1. The stages and the phases of analysis within each stage are illustrated in Figure 9.1.

TABLE 9.1 The four stages of analysis

Stages of the project (one video on the companion website for each stage)	Description of analytic activities
First Stage: Discourse analysis of initial posts to seven grief forums, each referring to a specific type of loss	Literature review and initial readings to identify the analytic focus, followed by several iterative cycles of in-depth readings and the selection, organization, and identification of patterns of discursive features to build and write-up an interpretation.
Second Stage: Refocus project to a single forum referring to one type of loss	Construction of a data set of threads to the forum that focused on "loss of a spouse, partner or significant other."
Third Stage: Discourse analysis of initial posts to the single forum	The analysis methods of the first stage were applied to all threads of the single forum. The findings were consistent with the first stage and were also extended and led to a published article.
Fourth Stage: Discourse analysis of first replies to initial posts to the single forum	The analysis methods of the first stage were extended to additional data, that is, to the first replies to newcomers' initial posts. Additionally, more of the analysis was performed within ATLAS.ti, including the merging of our individual atlas.ti-projects rather than comparing and interpreting our findings outside the program.

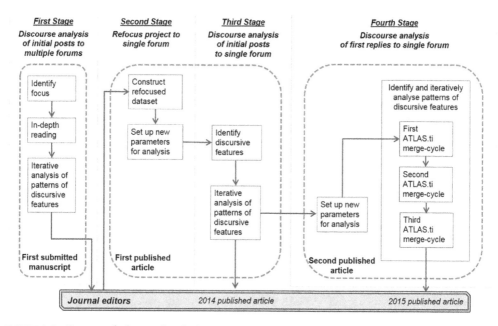

FIGURE 9.1 Stages and phases of analysis

First Stage: Discourse Analysis of Initial Posts to Multiple Forums

We began by undertaking a paper-based review of the literature on online support groups. The aim was to understand what is known about how such online groups provide unique kinds of support for those with, for example, rare medical conditions, stigmatized mental health conditions, and prolonged grief. We sought to understand how these groups had been studied in the past. We then familiarized ourselves with the content of one online grief support group by reading through recent posts and replies to the seven different online forums and making notes about what was being said. Each forum focused on a different type of loss—for example, loss of a parent or grandparent, loss of a sibling or twin, loss of a friend, loss of a pet, or loss of a spouse or significant other. As a result of reading and making notes we decided to focus on how loss is described by those posting in the forums. We planned to accomplish this by analyzing a selection of threads in all seven forums, taking a discursive psychology approach to analysis grounded in the view of grief as socially and discursively produced.

Our use of ATLAS.ti began at the point that we had identified the threads for analysis. During this stage we were using ATLAS.ti 6. We selected the 70 most recent threads from the seven forums and cut and pasted each thread from the website—consisting of the initial post and all the replies—into a separate internal DOCUMENT within ATLAS.ti, pasting the URL at the top of each DOCUMENT so we could easily access the original content from within the software. When all the data were within ATLAS.ti, we copied the ATLAS.ti-PROJECT so that each of us had a copy with all of the data to work on. Throughout this stage we worked separately on the data, each within our own ATLAS.ti-PROJECT, and met regularly to discuss our interpretations and plans for continuing the analysis.

We initially used the Word Cruncher feature to explore the content within and across the threads. Although this provided us with insight into the individual words that were used more or less frequently, it was not helpful in informing our thinking about the discursive features of the posts because individual words are only an indicator of content, not the structure of the talk. At the time ATLAS.ti did not include Key Word In Context functionality, meaning that we could not directly access the context within which frequent or infrequent words were used. We therefore abandoned this way of exploring the threads and reverted to a close reading of each thread in its entirety, as we had been doing before we added the material to ATLAS.ti. We each re-read the threads, this time making notes within ATLAS.ti to record our insights about what was discursively happening. These rounds of initial readings prepared "the way for a much more intensive study of material culled through the selective coding process" (Potter & Wetherell, 1987, p. 167). These initial readings led us to focus only on the initial posts rather than all the posts in each thread, to consider how newcomers establish and negotiate membership to the group.

We did not split the data to each work separately on just some data, but both separately analyzed all of the initial posts to each thread, going through several iterative cycles of coding, annotating, and writing about what we were seeing. In each cycle we separately analyzed the same set of approximately 30 initial posts. We met regularly throughout this process to discuss and identify what we came to view as the regularity and variability across the initial posts. We were each working on separate ATLAS.ti-PROJECTS, and during this stage we did not combine our work within the software by merging the ATLAS.ti-PROJECTS, but combined our separate work outside ATLAS. ti by showing each other what we had been doing, discussing the posts, and then making changes individually to each of our separate ATLAS.ti-PROJECTS. At this stage, therefore, we were using the software primarily to manage the process rather than to integrate our analysis, and our use of ATLAS.ti was straightforward. For example, we created one free QUOTATION for the full text of each of the 70 initial posts and linked CODES that were named to represent the interesting features we were identifying to all those QUOTATIONS where those features were present. We wrote notes about what we thought was going on in the initial posts using MEMOS.

This repeated process led us to iteratively identify what we called "discursive features" in the initial posts and to form tentative explanations as to what these various features were doing. A discursive feature is language that is used to enact a particular function, such as telling stories to display empathy. The final phase of this stage was to write up a detailed description of our analysis process and to demonstrate how we had derived the claims we were reporting. This involved several rounds of writing, in which we would meet to discuss the discursive features, each go off and write up an interpretation, swap our work, and edit each other's interpretation, continually moving back to the data to ground our claims. This process resulted in us condensing the eight discursive features we had identified into a four-part pattern, which reflected how newcomers were making a bid for membership to the group.

As is typical in discourse analysis studies, our findings are not organized by themes or by a description of what is being said, but instead focus on how language choices and discursive resources are used to accomplish specific tasks. We demonstrate our findings by presenting "one or more discourse excerpts, followed by their detailed analysis" (Wood & Kroger, 2000, p. 183) and by "going through the excerpt in detail in order to show how a claim is grounded" (p. 184)—in essence reproducing the analysis for the reader. In this way, our interpretive claims (the findings) are warranted by reworking the analysis of representative excerpts to show the reader what the language is doing, rather than by providing multiple examples. The reader then can decide whether or not she agrees with the analysts' interpretations.

This first stage culminated in an article submitted to a journal on how grief is constructed in an online support group. This stage of the project contained nine ANALYTIC TASKS. For ease of presentation in Table 9.2 and in the video demonstrations, we have grouped these ANALYTIC TASKS into three analysis phases. Figures 7.2 and 7.3, pp. 149–150, review the format and numbering system for stages, phases, and ANALYTIC TASKS. Note that bullet points in italics do not involve the use of ATLAS.ti.

TABLE 9.2 First Stage (Phases 1–3): Discourse analysis of initial posts to seven grief forums, each referring to a specific type of loss

Phase 1: Identify analytic focus	
1-A	*Review the literature*
	• We reviewed the relevant literature, focusing on methodologies and analytic focus of previous studies into online support groups, grief, and grief counseling.
1-B	*Become familiar with online grief forums to generate ideas for analysis*
	• We read posts in the forums of an online grief support group and identified five threads specific to a type of loss to consider in detail.
	• We repeatedly read each thread in detail, noting in a Microsoft Word file potential topics for analysis in relation to previous research.
1-C	*Reflect on data familiarization and plan analysis*
	• We discussed the ideas generated in 1-B and decided to focus on how loss is described by those posting in the forums.
	• We identified 10 initial posts from the seven forums that were specific to type of loss.
Phase 2: In-depth readings of initial posts	
2-A	*Create an analytic workspace to store discussion threads (initial posts and comments)*
	• We created and saved an ATLAS.ti-PROJECT
	• We created and named an empty DOCUMENT within the ATLAS.ti-PROJECT for each initial post and pasted the threads into them from the website.
2-B	*Become familiar with initial posts at a high level*
	• We counted all the words used in the DOCUMENTS, using the Word Cruncher feature.
2-C	*Repeatedly read and review posts to capture discursive features*
	• We read each post and made notes in MEMOS about the patterns and variation we saw.
	• We created QUOTATIONS out of passages that we found striking and surprising, and linked them to CODES that were named to reflect our thinking about the data.
	• We added COMMENTS to CODED-QUOTATIONS explaining why they were note-worthy.
	• We met regularly to review our work and to jointly reflect on the content of the posts. After each meeting we repeated the process, completing several cycles of reading, reviewing, and coding.
Phase 3: Select, organize, and identify patterns of discursive features	
3-A	*Identify patterns of discursive features*
	• In light of our joint reflections we re-read each post in its entirety and reflected on the CODES we had applied.
	• We re-read the MEMOS and COMMENTS we had previously written and added to our memos to draw out patterns and discursive features.
3-B	*Generate explanations and evidence them with data*
	• We identified the QUOTATIONS that had been most heavily written about in MEMOS and COMMENTS and linked to the CODES that related to discursive features identified in 3-A.
	• We retrieved these CODED-QUOTATIONS and reviewed them. As part of this interpretive process we collapsed the eight discursive features into a four-part pattern used by participants to construct their initial posts.
3-C	*Write up and illustrate our claims*
	• We outputted these CODED-QUOTATIONS, and in a Microsoft Word file we described and interpreted what was going on in the data in relation to the four-part pattern we identified in 3-B.
	• We reviewed each other's descriptions and edited them until we were in agreement about the interpretation.
	• We subsumed the write-up into an article, which was submitted to a journal.

Second Stage: Refocus Project to a Single Forum Referring to One Type of Loss

In the second stage we refocused our study in response to journal reviewers' comments to the article we had submitted at the end of the first stage. This involved focusing on the initial posts to just one of the forums on the online support group—the forum that involved discussion about the loss of a spouse, partner, or significant other. The rationale was to develop an interpretation of the discursive features employed by all newcomers to a forum on one type of loss, rather than to consider a sample of initial posts by newcomers to forums about a range of different types of loss, as we had done in the first stage. We chose this forum because it was most prolific at the time, with more threads than any of the other forums discussing different types of loss.

We visited the online support group and downloaded the most recent 107 threads from the forum. We created a new ATLAS.ti-PROJECT and followed the same procedure as in the first stage, cutting and pasting the whole of each thread—the initial post and all the responses—into a separate internal DOCUMENT, pasting the URL at the top of each one.

We decided to use the interpretation we had generated in the first stage to frame the way we would go about analyzing these 107 initial posts. We therefore set up the parameters of the analysis within an ATLAS.ti-PROJECT, this time using ATLAS.ti 7. This involved creating and defining CODES for the eight discursive features we had identified in the first stage and creating a MEMO in order to capture our thinking about any variety in how posts were constructed differently or the discursive features were functioning differently. Identifying patterns as well as variability in how discursive features are deployed is an essential part of discourse analysis approaches. In the same way as we had done previously, we created a free QUOTATION for the full text of each initial post so that we would each be applying all the relevant CODES to the whole of each initial post. This simplified the merging of both ATLAS.ti-PROJECTS and facilitated review and comparison of our individual coding.

We intended to undertake the analysis in the same way as we had done for the first stage in terms of both of us working on all of the posts separately and meeting regularly to discuss the analysis. However, we decided to use ATLAS.ti from this point in a more systematic way, as we were now more familiar with the software and realized it would be valuable to integrate the work we separately were doing within the software rather than each of us updating our own ATLAS.ti-PROJECT for agreed-on changes as we proceeded. We therefore set up user log-ins so that we would be able to easily track our contributions, and we decided that one of us would be responsible for managing the process of merging the ATLAS.ti-PROJECTS.

Table 9.3 displays this stage of the project, which contains four ANALYTIC TASKS grouped into two analytic phases.

Third Stage: Discourse Analysis of Initial Posts to the Single Forum

This stage involved analyzing the 107 most recent initial posts to the forum on "loss of a spouse, partner or significant other." The analysis process we followed was similar to the first stage, including several iterative cycles of in-depth reading, reflection on, coding, and writing about the posts. We sorted the QUOTATIONS by number of CODES attached to them to identify "rich" threads to do a close analysis of what was happening in those posts, and we met regularly to discuss our interpretations. However, this time we were looking for the discursive features we had identified in the first stage within the initial posts, and we wrote about the variance we were seeing in how the posts were constructed in the MEMO we had created for this purpose.

TABLE 9.3 Second Stage (Phases 4–5): Refocus project to a single forum referring to one type of loss

Phase 4: Construct a refocused data set	
4-A	Identify data for second-stage analysis • We accessed the online grief support group forum again and identified posts in the forum on "loss of a spouse, partner or significant other." This forum was chosen because it was the most active forum on the site. • We downloaded the 107 most recent threads from this forum.
4-B	Create an analytic workspace to store discussion threads • We created a new master ATLAS.ti-PROJECT and created user profiles and log-in details for each of us. • We created and named an empty DOCUMENT for each thread and pasted the content into them from the website. • We pasted the URL link to the thread at the top of each DOCUMENT to access the original content.
Phase 5: Set up parameters of the analysis	
5-A	Create and define discursive features to be used to analyze threads • We created the eight discursive features identified in the first stage as codes and defined them in CODE-COMMENTS. • We created a "Variable" MEMO in order to capture our thinking about posts that seemed to be constructed differently or functioning differently from other posts. • We created a QUOTATION out of the full text of the first post in each thread so that we would each always be applying CODES to exactly the same unit of meaning.
5-B	Duplicate the analytic workspace for each analyst • We copied the master ATLAS.ti-PROJECT so we each had an exactly the same ATLAS.ti-PROJECT to work on.

This resulted in identifying three additional discursive features that were integrated into the analysis. We also merged our separate ATLAS.ti-PROJECTS from time to time in order to integrate our interpretations before we finalized the analysis and developed a three-part pattern (telling unusual stories of loss, describing uncontrollable emotional and physical states, and troubles-telling) that we then used to write up our findings. The results were consistent with both the first-stage analysis of all seven forums and the existing literature, which served to validate the findings of the first stage.

This stage culminated in submitting an article to a journal, *Death Studies*, on how newcomers construct grief in this online support forum, which was subsequently published (Varga & Paulus, 2014). This stage of the project contained seven ANALYTIC TASKS grouped into two analysis phases as illustrated in Table 9.4.

Fourth Stage: Discourse Analysis of Replies to Initial Posts to the Single Forum

After completing the third stage we wanted to extend our understanding of what was happening in the forums by analyzing how members of the groups replied to the newcomers. Replies to newcomer messages in a group are important in validating them as members and remains an area with little research.

We duplicated the ATLAS.ti-PROJECT we had worked on in the third stage in order to undertake the analysis of the first replies. This meant that we had a record of the completed analysis of the initial posts that we could also use to inform our analysis of the replies. We already had the

TABLE 9.4 Third Stage (Phases 6–7): Discourse analysis of initial posts to the single forum

Phase 6: Identify discursive features in initial posts	
6-A	*Repeatedly read and reflect on all initial posts*
	• We read the initial post to each thread repeatedly and noted in MEMOS and QUOTATION-COMMENTS our thoughts about them.
6-B	*Analyze the initial posts in light of existing and emerging discursive features*
	• We linked the QUOTATIONS created in 5-A to the discursive features CODES created in 5-A.
	• Where we saw other discursive features in the data, we created new CODES and applied them to the same QUOTATIONS.
6-C	*Capture variance in the construction of posts and their discursive functioning*
	• QUOTATIONS for posts that were differently constructed or functioned differently than others were linked to the "Variable" MEMO.
6-D	*Combine team members' work*
	• We merged our two ATLAS.ti-PROJECTS several times throughout the process.
6-E	*Reflect on and refine analysis*
	• We retrieved the CODED-QUOTATIONS linked to each CODE in the merged ATLAS.ti-PROJECT, and we discussed the new CODES created in 5-A and defined them in CODE-COMMENTS.
	• We merged CODES created in our separate ATLAS.ti-PROJECTS that represented the same discursive features.
	• We reviewed the CODE-COMMENTS of all the CODES and refined them to ensure the definitions were accurate and precise. This process resulted in 11 CODES.
Phase 7: Select, organize, and identify patterns of discursive features	
7-A	*Prioritize the discursive features evident in the patterns*
	• We sorted the CODES list by number of CODED-QUOTATIONS to see which discursive features were most prevalent.
	• We reviewed CODED-QUOTATIONS at each of the most prevalent CODES.
	• We condensed the 11 discursive features CODES into a three-part pattern of the posts.
7-B	*Write up and illustrate our claims*
	• We identified the QUOTATIONS that had been most heavily written about in MEMOS and COMMENTS and linked to the greatest number of CODES.
	• We outputted these QUOTATIONS and those linked to the "Variable" MEMO.
	• *In a Microsoft Word file we described and interpreted what was going on in the quotations in relation to the 11 discursive features, including discussing variability from the pattern.*
	• *We reviewed each other's descriptions and edited them until we were in agreement about the interpretation.*
	• *We subsumed the write-up into an article, which was submitted to a journal*

first replies in the ATLAS.ti-PROJECT because we had pasted the whole thread to each post into a separate DOCUMENT in the third stage. In the same way as we had done for the initial posts, we created a free QUOTATION for each of the first replies to the thread, to which each of us would attach CODES. In order to distinguish the CODES created for the initial posts from those that we would generate to describe the replies, we colored the codes generated in the third stage blue and added the prefix "INITIAL POSTS" to all of them. We also created a few CODES that represented aspects of the replies that had struck us when familiarizing with the entire threads during the first stage of the project, for example, "Come back," "Extend sympathy," "Validation," and "You are not alone." We created two additional MEMOS: one that outlined our analysis process, so that we would both be following the same procedure, and the other that summarized our findings from the third stage to remind us of our original findings so we could use them to inform our interpretation of the first replies.

We then duplicated the ATLAS.ti-PROJECT and we embarked on the analysis, following a similar process of several iterative cycles as we followed in the first and third stages. However, in this fourth stage we used ATLAS.ti in a more sophisticated way, including cycles of merging our ATLAS.ti-PROJECTS that matched our iterative cycles of analysis. This has allowed us to more easily distinguish the separate analytic activities in each iterative cycle of analysis, and so this fourth stage of the project has a great number of phases and ANALYTIC TASKS.

We separately analyzed the same set of initial replies, approximately 30 replies in each cycle, reading them repeatedly, noting our thoughts in COMMENTS and MEMOS about the patterns and variation in the discursive features used, and creating, defining, and applying new CODES that represented the discursive features as we identified them in the replies. We prefixed the CODES we created during this stage with "REPLY" and colored them purple so we could easily distinguish them from the discursive features identified in analyzing the initial posts. After each cycle of analysis we met to discuss our interpretation, merged our ATLAS.ti-PROJECTS, and integrated our analysis before continuing with the next set of replies.

When we had analyzed all the first replies, we amalgamated all the notes we had taken during our separate analyses and during our meetings and sketched out our preliminary findings. We then decided to investigate the relationship between the nature of the replies in terms of the discursive features evident in them and the status of the individuals posting the replies. This involved revisiting the online forum to identify the status of each person who had replied, that is, whether they were a counselor, a guest, another newcomer, or an advanced member. We then returned to our merged ATLAS.ti-PROJECT and recoded each first reply to indicate the status of the person replying and generated a Co-occurrence Table to see if there were any meaningful differences in patterns of discursive features according to the status of the person replying. Although this co-occurrence analysis did uncover the interesting finding of many more replies posted by advanced members, this finding of "who is posting what" ultimately seemed antithetical to the concerns of discourse analysis and did not inform our main focus, which was the discursive features used in the replies to the newcomer posts. We therefore discarded this line of inquiry and returned to consider patterns of discursive features across the replies more generally. We ultimately created three CODE-GROUPS—"status of poster," "initial post codes," and "reply codes"—to organize the 33 discursive features CODES. This was in order to more easily navigate through the growing CODE list, but also to possibly run queries of how the poster's status was related to the replies.

At this point we followed a similar process to the first and third stages, sorting the QUOTATIONS by number of CODES attached to them to identify "rich" threads to do a close analysis of what was happening in those posts. The findings of this stage of the study were centered on showing how discursive features constructed validation and empathy through second stories, constructed grief through descriptions, and accepted bids for membership through giving advice and invitations to return to the group. This close analysis was done outside of ATLAS.ti, though now we would probably create a new ATLAS.ti-PROJECT, create new QUOTATIONS within the post, and pull them into a NETWORK view to illustrate the patterns.

This stage culminated in submitting a second article for publication, again to *Death Studies*, on how established members to an online forum respond to newcomers, which was subsequently published (Paulus & Varga, 2015). This stage of the project contained 17 ANALYTIC TASKS grouped into five analysis phases, as displayed in Table 9.5.

TABLE 9.5 Fourth Stage (Phases 8–12): Discourse analysis of first replies to a single forum

---

Phase 8: Set up the parameters of the analysis

8-A	*Prepare the analytic workspace for analyzing replies*
	• We duplicated the third-stage ATLAS.ti-PROJECT.
	• We created a QUOTATION out of each first reply to each thread.
	• We added the prefix "INITIAL POSTS" to all the CODES we had used in the second stage.
	• We created and defined CODES representing features we anticipated seeing in the replies.
	• We created a MEMO that documented our intended procedure for this stage of analysis.
	• We created a MEMO to record the results of the analysis of initial posts. Into this memo we pasted our findings from 7-B.
8-B	*Duplicate the analytic workspace*
	• We copied the ATLAS.ti-PROJECT so each of us had exactly the same structures in which to work.

Phase 9: First ATLAS.ti merge cycle of discourse analysis of replies

9-A	*Repeatedly read and reflect on first replies*
	• We read each of the first replies to the initial posts to each thread repeatedly and noted in MEMOS and QUOTATION-COMMENTS our thoughts about them.
9-B	*Analyze first set of replies for existing and emerging discursive features*
	• In our separate copies of the ATLAS.ti-PROJECT we each started coding the FREE-QUOTATIONS created in 8-A to the CODES that represented the discursive features we were interested in.
	• Where we saw other discursive features in the data, we created new CODES and applied them to the same QUOTATIONS.
	• As we read each post we made notes in separate variability MEMOS about patterns and variations we were seeing and coded the QUOTATIONS that we found striking and surprising.
9-C	*Combine analysis of first set of replies*
	• After we had each completed 9-B across the first set of replies (approximately 30 replies), we merged our two ATLAS.ti-PROJECTS to create one ATLAS.ti-PROJECT, which contained the coding we had each done so far.
9-D	*Reflect on and refine analysis*
	• We added the prefix "REPLY:" in order to distinguish the CODES created for the initial posts from those that we generated to code the replies. We also color-coded all initial posts CODES blue and reply CODES purple so that we could visually distinguish the two in the data.
	• We created CODE-GROUPS for the initial post codes and reply post codes in order to better organize them.
	• We discussed our coding processes and reviewed our separate coding by retrieving CODED-QUOTATIONS linked to each CODE.
	• We merged new CODES we had each created in our separate ATLAS.ti-PROJECTS that represented the same discursive features.
	• We defined the CODES using COMMENTS.

Phase 10: Second ATLAS.ti merge cycle of discourse analysis of replies

10-A	*Duplicate the refined analytic workspace*
	• We copied the ATLAS.ti-PROJECT we refined in 9-D so we each had a separate version we could continue working on separately.
10-B	*Analyze second set of replies to existing and emerging discursive features*
	• In our separate copies of the ATLAS.ti-PROJECT we coded the next set of replies (approximately 38) to the QUOTATIONS created in 8-A to the CODES that represented the discursive features we were interested in.
	• Where we saw other discursive features in the data, we created new CODES and applied them to the same QUOTATIONS.
	• As we read each post we made notes in memos about patterns and variations we were seeing and coded the QUOTATIONS that we found striking and surprising.
10-C	*Combine analysis on second set of replies*
	• After we had each completed 10-B across the second set of replies, we merged our two ATLAS.ti-PROJECTS to create one ATLAS.ti-PROJECT, which contained the coding we had each done so far.

TABLE 9.5 (Continued)

10-D	*Reflect on and refine our analysis*
	• We discussed our coding processes and reviewed our separate coding by retrieving CODED-QUOTATIONS linked to each CODE. • We merged new CODES we had each created in our separate ATLAS.ti-PROJECTS that represented the same discursive features. • We defined the CODES using COMMENTS.

Phase 11: Third ATLAS.ti merge cycle of discourse analysis of replies

11-A	*Duplicate the refined master analytic workspace*
	• We copied the ATLAS.ti-PROJECT we refined in 10-D so we each had a separate version we could continue working on separately.
11-B	*Analyze third set of replies to existing and emerging discursive features*
	• In our separate copies of the ATLAS.ti-PROJECT, we coded the next set of replies (approximately 38) to the QUOTATIONS created in 8-A to the CODES that represented the discursive features we were interested in. • Where we saw other discursive features in the data, we created new CODES and applied them to the same QUOTATIONS. • As we read each post we made notes in MEMOS about patterns and variations we were seeing and coded the QUOTATIONS that we found striking and surprising.
11-C	*Combine analysis on third set of replies*
	• After we had each completed 11-B across the third second of replies we merged our two ATLAS.ti-PROJECTS to create one ATLAS.ti-PROJECT that contained the coding we had each done so far.
11-D	*Reflect on and refine our coding*
	• We discussed our coding processes and reviewed our separate coding by retrieving CODED-QUOTATIONS linked to each CODE. • We merged new CODES we had each created in our separate ATLAS.ti-PROJECTS that represented the same discursive features. • We defined the CODES using COMMENTS. • We reviewed the COMMENTS of all the CODES and refined them to ensure the definitions were accurate and precise.

Phase 12: Select, organize, and identify patterns of discursive features

12-A	*Interrogate the relationship between post authors and kind of replies*
	• We identified the status of post authors from the website and created CODES to represent author status (Contributor, Guest, Counselor, Advanced Members, Guest, New Visitor). • We prefixed these CODES with "STATUS" and colored them red. • We created a CODE-GROUP for "STATUS." • We coded every QUOTATION created in 8-A with the relevant status CODE. • We used the Co-occurrence Table to interrogate the status CODES by the reply CODES.
12-B	*Prioritize the discursive features evident in the patterns*
	• We sorted the CODES list by number of CODED-QUOTATIONS to see which discursive features were most prevalent. • We reviewed CODED-QUOTATIONS at each of the most prevalent CODES. • We then condensed the 11 discursive features into a three-part pattern of the posts to report in the findings.
12-C	*Write up and illustrate our claims*
	• We identified the QUOTATIONS that had been most heavily written about in MEMOS and COMMENTS and linked to the greatest number of CODES. • We outputted these quotations and those linked to the "Variable" memo. • *In a Microsoft Word file we described and interpreted what was going on in the quotations in relation to the 11 discursive features, including discussing variability from the pattern.* • *We reviewed each other's descriptions and edited them until we were in agreement about the interpretation.* • *We subsumed the write-up into an article, which was submitted to a journal*

Stakeholders, Published Works, and Funders

We had no external funding for this project. Dr. Mary Alice Varga, Assistant Professor at the University of West Georgia, and Dr. Trena M. Paulus, Professor at the University of Georgia, completed the first three stages of the project while they were both at the University of Tennessee-Knoxville and completed the fourth stage after they had moved to their current institutions. Research design and data collection began in 2011, the publication resulting from the third stage of the study appeared in *Death Studies* in 2014, and the publication resulting from fourth stage of the study appeared in the same journal in 2015.

The dataset and the findings were also used as part of Yawei Shen's master's thesis at the University of Georgia, where she applied a Latent Dirichlet Allocation statistical model and text-mining techniques to ascertain how statistical models and discourse analysis approaches might be complimentary in understanding "big data."

Finally, this study is also serving as one of the primary cases in the forthcoming text by Paulus and Wise, *Researching Learning, Insight and Transformation in Online Talk*, under contract with Routledge.

References

Edwards, D., & Potter, J. (1992). *Discursive psychology*. London, UK: Sage.

Paulus, T. M., & Varga, M. (2013, January). Online groups as research context: Ethical dilemmas. *The Qualitative Report Fourth Annual Conference*. Fort Lauderdale, Florida.

Paulus, T., & Varga, M. (2015). 'Please know that you are not alone with your pain': Community member responses to bids for membership in online grief support groups. *Death Studies*, 39(10), 633–640.

Potter, J., & Wetherell, M. (1987). *Discourse and social psychology*. London, UK: Sage.

Varga, M. A., & Paulus, T. M. (2014). Grieving online: Newcomers' constructions of grief in an online support group. *Death Studies*, 38(7), 443–449.

Wood, L. A., & Kroger, R. O. (2000). *Doing discourse analysis: Methods for studying action in talk and text*. Thousand Oaks, CA: Sage.

Appendices

APPENDIX 1

Three Levels of Detail of Analytic Tasks

Common overly general ways for describing analytic activities	Appropriate level of detail for translation	Overly specific tasks requiring a sequence of similarly over-specific tasks
INTEGRATING Bring all our work together or Show differences in coding	Compare each team member's separate coding of each focus group transcript	Print out all data segments coded by each team member
	Review together the thematic and discursive coding of media representations of local politicians to identify overlaps and connections	Retrieve all the data coded to themes
ORGANIZING Revisit the analytic framework or Reflect on emerging codes in relation to theory	Review and refine codes and the coding scheme	Read names of codes
	Compare theoretical and emerging concepts and explain their similarities and differences	Prepare separate lists of theoretical and emerging concepts
	Refine the initial conceptual framework in light of the themes generated from the data	Prepare a representation of the initial conceptual framework
EXPLORING Find out what's going on in the data or Explore the data with regard to content and meaning	Read interview transcripts to identify potential concepts for coding	Read the first interview
	Search for evocative terms in newspaper articles	Prepare notes on meaning of evocative
	Watch videos of math lessons to identify types of interaction between students and teachers	Sort videos by student–student and student–teacher interaction
	Review field notes to summarize athletes' body language with same- and opposite-gender coaches	Highlight sections of all field notes referring to same-gender coaches
REFLECTING Think about differences in types of interactions or Show connections between concepts	Summarize differences in verbal and nonverbal interactions between doctors and patients	Prepare separate lists of types of verbal and nonverbal interactions
	Create and explain relationships between concepts	List each possible type of relationship
INTERROGATING Show relationships between themes and participants or Find out differences in attitudes expressed	Compare teachers' reactions to different kinds of bullying	Extract data for first teacher's reactions to bullying
	Identify related concepts by investigating co-occurrences among concepts in the data	List all the concepts used in the study
	Interpret media representations of local politicians in relation to attitudes expressed by focus group respondents	Separate media representations of local and nonlocal politicians

APPENDIX 2

Five Analytic Activities

Silver and Lewins (2014) developed a framework of five analytic activities independent of methodology to assist in developing analytic plans that connect a project's objectives with the detailed tasks to be accomplished. It is not a method of analysis to be adopted, as it does not consist of specific action steps. Rather, analytic activities are a high-level guide to thinking through the purposes of each element of a developing analytic plan in relation to other elements. Each activity has two or three dimensions, and Figure A2.1 illustrates the web of connections among the various activities.

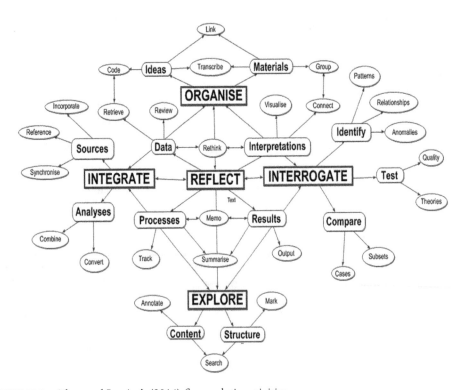

FIGURE A2.1 Silver and Lewins's (2014) five analytic activities

Silver, C., & Lewins, A. (2014). *Using software in qualitative research: A step-by-step guide* (2nd ed.). Thousand Oaks, CA: Sage, p. 45. Reproduced with permission.

The diagram is not a flow chart indicating a fixed sequence of activities, as projects engage in them in different ways, to different extents, and in different sequences. Once the purpose of a specific ANALYTIC TASK has been identified and the task written, it is no longer important which analytic activity it represents, and many ANALYTIC TASKS fulfill aspects of more than one activity. For example, the ANALYTIC TASK in Table 6.1 *Create and explain relationships between codes within categories identified in the literature* may have been the result of a *reflection* activity, but may also involve *organizing* activities. The purpose of the framework is only to stimulate thinking about the purpose and relationship of analytic activities. The following summaries introduce the five activities. For further details and their application to a number of case studies see Silver & Lewins (2014), p. 45.

Integration

The purpose of integration is to combine parts into a whole. This involves bringing together research materials, analytic methods, and the contributions of team members. Integrating materials may involve connecting data files related to the same respondent or setting or to synchronize media data with corresponding transcripts. Integration of methods relates to mixed-methods analyses, which may involve analyzing one dataset using two or more approaches, analyzing different sets of data using different methods, linking qualitative and quantitative data, or representing qualitative analyses numerically. Integration in team projects may involve combining and comparing the analytic contributions of different team members or refining the definitions of concepts used to reflect team members' multiple perspectives to ensure shared understandings.

Organization

The purpose of organization is to arrange something in a systematic or orderly way. This involves sorting data according to similarities and differences based on what is meaningful in relation to the objectives. Organizing may involve ordering similar concepts with a prefixing protocol, organizing a coding scheme hierarchically, or linking concepts to represent their relationships. Notations in transcripts may represent nonverbal hesitations, pauses, etc., or transcripts may be formatted to represent repeated structures, such as topic areas discussed, or track contradictions by linking contradictory statements with a named relationship. Sociodemographic characteristics may be used to group respondents, and metadata such as when social media content was downloaded, who the authors of journal articles are, or when articles were published may be used to organize materials.

Exploration

The purpose of exploration is to examine something in detail. This involves exploring both the content of data and its structure. Regarding the content, exploring may involve identifying surface features, such as counting how often particular words or phrases are used or identifying nonverbal interactions in video recordings. Another purpose looks beyond the surface features to the implicit meaning, such as developing detailed accounts, or "thick descriptions." Exploring may involve familiarization with a large volume of data before commencing analysis, such as by generating a high-level overview of words and phrases in the text. Regarding the structure of data, exploration may involve capturing repeated content, such as discussions about the same topics or responses from the same respondents.

Reflection

The purpose of reflection is to think deeply or carefully. This core activity in qualitative analysis involves thinking deeply about the data, the analytic processes, the interpretations generated, and the results to be presented. Two key reflective activities are writing and generating visualizations.

Reflection on data may involve summarizing or appraising its content by writing analytic notes or drawing diagrams. Regarding analytic processes, reflection may involve recording the progress of the analysis or visually representing the stages of the project or the contributions of different team members. Regarding interpretations, reflection may involve illustrating the validity of an explanation in terms of respondents' accounts. Regarding results, reflection may consider which data extracts are most illustrative or how best to represent an argument graphically.

Interrogation

The purpose of interrogation is to follow up what has already been done. This involves asking questions about, investigating, or visualizing in order to identify patterns, relationships, and anomalies in the data to test hypotheses or to generate theories. Patterns may identify similarities in how respondents discuss an issue or experience, relationships may establish connections within a concept or between respondents' accounts, and anomalies may find counterexamples of what appears to be a general trend or variances in how an event is experienced. Another purpose of interrogating may be to visually represent differences between established thought and what is emerging from a different context or setting.

APPENDIX 3

Examples of Units in Analytic Tasks

Types of units	Definition	Units (with examples of an instance of that unit)
Units of analysis	The entities that are the subject of the analysis. A project commonly has one major unit of analysis and several additional units.	Articles (e.g., a journal paper for a literature review) Artifacts (e.g., a historical document) Documents (e.g., a transcript of an interview) Individuals (e.g., a named respondent) Groups (e.g., a female participant) Organizations (e.g., a hospital) Regions (e.g., a county) Events (e.g., a political meeting) Settings (e.g., a church) Interventions (e.g., a health promotion effort) Programs (e.g., a science curriculum) Etc.
Units of data	The form of the materials or resources that comprise the data. Smaller units of data may be embedded within a larger unit.	Transcripts (e.g., a written record of a research encounter) Field note entry (e.g., a summary of an observed event) Journal articles (e.g., an academic paper on a specific topic) Survey responses (e.g., an answer to an open-ended question) Image (e.g., a participant-generated photograph) Video recording (e.g., a recording of a science class) Video clip (e.g., a segment of a film) Audio recording (e.g., a recording of a focus group discussion) Etc.
Units of meaning— concepts	A concept that is created because it is meaningful in the analysis. Several units of meaning may be identified for different purposes.	Concept (a general unit for all kinds of abstract entities) *Specific conceptual units defined by the methodology, for example:* Topics (e.g., a broad area of discussion) Codes (e.g., an evocative term used in a political speech) Categories (e.g., a group of related evocative terms) Themes (e.g., the persuasive effect of evocative terms across contexts)
Units of meaning— segments of data	Segments of data identified as being meaningful. Several units of meaning may be identified within the same unit of data.	Responses (e.g., an answer to a survey question) Speaker section (e.g., the comment of a respondent in a conversation) Interaction (e.g., a nonverbal communication in a video recording) Post (e.g., a response to a thread in an online discussion forum) Paragraph (e.g., an opening section in a news article) Phrase (e.g., a named theory discussed by scholars) Etc.

APPENDIX 4

Identifying the Units of Analytic Tasks

Analytic task	Units	Discussion of the rule of thumb
EXAMPLES OF INTEGRATING—COMBINING PARTS INTO A WHOLE *Overall purpose is bringing together the elements that make up a research project and thinking about how they relate to one another*		
Compare each team member's separate coding of each focus group transcript	• Team members • Codes • Focus group transcripts	This analytic task conforms to the rule of thumb from an analytic perspective, having one unit of analysis (*codes*) and one unit of data (*focus group transcripts*). However, the task requires three units because *team members* must be an additional unit for translation purposes in order to track each member's contribution in the software for comparing their work when the ATLAS.ti-PROJECTS are merged. Put another way, *team members* are not units at the strategy levels of the analytic plan, but they are units at the tactics levels of harnessing the software.
Review together the thematic and discursive coding of media representations of local politicians to identify overlaps and connections	• Thematic and discursive codes • Media representations	Two units jump out of the analytic task and conform to the rule of thumb. The context of the study is the media representations of local politicians' attitudes to a contentious issue (Brexit) in relation to the attitudes of local residents whom they represent to the same issue, captured in the focus groups. *Thematic and discursive codes* are units of meaning, and *media representations* are units of data. However, once units have been identified, the types of unit are no longer relevant for continuing the translation process.
EXAMPLES OF ORGANIZING—CREATING STRUCTURES RELATED TO OBJECTIVES *Overall purpose is creating structures that reflect meaningful aspects of the data in relation to project objectives*		
Review and refine codes and the coding scheme	• Codes • Coding scheme	Conforms to the rule of thumb, but we might prefer to think about *codes* and *coding scheme* as one unit if the purpose of the codes and the coding scheme are the same. We cannot know this without knowing the purpose of the analytic task.
Compare theoretical and emerging concepts and explain their similarities and differences	• Concept	Note that even though this analytic task has but a single unit for purposes of translation, it is by no means a straightforward task. The number of units affects the ease or complication of the translation process—the tactics—but has no bearing on the sophistication of the analytic activity—the strategies.
Refine the initial conceptual framework in light of the themes generated from the data	• Theme	As in the earlier example, this analytic task has a single unit for purposes of translation, but it is by no means a straightforward task.

Analytic task	Units	Discussion of the rule of thumb
EXAMPLES OF **EXPLORING**—*EXAMINING THE CONTENT AND STRUCTURE OF THE DATA* *Overall purpose is considering the inherent nature of data*		
Read interview transcripts to identify potential concepts for coding	• Interview transcripts • Potential concepts	Two units jump out of the analytic task and conform to the rule of thumb. *Interview transcripts* are units of data, and *potential concepts* are units of meaning. Now that these have been identified as units, the types of unit are no longer relevant for continuing the translation process.
Search newspaper articles for the use of evocative terms	• Newspaper articles • Evocative terms	Two units jump out of the analytic task and conform to the rule of thumb. *Newspaper articles* are units of data, and *evocative terms* are units of meaning. Now that these have been identified as units, the types of unit are no longer relevant for continuing the translation process.
Watch videos of math lessons to identify types of interactions between students and teachers	• Videos of math lessons • Types of interactions • Students • Teachers	This analytic task has four units, twice as many as the rule of thumb suggests. We could split the analytic task into two separate tasks—*watch videos of math lessons to identify types of interaction*, which contains the first two units, and *identify types of interaction between students and teachers*, which contains the last three. To bring this second task down to two units we could think of students and teachers as instances of a single unit—*participants*. Judging the wisdom of doing this comes with experience, depending on what we anticipate may come later. If students and teachers are expected to be analyzed in similar ways in future analytic tasks, considering them as instances of the single unit *participants* should be unproblematic. But if students and teachers are independent elements in other research questions or subquestions, then translating them as a single unit may not be the best way to go. Splitting the task may simplify translation, but it comes at a cost. It means identifying *types of interaction* first without regard to *students* and *teachers* and then going back to identify each type in relation to *students* and *teachers*. This is both cumbersome and implies easy separation of types of interaction from the people who are interacting. It may be best to think of these two dimensions at the same time as described in the original analytic task with four units and not worry about the slightly more involved translation. Thinking in this way might give you another idea. If it is unproblematic to think of students and teachers as instances of one unit—*participants*—then the original analytic task has only three units, not four. Maybe that is the best solution.
Review field notes to summarize athletes' body language with same- and opposite-gender coaches	• Field notes • Athletes • Body language	This analytic task has three units. *Field notes* are a unit of data because this is the form in which the data are stored; thus, it needs to be a unit for translation. The question is whether *athletes* and their *body language* are really two ways of expressing the same unit. This depends on the context—the objectives, methodology, and analytic plan. If the study is about self-identity in professional athletics, then *athletes* are the main entity of interest and would be a unit of analysis. Body language would be another unit, a unit of meaning. But if the study is about the meaning of different styles of body language in professional athletics, then the unit *body language* would be the main unit of analysis, and this analytic task might have only two units—*field notes* and *body language*—and the analytic task might better be expressed as *review field notes to summarize participants' body language*. Whether *athletes* would become a unit of a later analytic task is unknown at this point.

(Continued)

Analytic task	Units	Discussion of the rule of thumb
*EXAMPLES OF **REFLECTING**—CONSIDERING CAREFULLY AND DEEPLY* *Overall purpose is recording analytic insights and what is going on in the project*		
Summarize differences in verbal and nonverbal interaction between doctors and patients	• Interaction • Respondents	At first sight this analytic task could be considered as having four units—verbal interaction, nonverbal interaction, doctors, and patients. But the verbal/nonverbal distinction and the doctor/patient distinction refer to the action that will be taken, that is, summarizing differences. Unless the analytic plan suggests otherwise, verbal interactions and nonverbal interactions are instances of one unit that will be compared—interactions—and similarly for doctors and patients.
Create and explain relationships between concepts	• Relationships • Concepts	Two units jump out of the analytic task and conform to the rule of thumb. *Relationships* and *concepts* are units of meaning. Now that these have been identified as units, the types of unit are no longer relevant for continuing the translation process.
*EXAMPLES OF **INTERROGATING**—FOLLOWING UP WHAT HAS BEEN DONE* *Overall purpose is asking questions about data and the work we have done so far*		
Compare teachers' reactions to different kinds of bullying	• Teacher • Reactions • Kinds of bullying	This analytic task has three units, but is clearly not amenable to being split into two separate tasks. Reducing to two units requires thinking about whether any pair of these three units is really a single unit for the purposes of translation. As in the previous examples, this would depend on whether *teacher* is a unit of analysis in the study independent of the teachers' *reactions* to different types of bullying or whether they are a single unit. A similar issue is whether *reactions* to bullying and concepts about *kinds of bullying* are best represented as a single unit of meaning, or whether in subsequent analytic tasks they will have different purposes and require two units. How do we know all this from the analytic task as written? We don't. We know it from the analytic plan, which is conveniently displayed for reference in the ANALYTIC PLANNING WORKSHEET and that indicates the purpose of each analytic task.
Identify related concepts by investigating co-occurrences in the data	• Concepts • Data	This analytic task may seem to be at too broad a level of detail because the types of concept and data are not specified. But an analytic task is at the most helpful level of detail for translation purposes when the task naturally leads to the next task. In this example we know that the analytic plan requires finding out if there are related concepts and, if so, which they are, in order to then generate a more specific analytic task. In practice (rather than out of context in this table), this would be known from the ANALYTIC PLANNING WORKSHEET, which indicates what has gone before and what is anticipated to come next.
Interpret media representations of local politicians in relation to attitudes expressed by focus group respondents	• Media representations • Attitudes • Focus group respondents	The final example further illustrates the role of purpose in identifying units of analytic tasks. This task has three units, and the issue concerns media representations. The context of the study is the *media representations* of local politicians' attitudes to a contentious issue (Brexit) in relation to the attitudes of local residents whom they represent to the same issue, captured in the focus groups. Media representations are units of data, such as newspaper articles and online news clips, to be translated to components of the software. However, the purpose of the analytic task is to interpret these representations. These interpretations are concepts in the study to be translated to software components, but the interpretations are not units of the task. They are actions embodied in the purpose of the task. Therefore, although translation is always based on the units of the task, in some cases it is also based on the purpose of the task.

APPENDIX 5

Identifying the Purpose of Analytic Tasks

Analytic task	Purpose	Discussion of the rule of thumb
EXAMPLES OF INTEGRATING—COMBINING PARTS INTO A WHOLE *Overall purpose is bringing together the elements that make up a research project and thinking about how they relate to one another*		
Compare each team member's separate coding of each focus group transcript	One purpose: • To compare the coding undertaken separately by different team members	This analytic task conforms to the rule of thumb of containing one purpose. The action employed to fulfill the purpose is not evident in the way the task has been written, leaving us open to consider different ways of accomplishing the task.
Review together the thematic and discursive coding of media representations of local politicians to identify overlaps and connections	One purpose: • To identify overlaps and connections in the different types of coding	At first glance it may appear that this analytic task has two purposes: to review coding and to identify overlaps and connections between different types of coding. But the purpose of the task, why it is being undertaken, is to identify, and this is accomplished by reviewing the coding. Therefore, this ANALYTIC TASK, although complex because it has several elements, conforms to the rule of thumb.
EXAMPLES OF ORGANIZING—CREATING STRUCTURES RELATED TO OBJECTIVES *Overall purpose is imposing structures that reflect meaningful aspects of the data in relation to project objectives*		
Review and refine codes and the coding scheme	Two purposes: • To look at the codes that have already been created to check they are useful (review) • To make any necessary changes to the codes or their position in the coding scheme (refine)	If we stuck to the rule of thumb of only one purpose, we would have to split this analytic task into two: a) review the codes and coding scheme, and b) refine the codes and coding scheme. We could certainly do this, and we could translate each separate task with no problem. However, this would involve first reviewing the codes to decide what all the required changes are and then going back to make those changes as a separate activity. In practice this is not how people work—when we see a needed change we make it there and then. It therefore makes sense in this case to violate the rule of thumb and keep both purposes within one analytic task.

(Continued)

Analytic task	Purpose	Discussion of the rule of thumb
Compare theoretical and emerging concepts, and explain their similarities and differences	Two purposes: • To compare concepts • To explain the similarities and differences that are found	If we stuck to the rule of thumb of only one purpose, we would have to split this ANALYTIC TASK in two: a) compare theoretical and emerging concepts to identify similarities and differences, and b) explain the similarities and differences identified between theoretical and emerging concepts. As in the previous example this would separate activities that naturally happen together. In comparing the concepts we would identify the similarities and differences, and thus these insights would be at the forefront of our mind. To place them to one side would not only cost us time but also risk losing those valuable insights. This is therefore another example of when violating the rule of thumb is appropriate.
Refine the initial conceptual framework in light of the themes generated from the data	One purpose: • To refine the conceptual framework	This analytic task conforms to the rule of thumb of only one purpose. The action to fulfill the purpose is not evident in the way the task has been written, leaving us open to consider different ways of accomplishing the task.

EXAMPLES OF **EXPLORING**—EXAMINING THE CONTENT AND STRUCTURE OF THE DATA
Overall purpose is considering the inherent nature of data

Read interview transcripts to identify potential concepts for coding	One purpose: • To identify concepts that may be potential candidates for coding interview transcripts	This analytic task conforms to the rule of thumb of only one purpose. The way the task is written indicates that the purpose will be accomplished through the action of reading each interview transcript.
Search newspaper articles for the use of evocative terms	One purpose: • To find terms within newspaper articles that can be considered evocative.	This analytic task conforms to the rule of thumb of only one purpose. The way the task is written indicates that the purpose will be accomplished through the action of searching.
Watch videos of math lessons to identify types of interactions between students and teachers	One purpose: • To identify how students and teachers interact during math lessons	This analytic task conforms to the rule of thumb of only one purpose. The way the task is written indicates that the purpose will be accomplished through the action of watching.
Review field notes to summarize athletes' body language with same- and opposite-gender coaches	One purpose: • To summarize parts of field notes relating to body language	This analytic task conforms to the rule of thumb of containing one purpose. The way the task is written indicates that the purpose will be accomplished through the action of reviewing field notes and then writing summaries about body language.

Analytic task	Purpose	Discussion of the rule of thumb
EXAMPLES OF **REFLECTING**—*CONSIDERING CAREFULLY AND DEEPLY* *Overall purpose is recording analytic insights what is going on in the project*		
Summarize differences in verbal and nonverbal interactions between doctors and patients	One purpose: • To summarize identified differences	This analytic task conforms to the rule of thumb of only one purpose. The action to be employed to fulfill the purpose is not evident in the way the task has been written, leaving us open to consider different ways of accomplishing the task.
Create and explain relationships between concepts	Two purposes: • To create relationships between concepts • To explain why these relationships are meaningful	If we stuck to the rule of thumb of only one purpose, we would have to split this analytic task into two: a) create relationships between concepts, and b) explain relationships between concepts. We could certainly do this and translate each separate task without difficulty, but in practice this would be cumbersome. While creating the relationships we would necessarily be thinking about the nature of the relationships, and postponing the explanation would be inefficient—the purpose of explanation is inseparable from the purpose of creation. It therefore makes sense in this case to violate the rule of thumb and keep both purposes within one analytic task
EXAMPLES OF **INTERROGATING**—*FOLLOWING UP WHAT HAS BEEN DONE* *Purpose is asking questions about data and the work we have done so far*		
Compare teachers' reactions to different kinds of bullying	One purpose: • To investigate whether individual teachers display similar or different reactions to different types of bullying	This analytic task conforms to the rule of thumb of only one purpose. The action to be employed to fulfill the purpose is not evident in the way the task has been written, leaving us open to consider different ways of accomplishing the task.
Identify related concepts by investigating co-occurrences in the data	One purpose: • To identify concepts that are related	This analytic task conforms to the rule of thumb of only one purpose. The way the task is written indicates that the purpose will be accomplished through the action of investigating co-occurrences between concepts in the data.
Interpret media representations of local politicians in relation to attitudes expressed by focus group respondents	One purpose: • To interpret the relationships identified	This analytic task conforms to the rule of thumb of only one purpose. The action to be employed to fulfill the purpose is not evident in the way the task has been written, leaving us open to consider different ways of accomplishing the task.

INDEX

Page references to figures are shown in italics. Tables and boxes are shown in bold.